THE AIM of this book is to inform, educate and empower parents or carers of children and young people, about how drugs have the potential to damage their health and wellbeing. Many adults are particularly worried about the use of drugs by teenagers, and so they should be, but it is important to understand that drug use often starts well before adolescence for an ever-growing number of children.

It is written in a Scottish context because the author is a Scot and because Scotland has the unwelcome reputation of being more damaged by drug misuse than most nations. But the issues around drug misuse in Scotland are unfortunately duplicated across the world. So understanding our Scottish love affair with drugs – including the legal drugs, tobacco and alcohol – is as good a point as any to start from to find at least some of the answers to why people misuse drugs.

Another theme of this book is drug laws do not protect children. The current drug laws mainly protect businesses and adults. And yet urgent drug law reform, even a halfway measure like unit alcohol pricing, is painfully slow – politicians will only make laws that they believe the public will accept.

Fags Booze Drugs + children contains all the facts clearly set out and the intention of the book is to enable many more parents to do their little bit towards reducing the harm caused to children from drugs.

Those who profit from drugs can only do so if there is a market for their products. The misuse of drugs in society will only reduce when adults and children are well enough informed to realise that they do not need unnecessary drugs in their lives.

After qualifying as an engineer, **Max Cruickshank** changed course to youth work. He served for over 35 years enabling young people in various settings to meet the challenges of growing up. He has run thousands of workshops and training sessions for young people and their parents and sex education. He has been a leading you the Scottish Drugs Forum for over 20 years.

FAGS BOOZE DRUGS

+ children

What parents need to know to keep children safe

Max Cruickshank

ARGYLL ✤ PUBLISHING

Argyll Publishing
Glendaruel
Argyll PA22 3AE

www.argyllpublishing.co.uk

The author has asserted his moral rights.

British Library Cataloguing-in-Publication Data.

A catalogue record for this book is available from the British Library.

ISBN 978 1 906134 98 3

362.
29

Printing
Bell & Bain Ltd, Glasgow

To the thousands of children and young people who have attended my workshops and shared with me their wit, their youthful wisdom, as well as their confusion and ignorance of the harm that drugs can do. They have inspired me to use our shared experience to write this book for the benefit of others. Many of these children are themselves now parents.

I also dedicate this book to the thousands of parents and the many carers of children who have somehow successfully managed to keep children safe from the harm of drugs misuse. Their success is no mean achievement in a world where such enormous international commercial forces continually conspire to profit from selling harmful food, drink and drugs to children.

Once adults learn to listen to young people,
We will realise that they are like mirrors,
reflecting back to us,
What we have done to them.

Max Cruickshank
Youth Worker
28/8/96

Acknowledgements

I would like to thank my many friends and colleagues for the imaginative ways they have contributed to this book and for the support they gave me in my long hard struggle to write it.

Firstly my wife Pat for her great patience in proofing the text, and for all her quiet support especially as I often wrote on into the wee sma' hours.

Thanks to Dave Liddell the director of Scottish Drugs Forum for keeping my feet on the ground and focused on the important issues. His decades of successfully advising those working in the illicit drugs field and the politicians who make our laws has taught me that there are many ways of skinning a cat.

Thanks to Ann McClintock, a friend and psychologist who explained complex theories to me in a way that made them so much easier to explain to others.

Thanks to Ian Hamilton, my friend and visually impaired journalist, who can always see the bigger picture. He has inspired me to believe that I could write a book and that I had to share the decades of knowledge that I had worked so hard to acquire from thousands of young people.

Thanks to John Aurthur, director of Crew 2000, the youth drug advice charity. John has been a great source of grassroots knowledge and wisdom about young people and drug use. A man who knows how to listen to young people and not exaggerate what they are saying.

Thanks to Tony McGowan, counsellor and retired Health Promotion specialist who kept me right when I wandered off following some new theory or research that always needed further checking. His insights into the world of recovery have been invaluable to me.

Thanks to Stephen Cuffe – a man who can turn a complex myth into a wonderful cartoon that helps us all see things clearer.

Thanks to Dr Mike Fried, medical consultant and old friend. A good man to consult when you need a reality check on medical politics, pharmacology and a big injection of common sense, good humour and the energy to keep focused on the task in hand.

Thanks to Derek Rodger, who edited and published this book when others did not believe it had a market. Thanks for your utter patience in dealing with my ramblings and my dyslexia.

Finally my thanks to the many courageous people who have dared to share the story of their struggle with drugs with me. They have all made an enormous contribution to my education about addictions and to the contents of this book.

Contents

DEFINITIONS

Drugs are any substances that can alter the chemistry of our bodies; they may alter our moods, change how we think or feel as well as altering our physical or mental states.

In this book when drugs are referred to they include tobacco, alcohol, illicit drugs, prescribed and over-the-counter medicines, herbal remedies and substances commonly known as 'legal highs'.

I have used the generic term children instead of kids in this book to refer to both children and young people, under the age of 26 as is common in all of Europe.

SOME KEY FACTS

- The number of smokers in Scotland in the 16-74 age group is now down to 24.3% from a high of 30.7% in 1999 and nearly 70% in the 1970s and 80s. That is very good news. However a worrying number of children are still starting to smoke.

- In Scotland 10% of adult men and 14% of women reported that they did not drink alcohol at all. [SOURCE: NHS National Statistics 2011] This means that 90% of Scottish men and 86% of women drink alcohol.

- Between 1990 and 2000 the proportion of 12–15 year olds who drank alcohol the previous week, went from 14% to 21%.
  There was an increase in the proportion of school pupils who had drunk alcohol in the last week: from 11% in 2008 to 14% in 2010 among13 year olds and from 31% in 2008 to 34% in 2010 among 15 year olds. [SOURCE: SALUS]

- At least 65,000 Scottish children live in a home with a problem drinker.

- The consumption of alcohol, by adults and children, has reached its highest level ever recorded in Scotland.

- The damage to our health from alcohol is escalating to dangerous levels for all ages. That is bad news. Serious efforts are being made by the government to find practical solutions to this problem but so far it has not made a significant change to our national love affair with alcohol.

- Around 6-7% of the population of Scotland is known to have a serious problem with illicit drug use. The problem is likely to continue to grow, unless we can find ways of addressing it.

Foreword

THE AIM of this book is to inform, educate and empower parents or carers of children and young people, about how drugs have the potential to damage their health and wellbeing. Many adults are particularly worried about the use of drugs by teenagers, and so they should be, but it is important to understand that drug use often starts well before adolescence for an ever-growing number of children.

Facts empower us – Myths disempower us

Information is power. Parents who are well informed can make an enormous difference to what their children come to believe or understand about drugs. On the other hand, ill-informed parents can reinforce in children the many myths about how safe or unsafe their drugs of choice are. We should be aware that all of us can quite innocently pass on dangerous attitudes and unhelpful information about drugs to children. It is this sharing of ignorance, by trusted adults, that leads many children into dangerous drug use or misuse. Understanding the difference between facts and myths empowers parents and carers.

Statistics

The few statistics used in this book are there to give an idea of the scale of the drug misuse problem in Scotland but they do not differ very much in the rest of the United Kingdom or across the world. If anything things are worse in Scotland than in most other countries, so it is well worth learning from what went wrong in Scotland, so that others can benefit.

Also the main statistics used are to alert people to the fact that the media often use drug deaths and harm from drugs statistics in ways that do not always allow an accurate comparison to be made. The figures used in this book are from well-recorded, well-established official Scottish sources and research papers. Similar statistics exist for England & Wales, Ireland, Canada, Australia, the USA and Europe. They show very similar trends with some local cultural variations.

Scotland however, has the unwelcome reputation of being more damaged by drug misuse than most nations. So understanding our Scottish love affair with drugs is as good a point as any to start from to find at least some of the answers to why people misuse drugs. This can benefit us all.

Drug addiction

The fear of most parents is that their child may get addicted to drugs. There is a commonly held view that all drugs are addictive. This is not true. For the readers of this book the word addiction means a person's overwhelming involvement in using any drug (substance). This will means that they cannot function without regularly using their drug of choice. If they are a drinker they will be way past the stage of enjoying a drink occasionally, so need to drink most of the time, all day, or everyday, just to cope with normal living. People can be addicted to many things apart from drugs, e.g. work, sex, gambling, exercise, shopping or eating.

I have tried in this book to use the term addiction as little as I can as it is loaded with moral overtones, as is the even worse word, junkie. The problem is that because so many people see addictions as incurable, or something that they can do nothing about, this leads to a psychological acceptance of that problem, that allows them to feel comfortable with their condition. Such acceptance gives people the best excuse in the world for not addressing their problem drug use, which is the term I use as much as I can in this book.

Children are not adults

Young people are not physically fully grown until their late teens and early twenties. The bodies and minds of children can therefore be damaged physically, their emotional and intellectual growth can be retarded or permanently damaged by drug misuse. It is therefore particularly important that they should be discouraged from using any drug or substance that could harm them. The current laws on drugs do not protect our children enough. The reasons why are fully explained later.

Drugs and mental health

It is now thought that one in four of the Scottish population will suffer from some form of mental ill-health at some point in their lives. Children it seems, now suffer mental ill-health in almost the same proportion as adults. Research suggests that a very high number of the people suffering from all forms of drug addiction have deep-seated, undiagnosed and untreated mental health problems. It is not yet clear if it is these mental health problems that caused people to self-medicate with whatever drugs they think might help. However, it is clear that much of this self-medicating leads people into problem drug use, and can worsen their already fragile mental health. So for many people experimenting with and then using large quantities of drugs, when they do not already have a mental health problem, could be triggering such problems.

Drug Laws do not protect children

Another theme of this book is drug laws do not protect children. The current drug laws mainly protect businesses and adults, not children. The illicit drug trade continues to ignore and exploit all the laws. Drug law reform is urgent. MPs and MSPs only make laws that they believe the public will accept. Over the last five decades they have not radically reformed our drug laws because they do not believe the public would support them. Parental lack of understanding of all drug problems prevent them from giving our elected members the courage to make any real changes to the law. Campaigning based on the new facts and knowledge in this book could contribute to ensuring that drug laws are reformed to protect children.

Finally by way of introduction, there is a bit of repetition in this book. Because it is not the sort of publication that some people will read from cover to cover, to ensure that some essential points are not missed the author has repeated them regularly, e.g. that children are not adults until at least 19 years of age, that mixing alcohol and cocaine is highly dangerous, etc etc. I hope those readers who do study the book from cover to cover will please bear with the higher purpose.

1.

Your role as a parent or carer

What can you, as a parent or carer, do to reduce the harm to your children from drugs? Probably much more than you think.

When stories of parents appear in the media because their children use drugs, it is often presumed that they are not good parents. Well lets face the facts. The combined commercial forces of the tobacco, the alcohol and the pharmaceutical industries, and the international illicit drugs trade, are working daily against the best efforts of parents to keep their children safe from drugs. The drive to make a profit from these trades, is too often affecting the health of children and young people.

There is also a growing public concern that so many other industries are making huge profits from children. They include: food and soft drink manufacturers, the games industry, the clothing trade, the music and entertainment industry, the toy trade, mobile phone companies, television and video companies and many more are in on the act. All of them grabbing their share of the pocket money of children.

Very few parents are feckless or stupid. Even the most highly intelligent, well-motivated, loving parent, with a degree in childcare is no match for the relentless pressure that is exerted by big business, across the world, in pursing profit from children and young people. There is no doubt that some of their profit-focused activities are harming our children. The rise of childhood obesity alone is but one horrific example.

Countries such as Sweden, Finland and Denmark have made important changes to the rules governing television advertising, at peak times, of products such as those mentioned above which were being heavily targeted at children and young people.

Media reports of children as young as 10 or 11 smoking, drinking or using drugs horrify the public and leave many parents worried to death about the possibility that their own children may experiment with or start using drugs.

Parents want to know what they can do to protect their children from coming to harm from drugs. Well, the answer is that they can do quite a lot. One thing that we do know is that it is a complete waste of time burying our heads in the sand and hoping that the mantra of 'Just Say No' to drugs will work. Such approaches don't work. All they achieve is the avoidance of the problem, until parents are confronted with the unthinkable, a child with a drug problem they hadn't spotted.

It is very important to remember that your use of drugs as a parent, be it smoking, drinking or using an illicit drug, is observed, from a very young age by your children. This informs children's attitudes every bit as much as what they see in the street, in films, on television, through the internet or from their peer group.

It is now well accepted that investing heavily in the early years of children's lives has enormous benefits to the children and in cutting the costs of crime and ill-health to us all. Legislation has been passed to encourage all public services to make this a priority. It is estimated that for every £1 spent on early years up to £13 can be saved nationally. What positive things can parents and carers do?

Discourage children from smoking

Do everything that you can to discourage your child from starting to smoke tobacco. Remember that children from a very early age observe all your adult behaviour. Smoking around children gives out the message that smoking is a normal and safe thing to do. Smoking is now a habit of an ever smaller minority of people – only 25% of Scots were smokers in 2009, 23% of the Welsh and 21% of the English smoked in 2009. Smoking is certainly not a safe or healthy habit.

The age for smoking has been raised to 18 so if you are supplying fags to your children you are breaking the law. But, the law itself is a bit crazy – **there is no legal age at which you cannot smoke** – the law only prevents under 18s from buying tobacco products.

BUT – from April 1st 2011 it has become illegal for under 18s found in possession of tobacco products in a public place to refuse to hand over the tobacco to the police or to give their name and address. [Tobacco & Primary Medical Services (Scotland) Act 2010.] Park-keepers have always had the authority to confiscate cigarettes from children, but seldom used these powers.

Cannabis is the most common illicit drug used in the UK. Cannabis is most often used by smoking it with tobacco. If your children have an aversion to smoking tobacco, then this may put them off using cannabis, at least for a while. There are definite links between the use of different drugs. Some people do move on from tobacco to alcohol to illicit drugs, as when one drug fails to satisfy their needs they seek other solutions.

A cannabis joint can be equivalent to 5 standard cigarettes.

This is because the cannabis smoke is inhaled deeper into the lungs than tobacco on its own and is held longer in the lungs to get the maximum effect. This dumps higher loads of the carcinogenic (cancerous) elements into the lungs than from tobacco alone. This is not something to be encouraged.

myths & facts

Facts Empower us – Myths Disempower us

Information is power. Informed parents, can make an enormous difference to what children come to believe, or understand about drugs. On the other hand, Ill-informed parents and carers, can, unfortunately reinforce in children, the many myths about how safe or unsafe their drugs of choice are. We should be aware that all of us can quite innocently pass on dangerous attitudes and really unhelpful information about drugs to children. It is this sharing of ignorance, by trusted adults, that leads many children into dangerous drug use or misuse.

Discourage children from using alcohol as late in life as possible

Having spent many hours with parents who have a child using illicit drugs, one of the most common things I hear parents say is 'see if it had been alcohol they were using, I would have known what to do about it'.

This is misguided because they are not understanding that alcohol is an extremely powerful drug. There are hundreds of thousands of families affected by alcohol misuse across the UK. Without a doubt this situation is getting worse by the day. The Scottish Executive has revealed that in 2009 1:20 of deaths in hospital were alcohol related. We now have people in their early twenties being treated for liver damage, a problem that used to only be seen in people over fifty.

The whole situation with alcohol and children is very confusing because, believe it or not, **UK laws allow alcohol to be consumed from the age of 5**. The law also allows wine (table wine not wines like Buckfast), beer and cider to be ordered at the age of 16 & 17 along with a meal, in a licensed restaurant. They must be accompanied by someone over 18 who will pay for the alcohol.

At 18 we can legally buy and drink as much alcohol as we like.

The Alcohol etc.(Scotland) Act 2010 which came into force on 1st October 2011 requires those who sell alcohol to verify the age of those who they believe to be under the age of 25, using ID such as a passport, driving licence, Young Scot Card. This does not alter the fact that 18 is still the official age for purchasing alcohol.

Alcohol is the most likely cause of death in under-21 year olds, through road accidents and suicide.

myths & facts

Myth: The French allow children to drink watered down wine.

Fact: Having travelled to France several times a year, for decades I have seen no evidence that the French or other Europeans, regularly allow children to sample watered down wine from an early age. France is now reporting the same problems of binge drinking in young people as we have in the UK. So if it was ever true that this liberal approach was common, it does not seem to have worked. As with all drugs, the later children start to use them the less likely they are to develop problems with them later in life. In many countries 21 is the age for using alcohol.

Alcohol is 70% cheaper than it was 30 years ago, and cheap enough to be easily afforded by children today.

The Scottish and UK Parliaments are considering ways of increasing the price of alcoholic drinks. There is some doubt about whether the proposed 'minimum pricing by units of alcohol' will work. Young drinkers are very price conscious, so they will just switch to cheaper alcoholic drinks. Also the drinks industry is very clever at steering people to the drinks they want them to consume. An across-the-board tax rise could work, but regrettably, politicians do not want to annoy moderate, adult drinkers by raising the tax on all alcohol.

Since the majority of those over 16 use the drug alcohol regularly it is important for parents to have a sensible approach to this particular drug. Most children will experiment with it, some will use it regularly, and some will come to harm, if they don't understand the nature of the drug and learn to use it sensibly and in moderation.

Alcohol picks up on the our basic personality traits and moods. So if for instance a child is depressed – a normal state of mind for many at some point – and he or she uses alcohol to try to control their depression, they will end up even more depressed. Likewise if they are angry, hurt or feeling violent, these moods will usually be made worse by alcohol. Understanding this alone will help many children to avoid the worst side effects of this legal drug. If they are in a happy-go-lucky mood alcohol usually picks up that mood so they will normally have a good time.

It is well-known that many people with alcohol and other drug problems have a history of emotional, physical and sexual abuse. The way that many children have learned to cope with such abuse is by self-medicating with the drug alcohol.

Using any drug early in life lays down in our brains patterns of behaviour that stay with us. The later in life that children use alcohol, the better to reduce the possibilities of long term harm.

Even if children are allowed to drink alcohol in a safe social setting, such as within a family, they should still be discouraged if their moods are badly affected by it.

It is illegal to buy alcohol but not illegal to consume it, if you are over the age of 5 in the UK.

Encourage children to be responsible with money

From listening to the thousands of children who have attended drugs education workshops, one thing sticks out in my mind that parents should know – it is that many children have far too much pocket money. I have so often heard young people, including those who are unemployed, explain that their parents feel sorry for them, so do not expect them to contribute any of their dole money, or wages, to the family finances for their upkeep. Some parents may take £10 off their children for their upkeep, but this is then often borrowed back before the week is out, leaving young people with plenty of money for fags, booze and drugs.

Adults selling fags, booze and illicit drugs have no regard for the law, as they continue to dip into the pocket money of even the youngest of children.

Too many young people spend large proportions of their weekly income on fags, booze and drugs. We will be doing children a favour by asking them to contribute to their family finances. At the very least they could be paying for some of their leisure pursuits. This positive action will help children to understand what things actually cost. Parents would be making a serious contribution to cutting the funds to illicit drug dealers, the tobacco and alcohol companies, if they encouraged their children to be more responsible with money. They will also learn valuable lessons about being discerning consumers.

On a more positive note it seems that one of the reasons that fewer children are now smoking is nothing to do with heeding the health messages, but simply that they prefer to spend their cash on the latest technology that their pals have – mobile phones and iPods.

Learn what you can about illicit drugs

Using illicit drugs for some children will be just part of growing up. They want to try new things for themselves, as others may do with sex, stealing, driving fast, adrenalin-inducing extreme sports, dressing outrageously or just showing off.

In the last decade the range of illicit drugs available has increased to hundreds of substances, but at the same time the strength and quality of these drugs gets more suspect every month. Police regularly report that street cannabis can be as low as 2-3% pure, when it used to be 8-15% pure. Cocaine when imported into the UK may start off at 20% purity but often ends up as low as 2% pure when sold by street dealers. Speed, LSD and ecstasy have become so impure that they are fast going out of fashion. Children and young people hate to be ripped off, so many of them it seems are now turning away from the more common, illicit drugs to others about which much less is known.

If your child is using illicit drugs and you are able to talk to them about it, try to do so in a calm and non-threatening way. Check out the information in this book, go on the internet or call drugs help-lines to find out about the drugs they are using. Remember that alcohol is the drug most likely to seriously harm or kill children.

- The most important thing to remember about illicit drugs is that children have no idea what they are buying.

- **There is no quality control on illicit drugs.**

- Not all drugs are addictive but our bodies do build up a tolerance to most of them, so we may end up dependent on them or become a problem drug user.

- It is cocktails of drugs that do the most damage and cause most fatalities.

- Find out as much as you can about myths about drugs.

All too often children appear to know far more about drugs than their parents. Although much of what children know are common

myths, and seldom up-to-date or accurate. There is one vitally important thing you can do to prevent your children getting into serious
problems with drugs, Know as much as you can about the drugs and
the myths yourself.

Well-informed parents are better able to understand why their
children might want to use drugs, but they are also less likely to
freak out at the first hint that their children might be experimenting
with drugs. Whether we can accept it or not, it is natural for children
to rebel, to experiment with substances, sex, violence, stealing,
showing off and many other potentially dangerous activities.

A caring parent has to be there to pick up the pieces, comfort their
child who is making mistakes, and be able to calmly talk things
through with them. This approach reduces the harm that might have
been done; it offers a positive way forward, by supporting a child
through the minefield of problems that many parents never had to
deal with when they passed through adolescence.

Make sure your children are well informed

It is not enough that parents get themselves up to speed with what is
happening in society with drugs, they also need to do what they can
to ensure that their own children are fully aware of the hazards of
modern living. Find out what your children's schools are offering in
the way of drugs education. In my experience it will, even in the best
of schools, be very low key, probably well out of date and there is
never enough time set aside to go into the topic in any real depth.

Teachers are overloaded with trying to teach children about the
many social issues society thinks are important for child safety – sex,
abuse, bullying, obesity, violent crime, racism, money management,
AIDS, sexism and bigotry are all topics schools are trying to address.
Drugs education is another task added to the already full curriculum.
So don't expect your schools to deliver all that you desire for your
children about drugs as well. The range of drugs in common use
now include those that even the best-trained and most up-to-date
teacher has never heard of.

Watch television programmes and discuss press coverage of
anything to do with drugs with your children. This way you and your
children are learning together. With this approach, ground rules can
be discussed and agreed, taking on board ideas from your children.

This will reduce the chances of the dictatorial, I know best, because I am an adult, sort of rules being agreed that are a complete turn-off for children. Your child may just be desperate to hear some sensible advice from you as a trusted adult. Especially when they are going through the normal teenage stage of starting to make decision for themselves, and sorting out their own rules for life and codes of behaviour. You may have forgotten this, but adolescence is a very idealistic time of our development. It is when we form our own independent views on what is right and wrong in life for us. Exploring these issues with your children will let them see that you respect their views and their need to start to work things out for themselves.

The range of substances (drugs) available today has gone from around 40 to hundreds in the last decade. Some of the drugs you may have heard of or used yourself, but the new substances called 'legal highs' include herbal remedies, chemicals used by gardeners and bubble bath salts. They are now easily available on the internet, through 'head shops' and street drug dealers.

Many in the medical profession, pharmacists, drugs workers and even police drugs specialists, have little or no knowledge of many of these new substances. We just do not know if they are harmful or not. We do not know what side-effects they may have if used on their own, or in combination with other drugs, such as alcohol. It is not even possible at the time of writing this book to advise people where they can find reliable information on these substances. An internet search of 'legal highs' will throw up many dodgy sites of the suppliers of these substances. The information such suppliers provide is, to say the least, dubious as they are making their money from these substances. Many such dealers are operating just within the existing laws. It will be some time before laws are changed to control the selling of such substances.

Our current knowledge of 'legal highs' is not based on any reliable or substantial research.

Encourage your children to have healthy fun

Boredom is one of the most common reasons that children give for smoking, drinking and using illicit drugs. There is no known medication for boredom, but lots of myths about how drugs can cure boredom. But they are just that, myths.

The desire to try drugs or experiment is the most common route into drug use. Remember that when you were young your choice was probably a fag behind the bike shed or booze in the bus shelter. Children today are bombarded with messages, from the media and their peers, that promise instant fun, quick ways to make them confident, improve their sex lives, alter their moods to one that they think is acceptable. To achieve these altered states of mind your children can access a variety of at least ten of the 40 common illicit drugs, within 15 minutes, anywhere in the land. Even in our far away Scottish islands. It will be a very strong personality indeed who can cope with that temptation without at least having a few tries at something, just to see for themselves, what it is like. This is almost unavoidable, especially in our poorest communities which are heavily targeted by drug dealers of all sorts.

Parents today don't seem to get too upset if their children experiment with sex, even before they are legally allowed to, so why do they get so uptight about children trying drugs? Perhaps it is because they believe that drugs equals addiction or death and sex 'is natural'. The consequence of youthful sex may be an unwanted pregnancy or a sexually transmitted infection for the experimenters.

Children who have a wide variety of enjoyable social or educational activities to absorb them will have less time and perhaps less inclination to use drugs. That of course does not guarantee complete safety – some healthy sports and activities have their dangers. Driving scooters, motor cycles or cars is one of the most common killers of children.

Lower rates of young people with serious drug problems are to be found amongst those who have completed higher education, have a university degree, or who have highly satisfactory career plans and well-paid jobs. These are all things that give people challenging goals in life, good career prospects, a good salary, high status, self-confidence, as well as keeping them from boredom, because they are busy and have fulfilled lives. Alcohol related problems are an exception to this. It can be found across all of society including the professions.

The highest levels of problem drug use, from all substances, occur in the poorest communities, with the lowest educational achievement, the least job opportunities and the poorest provision for healthy social lives. It is also extraordinary though, that within these communities, many individuals and families seem to be able to avoid involvement in such addictions.

So, anything that a parent can do to encourage their children to study hard, get a time-absorbing career, a range of enjoyable interests and good social relationships, will to some extent, protect their children from the dangers of the most serous drug misuse. This of course is not easy at a time of exceptionally high youth unemployment.

Have good communications with children

'Families that pray together stay together', was a very corny phrase from the past when most families went to church regularly. Not a common situation today. Perhaps that idea could be replaced with, 'families that eat, talk and play together, stay together'. Such a simple thing as the different generations being able to communicate well, without falling out, or doing the adults-know-best routine, does pay dividends. If children know that they can trust you enough to share their worries, as well as their corny jokes and trivia, then it is so much easier to have a sensible, family discussion on the topics that concern all of you. Life, death, drugs, smoking, relationships, bullying, fears of failure, stress and depression are all things that children have to grapple with, as they go through the process of moving from dependent child to independent young adult.

Recent research tells us that families that regularly eat together, are more able to discuss issues such as drug use, sexual health and other matters that affect their growing children. The TV dinner eaten in the child's bedroom is something that should be discouraged to increase the amount of time in each day that families can spend together just catching up, talking and so improving their communications.

Where families have poor communications, the inability to talk, to listen, or to learn from each other can be the cause of children turning to the solace of drugs to cope with their worries, their loneliness and their misery.

Make sure children and young people get enough sleep

It is surprising how many children, young people, even adults today, sleep with a light on, or have a background noise in their bedrooms all night. It may be a television left on, a sound system playing music or the radio left on. This is not a good idea.

Growing children need 8–10 hours of sleep a night. During sleep the body relaxes itself, repairs the damage done during the day and energises us. Children who are sleep-deprived, are not able to function well at school or college and their work may suffer. This is because they will be tired, lacking in concentration, moody or grumpy. Teachers today know this only too well, especially on Monday mornings. Too many children have a bedroom full of sources of distraction or noise and the privacy to use it as they wish. Bad sleeping habits are often the result. This is one of the most important reasons for many children developing sleep deprivation problems.

Some sleep-deprived children turn to drugs for relief. Some doctors are not yet aware of this phenomenon, so are prescribing medication which is not appropriate when there are better, non-drug solutions. Do what you can as a parent to discourage bad sleeping habits. Sleep deprivation does children no good at all and can over time set them up for failure in education, stress related illnesses and into self-medication with drugs.

A sensible discussion with children about their sleeping arrangement is important and can result in ground rules being agreed that will solve the problem.

Recognise the importance of diet

There is enormous public concern about the diet of children today. Scotland and the UK is heading towards having one of the highest rates of child obesity in the entire world, almost matching America. It is well documented that our diets today are too high in unhealthy fats, sugar and far too much salt. A healthy balanced diet with a balance of the right foods, such as fruit, vegetables, fish, chicken, red meat and sufficient protein, carbohydrates and water, should provide a growing child with everything they need to be healthy and fit.

Overloading a child's body with excessive sugar, salt, caffeine and other stimulants stresses their bodies and leads to mood swings, lack of concentration and hyperactivity, none of which is good for children.

Research has shown that young offenders whose diets were changed radically and who were given daily doses of Omega 3 and Omega 6 fish oil supplements showed remarkable changes in their moods and levels of aggressive behaviour. These small changes made these young offenders more open to educational opportunities as well as helping these young men to gain control over their minds and bodies in ways that had never been achieved before. A good diet can clearly assist children to avoid some of the dangers of stress-related problems and mental ill-health, which can too often lead on to unhelpful drug use and misuse.

Recognise the importance of exercise

If an appropriate diet is followed children should not become obese. However we know that it is difficult today for children to resist all the sweets, the TV dinners, the micro-waved high salt and sugar meals, or the many treats that are on offer in many homes. Children's bedrooms are full of high tech entertainment options that do not offer any opportunity for exercise, unless you include super strength thumbs from playing hundreds of hours of computer games. Some of the damage from an unhealthy diet can be reduced by regular exercise.

There is little doubt that it is easier to get boys to participate in sport and exercise on a regular basis than it is to involve adolescent girls. Schools do work hard at this but lack of good facilities, limited specialist staffing and too few hours available in the curriculum, mean that most school children get less exercise than is essential. Research shows that many, if not most, adolescent girls drop out of regular exercise once they leave school. Young males are more likely to take regular physical exercise. There are, in most areas, many more opportunities for young males to participate in sport and fitness near home, than for young women. Exercise is important not just for physical health but also to control weight and to make us look good. Regular exercise is a sociable thing to do, because it gets us into other social networks. It also relieves stress, improves our mental health and improves sleep.

Exercise that is fun and suits a particular individual is more likely to be done regularly than exercise that we hate or are embarrassed to participate in. Walking, cycling, swimming and dancing are amongst the most useful all-round body workouts that we can do. Anything that you as a parent can do to help your children to exercise several times a week will be something that will help them socialise regularly and will keep them mentally and physically fit as well. It is recommended that we all exercise for 30 minutes on five days in the week. Walking a good distance to school or work is both a sociable and an excellent form of exercise.

Invest in time with your children

One of the regrets that busy parents have later in life is that they never set aside enough time to see their children growing up. Children only grow up once, so if we miss out on this we can never go back and retrieve it. Time invested in our children's development is never time wasted.

Most parents have no difficulty spending a great deal of time and energy with babies and small children, but when puberty arrives, many parents find it confusing and difficult to know how to spend quality time with their offspring. During adolescence children need massive support and love from their parents, but they also need time to be on their own or with their peers. Getting the balance right is never easy. Parents have to make a real effort to allow children space, but also to invest their own time and resources in trying to keep alongside their children as they face the journey through childhood into adulthood. If you are successful at this, then you will have done all that any parent could have done to build powerful, positive, parent-child relationships. This effort will take you and your children on through the many troubles that all of us will have to face for the rest of our lives.

Nobody should expect life to be a bed of roses. Life for all of us is more likely to be full of daily challenges that need confronted. We all have to learn from every mistake we make and children are no different from adults – they will make some big mistakes. The trick is to accept that the only thing you can do with your past or your mistakes is to learn from them and build on them to improve your life.

Accept that some children will still go off the rails

Regardless of how hard we work at it, or how well we think we have brought up our children, things will go wrong. The influence of others may be stronger than family ties at times and children may go off the rails for a while. Some children will develop emotional or mental health problems. This is not a time for parental guilt trips or tantrums. It is a time for a very cool head – you just have to keep strong and focused on what you believe is best for your child. Focus too on the many good things that have happened in your child's life. You have to continue loving your children, whilst they plough on making the mistakes you'd rather they didn't.

The UNICEF Convention on the Rights of the Child was one of the most important international declarations ever made. It reminds us that children have rights too, including the right to explore life, the right to try things for themselves and the right to make their own mistakes. We need to be able to stand back as parents and accept that we have all had to learn from our own mistakes, even if sometimes they have hurt us badly.

Few parents would stop their children playing team games or going rock climbing if they really wanted to. Such sports can cause disabling injuries as well as building a healthy team spirit, courage, a sense of adventure, the ability to assess risk and the self-discipline that is so important to have if we are to be able to overcome challenges in life. Allowing children to be involved in competitive swimming, athletics, dancing or talent contests will for some be a life changing experience, but for others a bitter disappointment if they don't make high grades. Young people who play in noisy bands may well become deaf very early in life if they do not heed advice about the hearing damage that is associated with such exposure to loud music.

Parents are usually delighted that their children passed a driving test for a scooter, motor cycle or car, yet having these important social skills can be highly dangerous in young hands. However, holding a driving licence can open up opportunities for work and pleasure. Some risks in life just have to be taken to learn more about ourselves.

The best help that parents can give to children at these transition points of life, is just to be there, as the solid, loving, caring, back-up person, for children to return to when they need this most.

The greatest harm to children from drug use comes from their ignorance, their immaturity and their inexperience at dealing with the consequences of what they are doing.

Realise that you are not on your own

The shock, trauma, embarrassment, guilt and pain you will suffer, if you find that your child has a drug problem, will inevitably make you feel isolated and alone. Perhaps you'll believe that you are the only parent in the world facing this problem. Well you are not on your own. The reality of modern life is that many more parents will have to deal with this situation. Don't despair, there is a vast range of help-lines, support groups, health specialists, youth workers, voluntary organisations, websites and publications around to turn to for help.

Having read this far, you will have realised that drugs of all sorts are around in every community, they are a serious health and social problem and they are not going to go away because we want them to.

There are whole industries across the world, whose only interest is in exploiting us all, including our children, by supplying quick chemical solutions to meet our every need.

In 2010 the UK government declared that virtually all the common children's remedies were no better than a placebo, did not cure anyone and were in some cases harmful, so should no longer be sold. Parents were to be advised by their local chemists about this. Within months the government abandoned that policy as they were so heavily lobbied by the drug companies who make vast profits from these useless drugs. So much for protecting children from drug harm.

From five decades of watching this situation grow I am convinced that we cannot depend on governments to solve the drug problems for us. There are so many vested interests pressurising politicians not to do anything that would harm their business interests – the tobacco companies fighting the government in the courts over banning cigarette machines, the alcohol industry and supermarkets finding ways to circumvent the banning of promotional offers are two examples. In fact it costs the Scottish government almost £6 billion a year of public money to deal with the consequences of all drug misuse.

As adults, we have a responsibility to do what we can to minimise the harm that can come to our children. The harm caused to children by the immoral behaviour and greed of the commercial organisations, such as the food, tobacco, alcohol, pharmaceutical industries and the illicit drugs traders, could be brought under control. But only by common sense, effective public education, regular community action, effective laws and sensible government policies to protect children and their families, instead of allowing commercial interests to ruin so many lives.

Individuals and communities can take action that will make a difference.

2.

What's going on?

KEY FACTS

- The world has changed a great deal for children of today, much of the change is good and some of it is not good.

- At least 59,600 children in Scotland live in homes where there is an illicit drug use problem.

- At least 65,000 children live in Scottish families where there is an alcohol problem.

- Drugs can damage children's brains and their mental development.

- 1 in 4 children are now believed to suffer from mental health problems at some point.

- The number of children seeking help because of feeling suicidal has increased seven fold in five years.

- Legal and illicit drug sellers conspire to dip into the pocket money of children, as do many other legitimate commercial enterprises.

- Religion is in decline, families are in crisis – poverty is worse and heavily linked to all forms of drug misuse.

- Current drug laws do not protect children.

- In Scotland, there are 24.3% of homes where smoking tobacco is still the norm. This is a great improvement but the impact on children of tobacco is still a big concern.

- The link between smoking tobacco and cannabis is important because for many children tobacco is the gateway into other substances.

- Alcohol misuse is now seen by the government to be far worse than anyone thought. With 1 in 20 deaths in Scotland caused by alcohol-related illnesses.

- The higher the levels of serious stress in any society, the higher the number of people who turn to drugs to cope with their lives.

- 40% of American children may be addicted to drugs prescribed by their own doctors.

Does environment push children into drug use?

Before we get into the topic of children and drugs in our society, it is important to reflect on how different the environment is today for children growing up. It is certainly a very different world from the one that most parents, grandparents and carers of children knew from their childhood. You can judge for yourself if it is a healthier or better world for children today than it was for you.

There is growing evidence that the more stressed a society is from violence or war, poverty, lack of employment, ill-health, natural disasters, high crime rates and other factors, the more that society turns to using drugs to cope with that stress. Research is building up a very strong picture of a child's environment being a major factor in whether they use drugs or not.

There are many improvements in life for children today

It is not all bad news. So we should acknowledge the many improvements that there are in the lives of present-day children . These include higher rates of survival into adulthood, the elimination of many of the diseases that particularly affected children, better housing, a bedroom of their own for many, serious hunger almost unheard of, fewer fatal accidents, education has improved, more access to sport and recreational activities, much lower crime rates as well as many more children enjoying a regular holiday.

We should be pleased too, that only a minority of children smoke tobacco, or use illicit or legal drugs. Regrettably, this is not true of alcohol, because the majority of children do use alcohol and far too many do so in very dangerous ways.

There are problems that many children have to face

This list may seem very large and out of balance with the positive things noted above. However, not all the problems affect all children. Great efforts are being made to deal with all of these issues, but some do not yet have the priority that they should.

It is important to understand the links between children being unhappy or miserable, their personal stress, depression, serious mental health problems and the kind of coping strategies that children use, as their way of dealing with their problems. In particular the impact of abuse, in all its forms, emotional, physical, mental and sexual, should not be underestimated.

Many children are no longer allowed to be children, for long enough
Many children are moving too fast through the natural stages from baby to child to teenager and young adult. With many forced into behaving a few years ahead of their actual chronological age, this does not allow them time to be what they are, children, not adults.

What are noted below are the things that create serious problems in the lives of many children. These are what most of us as parents would hope our children would not have to deal with.

Children affected by mental ill-health

Around 1 in 4 children in Scotland are now thought to have a mental health problem at some time. In adults this problem is now said to be as high as 1 in 3. The majority of those who have addictions to drugs in Scotland are also known to have undiagnosed and untreated, mental health problems. It is not clear which comes first, the mental health problem leading to addictions or if the addictions are causing the mental health problem. Clearly, children who are suffering mental illness at an early age are particularly vulnerable to drug misuse.

Can drugs damage the brains of children?
We are not full-grown physically until about the age of 19. Our brains are not fully wired up until a bit later, about the age of 21. Some recent research from Australia suggest that male brains may not be fully wired up until even later, perhaps around 25 years of age.

The inappropriate use of drugs by children is therefore something to be avoided. There is some evidence that children under 12 who smoke tobacco and use cannabis regularly are causing permanent damage to their brains and therefore their mental development.

There are known risks of permanent brain damage to children from alcohol use by their mothers, especially during the early stages of a pregnancy. For some mothers this results in baby suffering from foetal alcohol syndrome (FSA). The advice to women who want to get pregnant seems to vary from time to time, but it is moving towards a view that if women do drink alcohol and they plan to get pregnant, it is best to stop drinking alcohol before they get pregnant and throughout their pregnancy.

Thousands of very young children across the world are being prescribed powerful mind-altering drugs by their doctors. It is estimated that 40% of American children are addicted to medicines prescribed by their own doctors.

Drugs like Ritalin are often used to control difficult behaviour in children. Nobody seems to have stopped and asked why is it that we never had that level of behavioural problem in children a couple of decades ago? Medicating children with such problems may be the cheapest and easiest way to control their behaviour, but is it the best way? We do not really know why it is that so many more children today are suffering from hyperactivity, emotional or sleep problems, than in the past.

Messing around with a child's mind by introducing mind-altering substances, when they are still immature is something we must find ways to prevent. It is bad enough that some children are experimenting with drugs to solve their own problems, but quite another thing when professionals are involved in prescribing these substances. The power of the pharmaceutical industry to continue to come up with a pill for all ills, and all occasions, is at last starting to be questioned, and not before time.

Child abuse

Child abuse now seems to be very common or perhaps the public is just more aware of if than in the past. Such abuse includes emotional abuse, psychological abuse, physical abuse and sexual abuse. Social workers get a very bad press when such abuse ends in the death of a child, yet adults are often reluctant to report their concerns about abuse happening in their community. It may be significant that pornographic websites, including the violent exploitation of children, are the most visited on the internet across the world. Many children are abused to produce such pornography. Homes that have hundreds of television programmes and fast broadband internet encourage easy access to gratuitous violence and pornography of all sorts. Children are often more savvy about searching the internet that their parents. Many adults with addictions to alcohol and drugs report having suffered abuse as children.

Children viewing pornography

The Channel 4 series 'Sexperience' in 2009 exposed the fact that there are two and a half million pornography sites on the internet. They also found that two thirds of under fifteen year olds watched on average 90 minutes of pornography a week on the internet or on their mobiles. They reported that for many children this was their main source of sex education. The average age for first viewing pornography on the internet or on mobile phones was eleven years of age in the UK.

The internet can of course give access to some very good inform-ation and advice services, but because it is unregulated, there is also dubious information on health and drugs in particular. Just Google the word 'cannabis' or 'herbal highs' and see for yourself.

The 'Sexperience' programme also revealed that most parents had no idea what their children, or young people in their care, watched on television or on the internet, often in the privacy of their own bedrooms. Nor did most parents know how to use the facilities on their computer to prohibit access to stuff they did not want their children to see.

A campaign supported by Channel 4, PC World, BT and others has been launched to force those selling computers to preset computers at time of sale, to protect children. They are also collaborating with internet servers to act urgently on this issue.

Sexting

The social networking now adopted even by very young children has good and bad consequences. It can be fun, they can easily keep in touch with parents when they are out and about. On the down side teachers report regular disruption in classes, bullying by text and Facebook which has driven some children to serious mental distress and even suicide. A new and very dangerous aspect of this is when children as young as 12 think it is cool or fun to take pictures of themselves in sexual poses to send on to others so they can boast about their boyfriend's or girlfriend's sexy attributes. Some even photograph their sexual parts to share with others in their networks. This is what Sexting is about. Children's charities and the police are extremely worried about this new development as it is illegal to send such pictures publicly. Sexting can also lead children into the world of sexual predators who scour the internet daily for images of children.

Suicidal children

Considering what you have read already about the world that children live in today, it should perhaps be no surprise at all, that in 2007/08, over 500 children phoned ChildLine in Scotland, saying they were feeling suicidal – compared with 71 in 2003/04. This was seven-fold increase in 5 years. If your reaction to this is similar to that of many adults, 'that many of the calls must have been hoax calls', you are completely wrong. ChildLine is well used to distinguishing between hoax and genuine calls from its half a million calls per year. Of those callers who gave their age, 44% were aged 12-15 and 30% were aged 16-18.

Calls to ChildLine in Scotland about suicide are almost four times higher from girls than from boys.

Across the UK for the same period, 2007/8, a total of 2,925 children and young people rang ChildLine specifically about feeling suicidal (2,282 girls and 643 boys). This has risen from 910 calls in 2003/04. [SOURCE – ChildLine]

Childhood obesity

Children in Scotland are the second most obese children in the world, after children in the USA. Not an accolade that we should be proud of. The picture in the rest of the UK is not much better.

The long-term health damage to children from such levels of obesity hardly bears thinking about – diabetes, heart problems, vital organ damage or failure and a shortened life are the most likely outcomes. The associated bullying and emotional trauma of living with this completely preventable health problem may well add to the already growing stress and mental health issues mentioned previously.

According to research childhood obesity is established in children usually by the age of two. Childhood obesity is an example of where parents of children can be both the initiators of the problem but also the most vital resource we have to deal with it. However we must acknowledge that the power of the food industry seems to be working against even the most careful and concerned of parents. The food industry continues to market cheap, fast food that is stuffed full of sugar, fat, and salt, so that it can be frozen and quickly microwaved instead of cooked from fresh.

Encouraging children to walk to school instead of driving them there, is one small but very effective way for parents to reduce the incidence of childhood obesity.

Sugar in children's drinks

A small, 300ml can of Scotland's most popular fizzy drink Irn Bru contains 35 grams of sugar (29% of its contents) equivalent to 6 teaspoons of sugar. [SOURCE the producers or Irn Bru – A.G.Barr] How many parents would allow their children to have this amount of sugar in a cup of tea?

There is another worrying problem about children and weight. It is reported that nearly 50% of 15-year-old schoolgirls in Scotland skip their breakfast, for reasons that are not yet fully understood. The Edinburgh University Child, and Adolescent Health Research Unit completed the research in 300 schools. It could be the girls are sleeping late because of the disturbed sleep patterns, or they literally run out of time to eat before going to school by spending too much time on getting ready in the morning, putting on make-up, or dressing to look like celebrities. Others apparently think that if they skip breakfast they can afford to make up for these lost calories by having junk food later in the day. The research also notes that school children who do eat a proper breakfast everyday are more likely to have their school performance rated as 'good or very good'.

Many children are the main carers of adults

According to the Princess Royal Trust for Carers around 100,000 children in Scotland are the main carers of a parent disabled by illnesses, including addiction to drugs and alcohol. These parents need help with their personal care to be able to run their family home. Children who act as carers can miss out on crucial stages of their emotional and social development. These children often have a very short time to be a child. They lose out on what should be their normal social and emotional development. Acting as mum or dad when only 8–16 years of age is not a recipe for a fulfilled childhood. The stresses and strains on a child from being an unsupported carer is immense and can lead some of them into seeking solace from a variety of drugs.

Children cannot play outside

Over the last few decades, many local authorities have sold off playing fields to boost their shrinking budgets. Developers too often do not fulfill their vague promises to put back suitable recreational facilities into the sites where they build houses.

Most children are now getting less physical education at school than they used to. This impacts on their general mental and physical health.

Commercial companies are now providing many of the sports and leisure facilities. Children from the poorest most deprived areas are often excluded from such facilities because they simply cannot afford to use them.

Rules about child protection and health & safety have their down side too. So for instance, a parent cannot take more than one child under 5 years swimming without other adults helping them. This denies children in families with more than one child opportunities for good healthy, regular exercise and family fun-time together. The fear of being sued and the escalating cost of public liability insurance is what has forced local authorities to insist on these, anti-child regulations. It is interesting that there are legal solutions to this, used by commercial leisure providers, but not adopted by local councils. They simply display notices stating that they have no liability for any injury caused by them not having supervised swimming pools.

Voluntary youth organisations are now finding it very difficult to recruit male volunteers to work with children, as men are scared off by the ill-informed view that all men are potentially child abusers. Reducing play opportunities for children affects how well they socialise with others in their community as well as reducing the amount of exercise they lose out on. Reducing the number of positive male models in the lives of children is highly dangerous to their development.

Children wrapped up in cotton wool
As we get more affluent, many more children now have their own bedroom, stuffed full of things that parents think will keep them safe and away from the big bad world outside the safety of their own homes. The police and the media have reinforced the view, that the streets of our towns and cities are dangerous places for children to be. The reality is that children are losing the ability to socialise and to take even minor social risks, like walking to school or to the shops. It is noticeable that even paper boys and girls are now often driven around by their parents to deliver their papers, instead of walking on the paper round themselves, because parents fear for their safety. The real danger is massively overstated. Serious assaults and murders have continually decreased in the last three decades.

Too many children are leading very lonely lives, trapped in their bedrooms, where they have unsupervised access to the often-inappropriate influence of television and internet.

Teachers are now reporting that some children are becoming much more passive and better behaved in class, but also that this means that children are finding it harder to interact with others in discussions. Some children are using technology such as texting and social networking sites instead of engaging in the important personal and interpersonal verbal relationships they should be having. Fewer pupils are joining after school clubs. [source: Behaviour in Scottish Schools, 2009 Report]

Reducing the normal socialising activities that children used to do reduces the amount of time that children are in contact with other children. This can affect their self-confidence, makes them fearful of life outside their homes, and adds to their isolation and their ability to make and keep a good healthy network of friends.

Children's cash, a target for big profits

Multi-national companies are conspiring to dip into the pocket money of children, selling them sweets, junk food, and drinks with too much salt, fat, and sugar in them. They target children with expensive toys and games, mobile phones, music players, clothes and highly sexualised fashion items such as bras for 10 year olds, (now at last banned) very expensive sports equipment and sports clothing, inappropriate films and DVDs, health and pharmaceutical products they really don't need. Some governments, the Scandinavians in particular, have made a stand on this and are limiting opportunities for advertising aimed at children during peak viewing times.

Many teenagers are known to use all of their personal income, and their pocket money, to buy tobacco, alcohol, and drugs. Children are clearly an easy target. There are laws to prevent these purchases happening but the legal restrictions clearly do not work and are seldom enforced by the police or the licensing authorities.

Until 2008 there had not been a successful prosecution for selling tobacco to children in Scotland. Only since then have special efforts been made to prevent children accessing alcohol with limited success.

One positive and perhaps healthier change in children's spending patterns is that fewer children are spending money on tobacco, choosing perhaps to top up their mobile or buy music from iTunes instead.

Role models for children have changed

In the past many post school-aged children had apprenticeships or were in work situations where trusted adults mentored them. There were sports and film stars, entertainers and others who could offer a range of reasonably positive role models for children to admire, emulate and learn from.

Today the cult of celebrity offers children role models who live in the world of extraordinary affluence, living lives way beyond anyone's wildest dreams. Such lifestyles are only attainable if people were to win Big Brother, Britain's Got Talent or the National Lottery.

There are now so many negative role models around, including politicians fiddling their expenses, bank managers wrecking the world's economy, celebrities like Jonathan Ross earning millions of pounds a year for presenting a few radio and television shows, footballers in court for violent acts, cricketers and jockeys in betting scandals, fashion models ending up in jail for abusing their staff, entertainers booking themselves in and out of exclusive drug or alcohol rehabilitation clinics. All of this gives children and young people the quite false impression that it is easy to find a place in residential rehabilitation clinics, so therefore it will be easy to cure your addiction if you have one. This is very far from the truth.

The more realistic and more positive role models of a teacher, sports coach, music teacher, youth worker, priest or minister, a work colleague, aunts and uncles, are now less admired. This is a sad state of affairs because family and community-based role modelling is much more likely to offer long-term, positive mentoring for children, throughout their developing years and into adulthood.

Religion's influence on children has declined

Church attendance in the last 50 years has declined so that most families no longer belong to a church. Churches used to provide not just religious teaching, but social and moral teaching to children and adults as well. Today schools are perhaps the main organisation in the life of a child that regularly teaches about the rules for living a responsible life.

On the national, society-wide scale, the moral and social values in society are now more often driven by the media, as they lead the public debates on topics such as abortion, sexuality, binge drinking, assisted suicide, drugs, child abuse or violence in society. The tabloid press now drives public opinion through sensational stories on sex changes, crime, insurance fraud, dieting or health issues.

Sensational reporting about drugs and alcohol have done little to educate the public and often perpetuate the unhelpful and ridiculous myths about hangover cures, deaths from methadone, or the latest 'legal highs' to hit the streets. One example of this many years ago was the story run in many papers that children were using the drug LSD, supposedly by sticking coloured transfers on their skin. This was total nonsense and fantasy, but the story still ran for months. The lack of opportunity for children to discuss, debate and think about morality, rules for living, or what is right and wrong, with trusted adults, is leaving many children seriously confused and bewildered.

Family life is different now

We have just reached the point where the majority of parents in the UK, are no longer committed to each other through the formal or legal tie of a marriage. More children are born out of wedlock than within marriage. Single parenting is now the norm for a large minority of children, who are growing up in situations where divorce and family breakdown is very common. There is research that argues both for and against the likely effects on a child's development from living in a single parent family. It is becoming more common for children to be brought up in a family with two parents or adults of the same sex.

The proportion of single parent families in Scotland at the 2001 census was 28%. For Glasgow the figure is now 46.6% and the average for the UK is 25.6%. [SOURCE: Dr Carol Craig, author of *The Tears that Made the Clyde*]

The support systems of the extended families which aunts and uncles used to provide are less common. Grandparents are now often forced into playing a much more active role in child rearing for their own sons or daughters, because of their addiction to drugs.

Young people are also leaving home much later than in past generations and a growing numbers of them are then returning to their parents' homes, within a decade, after failed marriages or relationships. Bereavement, family break-up and conflict are often the trigger that children say was the starting point of their journey into addictions.

Poverty

The prediction in the 1960s that by 1984, the poorest people would get poorer and the richer people would get richer has, sadly, happened. Even after a long period of a Labour government, who promised that it would eliminate child poverty in the twentieth and early twenty first century, things are certainly no better. By some indicators poverty is much worse. The crash of world banking in 2008 is set to make the end of poverty a very long-term dream.

All the research into drug addiction points constantly to one glaring fact. That those most affected by addictions are still living where the highest levels of poverty persist. The incidence of all sorts of ill-health including addiction to tobacco, alcohol and illicit drugs, obesity, suicide and mental ill-health, cancers, heart disease and diabetes are all to be seen at their highest recorded levels in these most poverty-stricken and deprived communities.

Unemployment

When unemployment of adults and young people rises, so do all the problems of drug misuse. The UK is heading for a figure of 2.62 million and over 1 million youth are unemployed as I write. Long-term unemployment de-skills people, leaves them in despair and unable to participate fully in society. This is a recipe for mental ill-health and escape into alcohol, tobacco and drugs.

Drug laws protect adults not children

Laws designed to control the use and misuse of drugs in the UK are all set by the Westminster Parliament, but apply across the whole of the UK. None of the existing laws were designed to deal with the situation where large numbers of children and young people were likely to be using tobacco, alcohol, or illicit drugs, let alone using them in dangerous ways. The significance of this is best understood by just thinking for a moment about what the current drug laws state:

Tobacco

There is no legal age for using tobacco products, although you cannot purchase tobacco now until you are 18 years old. It was 16 years of age until 2008.

Alcohol

You can consume alcohol from the age of 5.

The law allows 16-17 years olds to order table wine, cider, beer to consume with a meal in a licensed restaurant. Although they must be accompanied by someone over 18 who can buy the alcohol.

You can buy any alcoholic drink you like at the age of 18.

From October 2011 those under the age of 26 will find it harder to purchase alcohol because new Scottish alcohol laws require those selling alcohol to ask for valid age identification to establish the age of the purchaser. **This is primarily a measure to protect businesses not children.**

The police can confiscate alcohol from those under 18 who are drinking in a public place, and report this to parents.

Illicit drugs

None of the laws on illicit drugs mentions age restrictions at all. 25% of children under 15 years of age have used tobacco, cannabis, and alcohol. Many do so regularly.

Existing drugs laws are designed to protect adults not children
They don't even protect adults particularly well. It seems though that politicians of all parties have no stomach for making major changes to the drug laws, to protect children. Lame excuses about the need to allow free enterprise to voluntarily ensure that children are not harmed have never stopped children getting access to tobacco or alcohol, let alone illicit substances.

One of the disadvantages of the internet is that there is no way of stopping those who are determined to buy drugs online. There seems to be a general acceptance that the international drug barons will just flaunt the laws anyway. This is no reason not to consider putting new laws into place to protect children, which will discourage adults from colluding with children and young people in their drug use.

Tobacco companies exploiting children

There were reports in some of the poorest countries in the world, that tobacco companies had been sponsoring school sports and providing equipment and books to schools. Laws in poorer countries make it easy to use such cynical marketing to hook in a new generation of young smokers, to replace the adult tobacco quitters they are losing in droves in affluent countries.

One brand 'Slim' cigarettes was clearly aimed at the young female market, the clever branding suggesting that smoking keeps you slim, which it doesn't. The company denied this saying the slim referred to the shape of the cigarettes and its packaging!

Even budget airlines are now in on the act, selling safe, smoke-free cigarettes on their flights, to help distressed smokers to cope with their journey. What message does that send out to children on these flights? Who I wonder produces these legal cigarettes?

The black market for cigarettes still persists with the man with the plastic bag in the pub and rogue market stallholders continuing to ply their trade. As tobacco tax rises the illicit and highly contaminated tobacco supplies from China and the Far East fills the gap.

Children's exposure to alcohol

A least 65,000 children in Scotland live a home where alcohol misuse is a problem. No real effort has been made to establish the actual number of children living in homes where an alcohol problem exists. It could be many times higher than this perhaps affecting 500,000 or more homes with children.

The UK government has at last acknowledged that alcohol is a major danger to children. There are serious efforts being made to change the laws to reduce consumption of alcohol, especially by the most vulnerable groups, such as children, young people, and irresponsible adult drinkers. Moves to increase the cost of alcohol is heavily opposed by the alcohol industry. As is the 'minimum unit pricing' of perhaps 45p or 50p per unit of alcohol. This is seen as a way of increasing the cost of drink to children, young people and the binge drinkers, whilst not increasing it to responsible drinkers.

The opposition by the drinks industry seems odd as it is estimated that if unit pricing of alcohol does go ahead, the alcohol industry in Scotland alone would gain at least £130m of extra income a year at no extra cost to them. The Chancellor would only gain a small amount in added tax revenue. This windfall to the drinks industry would certainly not be directed towards alcohol education or in supporting efforts to treat those damaged by excessive consumption of alcohol. However, a general tax increase on all alcoholic drinks could raise substantially more tax. It would also reduce alcohol consumption by everyone and could provide new sources of funding for the government to increase alcohol education and rehabilitation services.

Research is showing that it is not only children who are drinking dangerously, 20-30 year olds, the over 50s and pensioners are just as likely to be drinking alcohol dangerously.

The cost of alcohol-related harm is estimated at £3.56 billion to the Scottish economy annually.

Adults as well as children are utterly confused by the health messages on alcohol. There is confusion about what government advisers are saying is safe drinking, what is binge drinking, how alcohol endangers pregnancy, what age you can buy or use alcohol and much more.

A UK government health minister recently supported the idea that alcohol should not be given to anyone under 15 years of age at all. Nothing of course has followed this announcement – issued in an election year! What is clear though is that the existing laws cannot be used to enforce this proposal.

Clearly children can be badly damaged by consuming alcohol. We live in a bleak, northern hemisphere, with a cold climate and fewer hours of sunlight per year, all factors that research suggests leads to more depressive illness and more drug use of all kinds, especially high alcohol consumption and misuse. It has taken decades for our love of alcohol to develop, so it will take decades of law changes and public education to undo our harmful culture of heavy drinking.

Children's exposure to tobacco

Thousands of children in Scotland are still living in homes where smoking is the norm. Passive smoking is well-known to be harmful to growing children and to adults. There is a Scottish campaign to encourage smoke-free homes, which is gaining supporters by the day.

Recent research has confirmed that leaving cars windows open when smoking in the car with children on board in no way prevents them from inhaling the poisonous fumes. There are moves to ban the smoking of tobacco in all cars, even if there are no children in them.

Children's exposure to illicit drugs

In Scotland, 59,600 children live in a home where illicit drug misuse is a problem. These drug users are using many substances but heroin, methadone, cannabis, and cocaine are common. Many illicit drug users regularly use both alcohol and tobacco as well.

We do not know how many homes there are where cannabis is

smoked or used regularly. Cannabis is the most popular illicit drug used in Scotland. Like all illicit drugs it cannot be seen as a safe drug, and especially not safe for children.

Drugs education

3.

KEY FACTS

- Parents expect schools to provide drugs education, because they know very little about drugs.

- Most drugs education is only aimed at school-aged children.

- Drugs education is usually provided by teachers, who at best, have limited training in the subject.

- Primary schools often provide better drugs education than secondary schools.

- The police in Scotland have been heavily involved in the past in drugs education in schools, often replacing teaching staff.

- Most Scottish police forces have now stopped delivering drugs education in schools.

- Some drugs education has been provided by ex-drug users, and voluntary organisations who work in the drugs field.

- It has been seen as trendy to get pupils or young people to act as peer educators in delivering some drugs and sex education. It has not always worked.

- The main drugs education theme in the past had been 'Just Say No' to drugs. This has now been abandoned because it was too simplistic a message and did not work.

- Schools find it difficult to deliver what is seen as the more liberal 'Harm Reduction' message on drugs which is now seen as more honest and effective, especially for teenagers.

- Youth clubs, youth justice projects and workplaces with young people have provided some impressive drugs education to supplement the basic drugs education delivered, often many years before in school.

- Very few parents have had any drugs education themselves, so lack even basic knowledge. Parental ignorance can undermine the drugs education of their children.

- Much of the research into drugs education has concluded that it does not work. This has led to policy makers and politicians almost abandoning drugs education, a very big mistake when the harm caused by drugs in society gets worse by the day.

- Myths about drugs are dangerous and must be addressed through public education.

Why do we need drugs education?

- Every community in Scotland is awash with drugs which can harm children.

- We have laws to stop children accessing prescribed medicines, over-the-counter remedies and legal drugs like tobacco and alcohol.

- We know that legal substances such as tobacco and alcohol are regularly used by children from a very early age and are common in many homes.

- Illicit drugs, which include hundreds of different substances such as heroin, cannabis and 'legal highs' are sold on the streets in every community and on the internet. All efforts to reduce the sales of illicit drugs have resulted in only about 5% of them being removed from the streets.

- 25% of children in Scotland have tried illicit drugs by the age of 15.

- 25.6% of all adults report having taken illicit drugs at some point in their lives.

- 41% of 16-24 year olds had used illicit drugs in their lifetimes.

[last 3 points – 2008/9, Scottish Crime & Justice Survey]

The illicit drugs trade alone is thought to be the second or third, biggest business in the entire world. When the turnover of the legal and the illicit drugs businesses are added together it is thought that they could now be the biggest form of business in the world. Bigger than oil, wheat, salt, sugar or financial services.

The illicit drugs trade exploits the poorest of farmers in the world who provide them with the raw materials for a meagre few pence. These raw materials when processed are sold for pounds on our streets. The raw materials which cost the dealers a few pence generate thousands of pounds because the mark-up on drugs such as heroin, cocaine or cannabis is around one hundred fold.

The criminals who run the illicit drugs trade have no morals or scruples about who buys their products, child or adult. They operate their business 24/7 with no quality control to ensure safety of the drugs. No health instructions are provided on how to use the drugs safely. They have no public liability insurance to claim against if you are damaged or killed by their products. They have no call-centres with advisors to call if you want to complain about their service. Contaminated illicit drugs like heroin have spread infections such as anthrax. They have seriously damaged lives and are a drain on the the National Health Service. None of these costs can currently be passed on to the criminals operating this trade.

So the answer to the question why do we need drugs education is simple. If we do not educate our children and our nation to the dangers of using any of the hundreds of drugs readily available in our communities, then we have failed them. We will also be allowing the criminals and others who profit from selling drugs to carry on unimpeded. They will continue to exploit the ignorance and vulnerability of children and adults.

Confidentiality is a serious matter in drugs education

There is a problem with drug education that needs to be addressed – the issue of confidentiality. The problem arises if children are in a school, at a youth club, a social work care group, or in any organisation funded by the state, because if they talk openly about their own drug use during drugs education sessions they could find themselves investigated by the authorities. Such disclosure of confidential matter may trigger the child protection policies that are now the norm in any work with children under age 16.

Children are smart enough to understand that telling too much about their drug use could land them in it. So by not talking about the things that really concern children we are preventing them from getting the help they need.

Not allowing children to talk freely also prevents teachers and others from hearing about new trends and new myths and other information that can be used to enhance their teaching work.

We are not treating children with due respect if we are not offering them a high degree of confidentiality in our drugs education work.

This is a serious issue because, creating obstacles which prevent children from accessing the essential information that they need may be putting them in danger. Our obsession with child protection may mean children are missing out on one of the very few opportunities they may ever have of getting the help they need to understand the dangers of drug use and misuse.

We should remember that in law a child of any age has the same right to confidentiality as an adult when being treated by a doctor, even without their parents' consent. So why is it that those delivering drugs education cannot use a similar approach? **Failing to address this serious issue endangers very vulnerable children whose only opportunity of discussing their worries about drug use may be during a drugs education session.**

If we are not willing to treat our discussions with children and young people on drugs as confidential then we must make it clear to them that this is the case, so allowing them the right to choose what they reveal in such discussions.

How do children learn about drugs?
Children's first contact with drugs is often what they see in their own homes. If parents smoke, drink alcohol and pop pills all the time, a child's sees such drug use as normal. Then they are influenced by what they learn at school about drugs and from their peers or the media. So it is their environment that sets the scene for what children come to understand about drugs.

One important aspect of what they learn is that they pick up information from those around them, including the many myths about drugs that inform and misinform so many people. Across the land you will hear repeated the same myths about drugs. We need high quality drugs education because such myths are both very common and potentially dangerous for the lives of children and adults.

Why the myths about drugs are bad for children's health?
Drug myths are passed on around the country, and the world, from generation to generation, through our peers, siblings and parents. Even by teachers, health professionals, youth workers and the police

in their drugs education work. These common myths are believed by young and old, they are part of the tobacco, alcohol and drugs folklore. They include highly dangerous misinformation. Throughout this book these common myths are addressed. The most up-to-date facts are laid against these myths to help people to know the difference between a myth and a fact. Here are just a few examples to illustrate why it is so important to know what is a fact and what is a myth about a drug.

myths

Myths:
Smoking tobacco calms you down.
You can drink yourself sober.
Tobacco keeps you slim.
You get a better buzz from 5-10 ecstasy than just one.
Men's livers are different from women's, so men can heal their livers if they drink too much.

Remember these are all myths. These myths are difficult to correct without expert knowledge of the human body and an understanding of these drugs.

Here are the answers to a few more myths. Many others are featured later.

myths & facts

Myth: Alcohol is not a drug.

Fact: Alcohol is a very powerful drug, which when used to excess can damage many of our body organs and can kill us through accidents or through long-term heavy consumption. 1 in 20 deaths in Scotland are alcohol related.

myths & facts

Myth: Cigarettes are not as dangerous as illicit drugs.

Fact: Cigarettes contain nicotine which is certainly a dangerous, highly addictive drug. Cigarette manufacturers have added up to 4,000 different chemicals to cigarettes, across their product ranges. Tar is a particularly nasty ingredient, which over the years of smoking, deposits black tar in our lungs, leaving us eventually unable to breathe. If we are a heavy smoker we have a 1 in 2 chance of getting cancer of the mouth, throat, esophagus or our lungs. There are around 13,300 smoking related deaths a year in Scotland.

myths & facts

Myth: Cannabis is natural, because it comes from plants, so it is harmless.

Fact: Yes, cannabis comes from a plant but so does tobacco, heroin, cocaine and most other drugs. During production many other substances are added to illicit drugs to make more profit. Powdered glass can be added to skunk to make it look high quality. Cannabis itself is not addictive but the tobacco it is smoked with is. Heavy smoking of cannabis along with tobacco increases the cancer risks enormously .

What parents want from drugs education may not protect their children

No parent wants their child to be harmed by drugs. Most parents' knowledge of drugs is very limited indeed, so they live in hope that they can trust schools, or someone else, to address this difficult subject for them. The same is often true of sex education.

When most parents think of drugs they are usually referring to illicit substances like heroin, cannabis or cocaine. They may not have realised or understood that cigarettes are one of the most powerful drugs, containing thousands of different chemicals or that alcohol is a very powerful drug. Both are legally available to children of certain ages. Tobacco and alcohol caused 14,775 deaths in Scotland in 2008, compared with illicit drugs, which accounted for 574 deaths. [source Scottish Government]

Parents still seem to want their children get the message that all drugs are dangerous and will kill you, when the fact is that not all drugs kill, but can cause health problems if used heavily.

It certainly is true that occasionally a child gets his or her hands on drugs in the home and overdoses on them. This may be a drug prescribed by a doctor to an adult, it could be something they bought in the chemist, and it could be methadone or alcohol. Such drug-related accidents are extremely rare. Children do however die in road traffic accidents, where the drivers were drunk or under the influence of drugs, including prescribed drugs. Stabbings and acts of violence in the street are often fuelled by alcohol or drug use.

So what should the drugs education message be?

We need to be sure that the information and the message that we give to children of all ages about drugs are appropriate for their age, are factual, accurately inform them, are honest about both the good and bad consequences of using drugs, are as up-to-date as they possibly can be, and are explained in a way that can be clearly understood by children.

There is no place in drugs education any longer for the emotionally charged scare stories, the half truths, the passing on of ridiculous myths, nor for only telling children what we want them to hear, rather than what they need to know to keep themselves safe.

All of this is a very tall order. Many parents will have difficulty accepting this approach because they think that we can still scare children into avoiding life's nasties. The reality of modern living is that because of all the viewing of violence and aggression on televisions and elsewhere we are now de-sensitising children against believing in such scare messages.

Myth: Some batches of heroin have rat poison in them.

Fact: About 40 years ago the police did find evidence of rat poison in street heroin. That was a one-off and the story is repeated often as if it is common today.

myths & facts

Many parents would dearly like to believe that if you tell children often enough, the message of the 'Just Say No' campaign, you will be keeping children safe. That message was the one sent out by Scotland Against Drugs (SAD) with the very strong support of politicians and the police. At the time this was thought to be good drugs education. That approach failed in the USA and it has been abandoned here because we do not believe that it worked.

The 'Just Say No' approach was a form of propaganda. It left no opportunity for children to consider or discuss the pros and cons of drugs. It did not listen to their views and experience in a safe and non-threatening way. It did not even include smoking or alcohol as drugs and it demonised illicit drugs as always bad, highly dangerous and always having fatal consequences, which is not always true.

This was also an insensitive approach, as it did not allow for the fact that many children are living in communities and in families where the use of drugs is common or condoned, or seen as a very normal way of dealing with life's problems. This created great anxiety in some children who had to live with this daily, because their own families were regularly consuming a variety of drugs.

This flawed message also caused great confusion and created a distrust of the adults who delivered that message to children. Myths like 'cannabis and ecstasy kill' were commonly churned out, yet no deaths have been recorded directly from using cannabis. At the same time when the annual deaths from ecstasy averaged one per year, children no longer trusted anything that the drugs educators were telling them.

The 'Harm Reduction' approach is quite radically different.
It ensures that children are knowledgeable about the many substances that they may encounter in their community. It also allows for open discussion of the good and bad aspects of drug use. It explores how drugs affect the mind and body. Children are also helped to find ways of dealing with problems, that will work for them and which do not require them to use legal or illicit substances. So tobacco and alcohol are always included along with illicit drugs, in this approach.

What is the aim of drugs education?

Drugs education should be based on three broad educational aims that underpin the teaching of other subjects:

1. To increase children's knowledge and understanding of drugs, drug use and the issues related to it.

2. To explore a range of opinions and attitudes towards drug use and so enable them to come to their own well-informed views.

3. To help children to develop a range of skills relating to drug use and enable them to make their own informed decisions about drugs.

'Knowledge of drugs needs to be based on information that is accurate and acknowledges both the benefits and risks of drug use. Attitudes towards drug use vary greatly and there is no one 'correct' view of drug use. This raises complicated issues which need to be debated and explored from different angles. Encouraging young people to make their 'own, informed decisions', it means just that, and does not mean telling young people what decisions they should be making.'

The International Journal of Drug Policy, Vol.7 No. 3. 1996

It is worth noting that this particular report was withheld from publication by politicians when it was first available.

Many people naively believe that good drugs education will stop children from experimenting with drugs or from using drugs regularly. The fact is there are now hundreds of different substances available within minutes anywhere in Scotland. To hope that good education alone will stop children accessing drugs is foolhardy.

However, like all good education, if drugs education is done well, it will assist children to know the difference between facts and fiction, between myths and common sense. It will help them to understand that any substance that they allow to enter their bodies could be good for them, or cause them harm. It will alert children to what is going on in their world and where things do not seem right. This approach helps children to understand how their minds and bodies work, what makes them sad or happy, what keeps them awake or makes them sleepy, how what they eat and drink as well as how much exercise they do can also affect their moods. They come to understand that drugs affect how we feel and think.

This is the essence of what is called the **Harm Reduction Approach** in drugs education. If delivered well, by competent teachers or others who can engender in children trust and empathy, it can achieve the aim of keeping children safe from the harm that drugs can do to them.

If we do not provide high quality drugs education such as described above to children, then we must accept the consequences which are that a child's knowledge and understanding of drugs, will depend entirely on myths and misinformation, passed on to them by their families, their peers, the media and those selling them drugs for profit.

Ask yourself if you can trust the tobacco or drinks industry to teach your children about using the drugs that they are selling? Most people do not realise that the Drinkwise website and alcohol education materials are funded by the alcohol industry.

Are you happy to live with the fact that illicit drugs dealers tell people what they think they want to hear about the substances that they are buying?

The best drugs education of children in the world is of little use if parents too are not much better educated about drugs. **Parents must be included in drugs education** so they can support their children more effectively.

Drugs education should not stop when children leave school

Leaving school is one of the important transition points in life, when children experiment with all sorts of behaviour that they may not have tried earlier. There are some efforts made through youth organisations and work places, to top up the drugs education that children had at school. When we consider that the most dangerous time for using drugs for most people is going to be in their late teens and early twenties, it is essential that this age group be given access to high quality and appropriate drugs education.

Politicians have been the main barrier to good drugs education!
Because politicians cannot make up their minds what the message should be, drugs education has been very ineffective so far. The government is terrified of sending out the 'wrong' message. In the past politicians have fully backed the failed 'Just Say No' approach to illicit drugs education. There has been little or no education on smoking or alcohol. Politicians are not all convinced that the 'Harm Reduction' approach works. As always, they look longingly to America and other countries to give us a lead. Yet we know that importing ideas from other cultures do not always give us the results we hope for. 'Just Say No' came from the efforts of Nancy Reagan to support Ronald Reagan's presidential campaign. The USA still has as big a problem of drug misuse today as it did then.

The government's own publications with advice on tobacco, alcohol and illicit drugs are often confusing, badly written, out of date and not comprehensive enough to educate the range of readers that they are aimed at. The audience for such material includes people who have real problems with literacy as well as those who have a university level of education. No publication can ever hope to meet such a diverse audience. We need a wide variety of approaches, appropriate to the target audience.

Many prisoners have major problems with literacy and numeracy, so sophisticated beautifully designed and printed government leaflets on drugs are often unreadable for them.

The Scottish government's current drugs leaflets are all aimed at adults and none are any longer produced to educate children or young people. This is partly because they cannot agree what the message should be to children.

There are government-supported helplines and internet sites that are a little more effective and are much easier to update when new drug use trends come along.

In general, primary schools are now doing a fairly good job of educating children about drugs. Their approach is about helping young children to have a good understanding of how their bodies and minds work and what drugs are used for. They do not usually go into the finer details of the range of drugs used in society. This approach has provided a good basic background education on drugs for children.

It is when secondary school takes over that the quality and quantity of drugs education starts to go badly wrong. Again the problem lies in getting a consensus on what the message on drugs should be for children, young people and adults. Different messages may be required for different ages and stages of people's lives. Exactly the same problem of confused political messages exists in sex education for children and young people.

The debate goes on. Hopefully some parents reading this book may contribute to that debate by raising some of these concerns with MSPs and MPs. This could make a real difference here.

Who is the best person to provide drugs education to children?

Good drugs education requires both the right knowledge and the special skills to deliver that knowledge effectively to a wide variety of recipients with very different needs.

Trained Teachers

Trained teachers should in theory be well placed to provide drugs education. Dozens of drugs education programmes and packs have been developed to support teachers in this task. Teachers like these drugs education packs, but often do not use them in the way that they were designed to be used. Instead they take from the packs the bits that suit their particular philosophy or approach and discard the rest. This can mean that they miss out some of the key messages in these teaching materials.

Other problems have prevented some of this work succeeding. Drugs education is one of the many 'add-on' tasks that society is asking hard-pressed teachers to deliver. Pressure from the authorities to deliver drugs eduction leads to a lot of box ticking with only the minimum required hours of drugs education being achieved. Schools sometimes deliver their 'annual' drugs education sessions in the last few weeks of the summer term, perhaps as part of a health fair or fun day. **This is token drugs education** and a waste of time, but it allows the schools to tick the boxes. Politicians then believe that they have done their duty in providing the targets for the delivery of this part of a child's education.

Not enough time has been given to training teachers in drugs, or to updating them regularly as the information and drug problems evolve and change almost weekly. This means that teachers quickly start to lack credibility with their pupils and never have enough time to cover this very important health topic comprehensively. Many teachers feel seriously deskilled in this area of their work.

Parents groups, school councils and the governors of many private schools still favour the failed 'Just Say No' approach. Schools have too happily allowed others, such as the police, outside agencies and other non-teachers to deliver part or all of their drugs education, believing them to be more skilled or more up-to-date in their knowledge.

The Police and drugs education

The police in Scotland for years spent a lot of time delivering drugs education in schools. Parents and schools trusted the police to do this, but it is only evaluated and monitored by the police themselves and not all of it has been positive.

Many Chief Constables are now withdrawing the police from schools drug education, having accepted that there are too many problems with it. One of the strongest reasons for not allowing the police to deliver drugs education directly to children is that they, in their role as upholders of the law, cannot ignore what they hear in such sessions with children. Police are trained to gather intelligence in all their work. They cannot ignore law breaking if they hear of it which means in drug education they cannot offer even the basic need for confidentiality. Most chief constables in Scotland have now accepted that this conflict of roles of police officer and drugs educator is untenable.

The police authorities in England have long ago accepted that there were problems for the police in drugs education. Their concern was about why they were involved in drugs education. Was it for surveillance purposes? Or to reinforce the authoritarian drugs-will-kill propaganda? Or was it just for good police public relations reasons? None of these are good motives for providing drugs education to children.

There is a national police-led drugs education initiative aimed at 12 year olds in Scotland called the 'Choices for Life Project'. It is run each summer across Scotland attracting around 22,000 pupils and school staff to spend the day having fun whilst they consider messages about drugs from well-known actors, entertainers and musicians. Although originally led by the police they now take a low profile working with others to deliver a fun day out about drugs.

The hope is that this high profile raising of the drugs issue with primary seven school children will be built on back in schools. Teachers have been given access to a range of resources online to back up these events. However because these drug education days are delivered near to the end of the school year in June it is often difficult for teachers to follow up what was learned until much later in the year, long after the impact of the event has gone from the minds of children.

I accept that the police can make a useful contribution to the training of teachers and perhaps even parents about drugs. But I do not think that the police should be involved in delivering drugs education to children in schools.

Using ex-drug users to educate children

Inviting in ex-drug users, alcoholics and reformed smokers to shock the children with their stories has also been very popular with some schools and some parents. Serious questions have been asked about how wise this approach is. In these sessions children often see a young, healthy, drug-free ex-problem drug user with a new purpose in life, presenting themselves as glowing role models. Research shows that what many children take from that approach is that they wonder what is the problem with drug-taking? When they see before them evidence that if you get a drug habit, like the presenter of the session, then you can just as easily recover, just like the problem drug user before you has successfully done. It was also found that the ex-users often seemed to glorify, for some pupils, the criminal behaviour associated with illicit drug use.

Peer Education

Over many decades politicians and education authorities have been interested in using peer education to deliver drugs education. In over 40 years of observing such an approach I have seldom seen it delivered well. There is a problem when using Peer Educators, who by their nature, are usually young volunteers, not much older than the pupils they are educating – it is not very efficient. If 30 Peer Educators are trained it is not unusual to find that only 5-10 of them stay the course long enough to complete the training and even fewer go on to deliver any of the drugs education to children.

The fact that they are young in itself means that they cannot be all that experienced in life, or in the topic they are delivering, so they tend to rely heavily on cool communication skills to cover their inexperience. The lack of credibility in young Peer Educators is particularly obvious when they are trying to deliver sex education. Even the most streetwise 16 to 18 year old Peer Educator can only have a very limited personal experience of sex in order to convincingly cover this very complex topic in any real depth.

Only where Peer Educators have been very well trained and are paid to deliver their sessions over long periods of time, a year or more, can we hope to see this approach having more success. Such an investment in peer education simply does not happen in the UK, although it has been done in the USA. That does not mean that we should abandon this approach.

There is an added danger with Peer Educators which is that the people who fund this work can just stand back and blame the youth and inexperience of the Peer Educators for not successfully delivering effective drugs education. Funding is often limited to a 2-3 year period so there has been very little opportunity to develop this approach fully in Scotland or the UK.

Drama, DVDs, Videos & other technologies

The use of drama productions, touring drugs plays, videos, educational DVDs, computer programmes to deliver drugs education has had mixed success.

Touring drama productions can be effective in themselves in opening up a lively discussion and getting useful messages across. However the value is lost if there is not an immediate opportunity to discuss the presentation with the audience, so maximising the effect. Too often the actors do this themselves. This seldom works because of the actors' lack of real and up-to-date knowledge about drugs. These discussions should be led by trained drugs workers or teachers who have the drugs knowledge and the groupwork skills needed to handle such a task. Very large audiences make meaningful participation in the discussion very limited, except for the most articulate of the children. Because this approach is costly to put on, they need large audiences to view the performances to justify the high cost. This is a very expensive way of getting over very limited messages that could be delivered better in other ways.

Using DVDs, videos, and computer programmes is another expensive medium that suffers from similar but different problems –

the material dates very fast, so they usually have a very limited shelf life. If they are really well-produced they can support other parts of a drugs education programme. The teacher or trainer must know the material very well, be sure that it is appropriate for their audience and must be well-prepared to maximise the learning that can come from these materials. There are also drawbacks from using material from a culture different to those who are viewing it. For example American or Australian material or material that contains very strong broad Birmingham, Welsh or East End of London accents can be problematic for a Scottish audience. Unusual jargon, street names of drugs or even jokes can diminish the effect that such materials might have.

So who can deliver the most effective drugs education?
We do not live in an ideal world, but if we did then clearly highly trained specialist teachers would be our first choice for delivering drugs education to children. There are others who can deliver equally as good a service. There are many good examples of voluntary organisations specialising in drugs education work. Youth workers, health education workers, prison staff, and social workers have done good work in providing drugs education.

To extend drugs education to those who are out of school and to parents we should consider creating a team of drugs education specialists who have the knowledge, the skills, and the resources to go out across the land and develop effective ways of providing top-up drugs education to post-school young people and adults. If such a major programme of preventative education were successful then we would within a few decades have a population that was so much more aware of the problems and more able to influence and educate their children.

How could we fund this approach?
The Scottish government has estimated that the annual cost of alcohol misuse is £2.25 billion and drug misuse costs are £2.6 billion. The cost of mental ill-health is £8 billion. This makes a staggering total of £12.85 billion. These are all negative social costs to society, some of which could be reduced. We know that there are links between mental ill-health, alcohol and drug misuse, so surely there is a strong case for investing substantially in exploring the most effective ways to

educate not just children, but also adults, and especially parents about drugs and mental health. We could potentially save billions of pounds every year.

How do we know that drugs education works?
Hindsight is a great thing and no doubt if we knew how to measure our progress over decades we may find that drugs education has been more successful than we think. After all, the number of people who are using the most dangerous of the illicit drugs is 59,600 in 2011 in Scotland, when it should have been very much worse after nearly 5 decades of illicit drug use in our society.

Tobacco use by children is moving downwards, although the current trend is that young women are now more likely to smoke than young males. Smoking education has supported the reduction in smoking.

Alcohol misuse is at an all-time high, so clearly not including alcohol in most of our drugs education programmes, has had serious consequences.

Research says most drugs education does not work!
The academic research into drugs education seems to suggest that the main outcome of school-based drugs education is that it shifts forward the age at which children experiment with drugs by about 2 years, rather than stopping them from using drugs altogether, or changing their general attitudes to using drugs. **Shifting forward by 2 years the time that children start to use drugs is not a failure in drugs education, it is a success.** We should be building on this success not abandoning it.

Most of the research has concentrated on school-based drugs education, delivered mainly by teachers, who have had very limited training in the subject, and whose knowledge is often out-of-date. What teachers are trying to teach children is a very complex subject, with difficult concepts, loads of jargon including street names for drugs unknown to them which change regularly, leaving some teachers unaware of what children are talking about.

The main drugs education message for years was 'Just Say No' to drugs, which is not a message that many children, and very few young people, wanted to hear. Added to that, very few teachers are aware of the plethora of myths about drugs that are firmly embedded in the minds of those that they are trying to teach. So we really do need to think long and hard about what the academic research about drugs education failing really tells us, and how relevant it is now. If being able to prove that a drugs education programme has stopped children using drugs is the aim, it is doomed to failure. **It is also utterly unrealistic for us to think that education alone can affect enormous changes in human behaviour.** However good education helps people to think for themselves and to seek the information they lack.

Drug misuse as we know it today has been developing for decades. Hundreds of new substances have hit the streets in that time. The myths and misinformation about these substances has grown like topsy leaving people very confused. The public urgently needs educated about these often dangerous substances, otherwise society will be completely swamped by the fall-out from this.

Governments respond successfully to other health problems such as Mad Cow Disease, Aids, Anthrax, or Hepatitis with major public health education efforts. So why should we think that abandoning drugs education is sensible?

Educating thousands of people to quit smoking has had positive results. However its success was supported by changing and enforcing the law on smoking in public places, so forcing people to learn the facts about the dangers of smoking and helping them to quit.

It has taken well over 25 years to educate most drivers to accept that drinking and driving is unhealthy, anti-social and criminal. Public education and law changes together triggered this change in public behaviour.

It may be difficult to prove that drugs education works, but that should not stop us working harder to find the approaches that do work. Not to do so is to allow commercial enterprise to continue to avoid its responsibility to inform and educate the public of the dangers of misusing their products. It also fails to raise awareness of the dangers of illicit drug use

Targeting the most vulnerable with drugs education should be a priority

There would be real benefits to be gained by making special efforts to educate the most vulnerable children and young people about drugs, many of whom are to be found in the most deprived of communities. We should also be concentrating on those held in young offenders institutions and prisons. According to the Prisoner Survey (2011) approximately three-quarters of prisoners (73%) test positive for illegal drugs on admission to Scottish prisons. This should be a very high priority, especially if more unnecessary deaths are to be avoided.

Action parents can take

Parents should make enquiries at schools to find out what drugs education is being offered. Parents can do a lot to support schools in delivering the best drugs education possible. Where parents are not happy with what their children are receiving, they will need to find alternative resources on drugs education to support their children.

What about drugs education for older young people and parents? Since most of drugs education is aimed at school children – an age group where the least serious drug problems are recorded – it leaves a much larger group of the population, post-school children, older young people and adults, ill-educated about drugs. This is not a sensible approach when we look at the fact that 31% of adult men and 20% of adult women report having used drugs in their lifetime.

Most adults will have responsibility for children at some point in their lives. So educating adults about drugs is essential if we are to continue to help children avoid this problem.

Top-up drugs education

It is likely that even with the best drugs education, many children will have forgotten much of what they learned or they may not yet have been at an age where they could see it as relevant to their lives. So top-up drugs education for adults should be a very important part of the strategy for keeping people safe from the misuse of drugs. Those over 16 years of age are after all still the most likely group to come to harm from drug misuse.

Almost all drug related deaths in Scotland are in the 25-50+ age group, not children or young people. Of the 485 drugs-related deaths in 2010 it was found that 33% were aged between 25-34 and there had been a fall in the number of deaths in under 25s.

The most likely cause of death of anyone under 25 in Scotland is a road traffic accident where alcohol and sometimes drugs are involved.

Universities, colleges, work places youth projects, youth organis-ations, prisons and young offenders institutions are all places where there are opportunities for top-up drugs education. Good work has been done by Crew 2000 in Edinburgh in nightclubs, at music festivals and other public events, to keep young people informed. There is much more that should be done in work places.

Some of the heath information campaigns in the media do work and have had some success with this age group. There are however limitations to their success because much of the material is mainly shown on commercial television, in cinemas and through adverts on busses or taxis, so they miss out on some sections of the population. Since young people and adults are those most likely to be using all drugs, much more needs to be done to widen the range of oppor-tunities for educating them.

Mixing alcohol and cocaine is a good example of the need for urgent public education. This is a new trend that in a matter of 3-4 years has seen many young people and adults dying. Most of these particular drug-related deaths were not of people who would normally be seen as a typical problem drug user. They were people in pubs or partying with friends, who decided to try this particularly dangerous cocktail of drugs. **Of the 574 deaths in Scotland from drugs in 2008 there were 79 from cocaine often mixed with alcohol.** There were no such deaths recorded 4-5 years earlier.

Education is also urgently required when it comes to the new and lesser-known substances such as the 'legal highs'.

An important spin-off from adult drug education is that good, reliable research can be done, from those who are involved in this approach to drugs education, by gathering knowledge about new trends in drug use. This can be used to improve future work with this age group.

Drug education for parents has had little success, so far

Considering that most children do not smoke or use illicit drugs some credit must go to parents of these children. It may have been that as role models, their good example has worked or perhaps they were well enough informed to be able to not only discuss this with their children, but also that they successfully persuaded them not to start these unhealthy habits.

Parents are clearly a very important influence, along with schools, on how children view and understand drugs. The growing problem of alcohol misuse is clearly an area where parents have been less successful.

The confusion amongst parents about cannabis and other illicit drugs is well known. There is good reason to believe that if more parents were better educated about drugs, then in the long-term this would help their children and the whole nation. This reinforces the case for urgently finding ways to provide parents with the drugs education they need to support their families.

Such an idea is easier to wish for than to deliver because many parents are very resistant to attending drugs education sessions as they do not believe that this is an issue that affects their family. Other parents are worried about what others will think about them if they are seen attending such sessions – will people think that they must have a drug problem in their family? Many parents do not see smoking and drinking alcohol as being a drug problem. They are put off attending drugs education sessions by their limited understanding of what are the problem drugs.

Allowing for all of these difficulties, ways must be found to bring parents up-to-speed with the reality of drug misuse in our communities. Larger workplaces, churches, school parents groups and other opportunities should all be considered as places to start this very important work. Parents who are well educated in the drugs issue are better placed to pressurise politicians to make the necessary changes to protect us all.

Understanding the problem of drugs misuse for society

4.

KEY FACTS

- The reasons why children use drugs are no different from adults.

- Most drug deaths are from cocktails of drugs, not a single substance.

- There are now hundreds of drugs available to any of us within 15-30 minutes anywhere in the land.

- New drugs are now being bought on the internet and posted directly to people. Even drugs workers know almost nothing about these 'legal highs'.

- We live in a society that has come to believe that there is a magic pill to solve all our problems.

- Criminal and legitimate international businesses exist to meet the demands that we create.

- Legal substances such as tobacco and alcohol affect the lives of many more families in Scotland than illicit drugs do. Only about 6-7% of the population have an issue with illicit drugs.

- There is no quality control on illicit drugs, no instructions on how to use them and no come back to the sellers if they harm us.

What are drugs?

Drugs are any substance that can alter the chemistry of our bodies; they may alter our moods, change how we think or feel as well as altering our physical or mental states.

Drugs can make you feel high or low, full of energy or sleepy and lethargic. Drugs can calm you down or make you very anxious, nervous, or even paranoid.

Our physical state of health, the mood we are in, and our general state of mind when we take a drug can affect what a drug does to us.

Drugs are introduced into our bodies by sniffing, smoking,

swallowing, eating, drinking, or by injecting them. These different methods of administering a drug can alter how our body reacts to the drug, faster or slower. All of these factors can result in different outcomes, even from the same drugs, taken at different times.

The purity and dose of any substance can vary enormously so the consequences of using any drug can have very different effects on our bodies and minds. This is particularly true of illicit drugs.

Drugs that are prescribed by doctors are well tested before they are allowed to be prescribed for human use. They are supplied to us in the doses suitable for our age and our medical condition. If taken as prescribed these drugs should not harm us, although all drugs have some side effects. Read the notes accompanying any prescription drug – it may surprise you. They often list twenty or more possible side effects, all of these are constantly monitored nationally and internationally, to ensure that any dangerous effects are fed back to the manufacturers and to doctors. When a doctor offers you a prescription they should explain any known side effects and instruct you in what to do if you have adverse reactions. **No such duty of care applies to those selling illicit drugs or tobacco and alcohol.**

Some drugs are legally available
Some drugs are legally sanctioned by the government and available within certain controls. These include tobacco, alcohol, many herbal remedies and over-the-counter medicines from a chemist a super-market, a health food shop, or corner shop. We need to be cautious though, because if we are using these legally sanctioned drugs, in combination with prescribed, or illicit drugs, this can often cause us unexpected side effects. This is why it is important that your doctor must abide by a strict code of patient confidentiality, allowing you to share with them information about how much you smoke and drink, what illicit drugs you may take as well as any other health food supplements or medicines that might be important to know about. For example, weight lifters using excessive amounts of steroids risk serious blood pressure and heart problems, which can be fatal.

Most recorded drug deaths are from cocktails of drugs, not from the overdosing on one drug alone.
Today there are drugs available from market stalls, sex shops, back street traders and the internet. As one illicit drug goes out of fashion

or people believe that they are being short-changed, new ones are appearing called 'legal highs'. Only a few of them have so far had legal restrictions put on them. The minute they are brought under legal restrictions the formula for manufacturing them is changed to get around the law. These drugs are so new, and so uncommon, that very little is known about them. Some are legal substances such as gardening products, which nobody thought would ever be used by humans. Mephedrone is one of these new drugs, a plant fertiliser is another.

Children and young people are more vulnerable to harm from drugs
Adolescence is a time of physical, emotional, and intellectual development. It is during this time that our brains start to put in place the hard wiring that gives us much more control over our actions and behaviour. We don't for instance have much sexual feeling before puberty but then sexual awareness and behavour become active . It is true too that young males in particular seem to be quite reckless in their behaviour, doing highly risky things like driving fast cars or motor cycles, indulging in extreme sports and other things to seek thrills. This may be partly about their inexperience or because the areas of the brain that control their ability to assess risk are not yet fully developed. Because drugs can alter our emotional states and how much control we have of our bodies and minds they are a particular danger to growing children. For example, boy racers can be killed when driving under the influence of drink or drugs; young women can get pregnant when drunk.

Most children have little understanding of death. They do not always see the link between their behaviour and the possibility of ill-health and death. Fear of death in adolescence is very low, with children and young people believing that it will never happen to them, only to adults. This leads to many children taking serious risks with drugs, by binge drinking or mixing large quantities of a variety of drugs together, to show off or try to prove their superior drug knowledge to others. One recent fashion is the mixing of alcohol and cocaine, which has had fatal consequences for some people.

Buying drugs from an internet website and from abroad can be dangerous, as they come with no consumer protection standards, such as you would have from those supplied by shops or chemists.

Why do people use drugs?

History tells us that across the millennia, humans have used a variety of drugs for different social purposes. In ancient times, herbs and potions were used in religious rituals, or to psyche up warriors before going into battle. In religious orders, monks made alcoholic drinks to ward off diseases when the water supplies were unreliable. Buckfast Tonic Wine is one of the more recent examples of this. It is made by the monks of Buckfast Abbey in England. This strong alcoholic drink is heavily featured in excessive binge drinking in some of Scotland's poorest communities.

As the centuries have rolled on we see the use of drugs changing, from use in religious ceremonies, for rights of passage ceremonies for young men and women, to being part of community celebrations such as births, marriages, deaths and festivals.

In more recent centuries, tobacco, then alcohol were developed as commercial products. These industries have created a massive number of jobs, enormous profits for multi-national companies and a very steady, reliable stream of tax revenue for governments.

World travel has taken people to places where other drugs such as cannabis, heroin, cocaine and even poisonous frogs are the drugs of choice. In the last 50-60 years the sale of these substances has developed into an extremely lucrative international business. The only differences between that illicit trade and the government-sanctioned drugs – tobacco and alcohol – is that the government controls the quality of these substances. They also decide who can buy them and they gain enormous amounts of tax revenue from them.

UK tax take from tobacco in 2009 was £8.2 billion and from alcohol it was £5.7 billion making a total of £13.9 billion that year.

There is no quality control and no tax income from illicit drugs. The drug barons are criminals who have no interest in our health, it is of no concern to them that the rain forests are being destroyed to plant more areas to grow their drug supplies. These criminals are under nobody's control.

Even in a good year less than 5% of illicit drugs are captured by the police and customs officers in the UK. So part of the answer to why people use drugs is because they are there, and there is a massive profit to be made from them.

Who uses drugs?

There are now hundreds of drugs available in Britain. Drug use and misuse of all kinds is massive. From cradle to grave drugs are being used by children and adults. Self-medicating on drugs is almost a national pastime. So the answer to the question 'who uses drugs?' is simple – almost everyone. Remember that tobacco and alcohol are drugs along with the illicit substances and those produced for medicinal purposes.

There is nowhere in Britain that we cannot buy illicit drugs within 15-30 minutes, even on the remotest of Scottish islands, such as Barra, Shetland or Orkney. Ironically it will soon be harder to buy tobacco and alcohol in some communities, especially for those under the age of 21 or 25, as the new Scottish laws require ID for all sales.

I have run health workshops for children for over 30 years and listened to thousands of children and young people talking about their reasons for using drugs. It turns out that the reasons children give are no different from those that adults report.

For many it is just something they want to try for themselves or because they are bored. For others it is to combat problems or pain in their lives, such as abuse, emotional problems, physical pain or a poor social life. Some believe it boosts their confidence; makes them more creative, some just like the feelings they get. Others find it hard not to join in when their friends are using drugs. Some think that drugs will keep them slim or increase their muscles and give them athletic strength to compete in sports or work long hours without sleeping. For others drugs help them to sleep, to handle a bereavement or the stress in their lives.

Some drug use is about taking the human mind into realms they have never been to before. For some, using drugs is just a bit of fun, a good laugh and something that for them and their peer group is socially acceptable – even normal. This is especially true of alcohol, cannabis, ecstasy, speed, and cocaine use amongst young people.

The highest rates of drug misuse are amongst those living with the most poverty, where they have no hope of any way out of it.

Any of these reasons we may consider to be good or bad. Whatever our view is, the fact is that people today have come to believe, wrongly, that there is a magic pill out there to solve all our problems. Whole industries have been created to serve our insatiable appetite for drugs.

So what harm does drug use do?
Because of the massive scale of all drug use in society, it is inevitable that some people will over-indulge, becoming dependent and eventually become problem drug users.

Governments across the world are slowly accepting that drugs, legal and illicit, are here to stay. The cost of stopping people using drugs is escalating to such a level, that it is now economically more sensible for governments to concentrate on trying to control access to legal drugs and to go only after the big time illicit drug dealers, because every time the police pick up a street level dealer another quickly takes their place.

It is now more generally accepted that we need to provide appropriate ways to support and treat all those who need help with the drugs they are misusing.

Drug prevention helps to reduce the escalation of the problem
Prevention of misuse is so far mainly to do with tinkering with laws about sale and distribution or with police and customs activity to capture the supplies of illicit drugs.

Prevention is also about public education, to reduce the attraction of drugs, to protect children and the most vulnerable in society. All of these activities have mainly only addressed the use of illicit drugs and have allowed politicians to take their eye of the ball regarding the enormous problems of tobacco and alcohol misuse. This is at last starting to be addressed and there is a growing acceptance that the misuse of all drugs in society must be dealt with.

The biggest drug problem in Scotland and the UK is alcohol.

Main facts about alcohol, tobacco and other drugs

5.

Here are the basic facts that parents need to know about common drugs. The facts below could be used for a family quiz – a fun way to increase everyone's knowledge and understanding of drugs.

Main facts about smoking

facts

- When tobacco was first introduced to Britain in the middle of the sixteenth century, it was believed to be an amazing substance that could cure just about every ill known to man. We now know differently. 50% of smokers die from major cancers.

- The nicotine in tobacco is a stimulant.
  Stimulants speed up our hearts, make us hyper and high, minutes later the effect wears off and dumps us back down. Smokers don't like that state so they smoke more of the stimulant to get high again. This traps them in a circle of addiction to this stimulant, which continues until they stop using the drug.

- What else is in a cigarette?
  There are around 4,000 different chemicals and gasses to be found across the different brands of cigarettes. Would you buy your children sweets, drinks or food that you knew were loaded with so many unknown chemicals?

- Smoking has no known health benefits.

- You can smoke at any age.
  This is true, but you cannot buy tobacco products until you are 18 years of age. It used to be 16.

- The police can confiscate tobacco from those under the age of 16 and report them to their parents.

- How many smokers in Scotland?
  24.3% of the 16-74 age group still smoke.
  Around 30% of 16-24 year olds still smoke.
  Amongst 15 years olds, 11% of boys and 14% of girls are smokers. [SOURCE: SALUS 2010]

- Children become addicted to nicotine very soon after

starting to smoke. Around 3-4 cigarettes is enough to hook them in. It used to be thought that it took much longer.

- Smoking is a learned behaviour.
  We were not born to smoke. If we had been, we would have had a chimney in our heads to let the dangerous gasses out. We can, with the appropriate help, unlearn any bad habit such as smoking.

- Smoking does not calm you down.
  Tobacco is a stimulant drug so it cannot calm you down. Inhaling tobacco only calms down your craving for the nicotine and the other drugs in cigarettes.

- Smoking does not keep you slim.
  If you quit smoking you may put on some weight, this is partly because heavy smokers do not always eat well. Also, when we stop smoking our taste buds perk up again, so we enjoy food more.

- Smoking does not cure boredom.
  There is nothing in tobacco that cures boredom, but smokers come to associate their habit of using tobacco with the breaks in the day when they smoke. Non-smokers may have a coffee or tea in these breaks but that does not mean that these drinks cure their boredom. It is just escaping from a boring task that relieves the boredom.

- Passive smoking.
  Children living in homes where adults smoke have many more health problems such as glue ear, chest infections, asthma and sore throats. Leaving car windows open so you can smoke does not reduce the poisonous gasses inhaled by children in a car.

- Smokers are more likely to get cancer.
  Cancers of the mouth, throat, lungs as well as heart problems are all associated with heavy smoking. These are killer diseases. Smoking tobacco along with cannabis increases even more, the risk of getting all cancers.

- Public smoking controls.
  In March 2006 the Scottish Government banned smoking in all public places, this now applies across the UK and in many other countries. One of the good things to come from this is that fewer people now see smoking as a sociable activity associated with drinking alcohol.

Smoking Costs 2012

The table of costs of smoking is calculated on the average cost of cigarettes being £6.92 for a twenty pack of the most popular brands bought legally. Many cigarettes are now bought on the black market. One cigarette now costs 35p. The projected cost over ten years include an allowance of 6% per year for tax and other price rises.

Government tax on tobacco products is about 80% of the purchase price which would on average be £5.54 on a pack of twenty.

cigarettes smoked per day	cost per day	cost per week	cost per month	cost per one year	cost over 5 years	cost over 10 years	what you can buy for this
5	£1.75	£12.25	£53.23	£638.75	£3,611.49	£8,418.66	
10	£3.50	£24.50	£106.46	*£1,277.50	£7,201.38	£16,838.42	* cost of a holiday
15	£5.25	£36.75	£159.69	£1,916.25	£10,801.87	£25,257.08	
20	£7.00	£49.00	£212.92	*£2,555.00	£14,402.78	£33,676.97	* run a car for a year
25	£8.75	£61.75	£266.15	£3,193.75	£17,585.19	£42,095.63	
30	£10.50	£73.50	£319.38	£3,832.50	£21,603.76	£50,514.16	
40	£14.00	£98.00	£425.84	*£5,110,00	£28,805.56	£67,353.94	* pay towards a mortgage

- Tobacco advertising.
  Advertising of tobacco is no longer allowed except at the point of sale. This is to be changed soon when sales points will have to remove all advertising and fix curtains or shutters over the shelves to hide the packs of tobacco. The tobacco industry lost this battle in the courts. Plans are also in hand to plain wrap all tobacco packets, removing logos and branding.

- Cigarette machines.
  There are plans to ban the sales of tobacco from vending machines. The tobacco industry has lost this battle in court.

- Tolerance.
  Young smokers soon build up a tolerance to tobacco and need more to satisfy them.

- Smoking and pregnancy.
  Women are now advised that they should not smoke when trying to get pregnant and during their pregnancy.

- Tobacco and Cannabis.
  We do not know how many people smoke cannabis with, or without using tobacco. One cannabis roll-up is equivalent to 4-5 standard cigarettes, because of how it is smoked. The combined tobacco and cannabis smoke is sucked deeper into the lungs and held longer to maximise the effect. This causes additional damage to that already done by smoking tobacco alone.

- Smoking dumps droplets of tar into your lungs.
  Tar from tobacco smoke is propelled in tiny droplets into our lungs, where it solidifies and builds up in lumps in the lungs, so that eventually we cannot breathe properly.

- Dying from smoking.
  In 2004 there were 13,473 deaths from smoking in Scotland. That was 24% of all deaths. There are around 114,000 deaths from smoking in England and Wales each year.

- Cost of smoking.
  Cigarettes cost about 35p each. If you smoke 10 cigarettes a day it costs £24.50 per week, £106.46 per month and £1,277 in a year. Twenty a day costs £2,555 in a year.

- Tax on cigarettes.
  The tax on cigarettes is almost 80% of the cost. So £4 out of every £5 spent on cigarettes goes straight to the government in tax and only £1 to the tobacco companies.

- Quitting.
  Quitting smoking is the best thing a smoker can do to improve their health and that of their family.

- How addictive is tobacco?
  Nicotine, the main drug in cigarettes, is highly addictive but it is eliminated from our bodies in 3 weeks. This is probably why many people have managed to quit with very little help. The main reasons that people find it difficult to quit is psychological not physical addiction. So learning to convince your mind that you do not need tobacco is the key to success if you really do want to quit. There is plenty of help available to support quitters.

- Seek advice from your doctor or call:
  SMOKELINE Tel: 0800 84 84 84 (12 noon to 12pm) for information, advice, counselling and support to quit smoking.

Main facts, about alcohol

facts

- Alcohol has been produced and consumed for centuries in societies all over the world.

- Alcohol is classified as a depressant drug (a downer).

- Alcohol is a depressant drug, but this does not mean that it always makes us feel depressed. It is better to think of alcohol as a disinhibitor; it loosens off our inhibitions, causing us to lose control over our body and mind.

- You can drink alcohol from 5 years old. In the UK, you cannot give a child under 5 years of age alcohol, so although you may find this hard to believe – legally children can consume alcohol from 5 years of age.

- Alcohol at 14. A child can be in a licensed bar as long as they don't buy or drink alcohol.

- Alcohol at 16-17. If you are aged 16 or 17 you can legally drink cider, beer, table wine to drink along with a meal, in a licensed restaurant. You must be accompanied by someone over 18 who can buy the alcohol. Licencees always have the right to refuse anyone alcohol without stating why.

- At 18 you can drink what you like.

- The Scottish and UK governments are seriously considering increasing the age at which alcohol can be bought. Perhaps to 21 as is common in Canada, the USA and many other countries.

- Buying alcohol in off-licences and supermarkets.
  The laws noted above have not been changed. However new laws in 2011 require supermarkets and off-licences to ask for ID documents to verify the age of those under the age of 26. Many bars and restaurants also demand ID from young people.

- Alcohol is a very powerful drug.
  Yes it is a drug, it has the potential to cause great harm if misused. Alcohol-related harm is costing the Scottish economy £2.25 billion a year.

- Alcohol-related deaths.
  In Scotland) there were 1,282 alcohol-related deaths in 2009. In 2010 it was established that 1 in 20 deaths in Scotland are alcohol related.

- Alcohol, like any drug taken in large quantities, will poison you. If you drink a large amount of alcohol you will get sick and may damage vital organs in your body, including your brain. Alcohol poisoning is one of the officially recorded categories of death.

- Tolerance to any drug increases our consumption. Our bodies gets accustomed to drinking alcohol, so we build up a tolerance to it. This is not a good thing. As our tolerance of alcohol increases, so do all the side effects you don't want; getting fat, finding you need more alcohol to get the effects you had when you drank less, spending more of your cash and falling out with friends and family.

- Drink safely – understand what units of alcohol are. Units of alcohol are an easy way of understanding how much we drink. On average, in a fit fully grown adult, it takes one hour for one unit of alcohol to leave the body, e.g. a bottle of Buckfast has 11.3 units of alcohol; a bottle of spirits like vodka has 27 units; Alcopops have 1.4 to 1.7 units, pint of beer (575 ml) at 4% is 2.3 units of alcohol. The government recommends that women consume no more than 14 units of alcohol each week, with two days alcohol free. Men should consume no more than 21 units with two alcohol free days.

- How many units of alcohol are in the drinks you like. Multiply the volume of the drink (mls) X the % of alcohol and then divide that by 1000 e.g. Buckfast 750mls X 15% alcohol divided by 1000 = 11.3 units of alcohol. So it will take 11 hours for all these units to leave the body.

- Alcohol affects our moods. If you are in a happy high mood it will make you feel good. If you are in a stressed out, anxious, low mood, or are feeling angry or depressed, then it will pick up this mood, making you feel worse. If you are someone who tends towards low moods and depression, alcohol is not a drug that will do you any good. This drug tends to pick up our personality traits and multiplies up the strong and negative aspects of them.

- Female bodies cannot process alcohol as well as male bodies. The reason for this is because females have less water in their bodies to dilute the alcohol. Females who drink like males damage their health more quickly than males. Men have 62% and women 52% of water in their bodies.

- Children are not adults.
  Humans are not physically fully grown until they are about 19 years of age. Our brains are not fully developed until at least 21 years of age. The earlier in life we use all drugs the higher the risk of us developing problems with them.

- Alcohol and brain damage.
  Heavy drinking of alcohol can prevent our brains from developing fully. This explains why babies born to mums who drink heavily during pregnancy can suffer physical and mental damage from Foetal Alcohol Syndrome. Problem drinkers (alcoholics) can suffer from diminished brain function.

- Alcohol is very high in both sugar and calories.
  If you are concerned about your weight, you need to think about how much alcohol you drink.

- Drinking alcohol makes you pee a lot.
  Alcohol causes dehydration which means that your body does not have enough water to keep you healthy. Every cell in the human body needs a large amount of water to function well.

- Free water in licensed premises.
  Drinking water between alcoholic drinks will save you money and reduce your chances of having a hangover. In 2010 law changes in Scotland support the idea of drinking water regularly when you consume alcohol. If you ask for it you must be given free water in any licensed premises, including licensed restaurants. You do not have to pay for tap water only the bottled varieties. **You would be doing our nation a great favour if you encourage others to speak up and ask for free water in licensed premises.**

- A hangover is your body telling you that you have had too much alcohol. In this state you are both dehydrated and poisoned, so your body needs help. A pint of water before you go to bed and a good night's sleep are the only reliable cures. No – Irn Bru, hot sweet drinks, a fry-up or more alcohol will not help, nor does fresh air or jogging round the block.

- Heavy drinking of alcohol does not improve our sex lives. Drinking small amounts of alcohol can make us more confident and relaxed, so may improve our chances of having sex with someone. Loading up on alcohol makes males lose their sexual function (brewer's droop) and many young women get pregnant when they are drunk. Both sexes risk picking up sexually transmitted diseases when drunk.

alcohol's route through the body

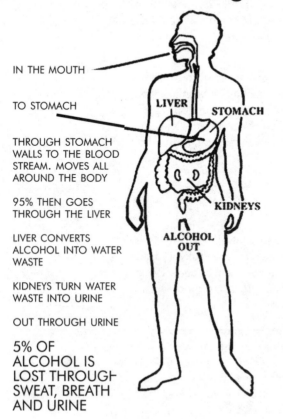

IN THE MOUTH

TO STOMACH

THROUGH STOMACH
WALLS TO THE BLOOD
STREAM. MOVES ALL
AROUND THE BODY

95% THEN GOES
THROUGH THE LIVER

LIVER CONVERTS
ALCOHOL INTO WATER
WASTE

KIDNEYS TURN WATER
WASTE INTO URINE

OUT THROUGH URINE

5% OF
ALCOHOL IS
LOST THROUGH
SWEAT, BREATH
AND URINE

LIVER

STOMACH

KIDNEYS

ALCOHOL
OUT

The chart shows the
route taken by alcohol
from the mouth to the
stomach and from there
it is absorbed very
quickly into the
bloodstream and then
moves all around the
body.

The diagram shows approximately
the areas of the brain where different
activities occur. The area of the brain
which controls our automatic
functions is hidden deep in our heads
to protect it from damage. When
alcohol is consumed it affects all the
brain activities noted on the chart.
When we binge on massive doses of
alcohol it can literally shut down the
area of the brain that controls our
automatic functions and so kill us.

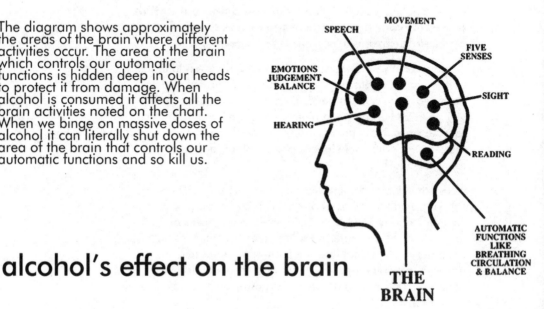

SPEECH

MOVEMENT

FIVE
SENSES

EMOTIONS
JUDGEMENT
BALANCE

SIGHT

HEARING

READING

AUTOMATIC
FUNCTIONS
LIKE
BREATHING
CIRCULATION
& BALANCE

alcohol's effect on the brain

THE
BRAIN

HOW MUCH IS TOO MUCH?

Alcohol has different effects on different people, but as a general guide, these maximum weekly limits are advised for least risk to your health:

alcohol limits

It is best to have two alcohol free days in the week to allow the liver to recover. Readers will often see the units expressed as daily totals of 2-3 units for women and 3-4 units for men. That could be seen as being 21 units for a woman and 28 for a man in a week, including two alcohol free days, which is not what the government intended. It is best to stick with 14 and 21 units.

ADULT WOMEN UP TO... **14** UNITS
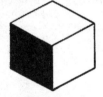
PER WEEK

ADULT MEN UP TO... **21** UNITS

PER WEEK

THESE LIMITS ARE FOR AVERAGE BUILD ADULTS

BUT NOT ALL ON ONE NIGHT!

alcohol low risk/ high risk

It is important to understand that as we push up our weekly intake of alcohol we also increase the harm we are doing to our bodies.

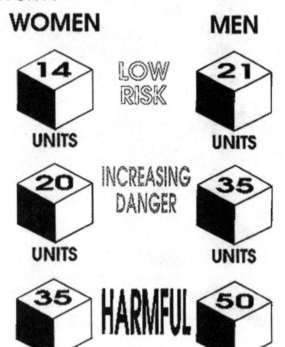

WOMEN — MEN

14 UNITS — LOW RISK — 21 UNITS

20 UNITS — INCREASING DANGER — 35 UNITS

35 UNITS — HARMFUL — 50 UNITS

alcohol
effects / reactions

The chart should be read down the left side first. It is a good way to remind ourselves that as we consume more alcohol things can easily go from a nice controllable situation to one that puts us in great danger.

The notes on the right side of the chart offers some other useful tips.

LOOSENING UP
You start to feel relaxed, loosened up. Alcohol is putting to sleep the parts of your brain that control your behaviour. You feel less inhibited.

RELAXED
Feeling merrier or sadder.
Acting louder than usual.
Judgement gets weaker.
The accident risk increases.
Now in the danger zone for driving.

WOBBLY
Ability to make sensible choices is fading. You find yourself doing or saying things you later regret. Walking and talking becomes more difficult.

MEMORY LOSS
Next morning and you can't remember what you did. Speech is probably slurred. You can't walk or see straight.

LEGLESS
You may not have passed out yet, but you're very near to it.

COMA
Alcohol starts to affect some of the body's basic functions that keep you alive – your breathing and heartbeat. Body slips into a coma.
Drinking to this stage can be fatal.

WHY EACH OF US CAN HAVE DIFFERENT REACTIONS TO ALCOHOL

SEX
Women are more strongly affected because their bodies have more fat and less water to dilute the alcohol.

WEIGHT
A lighter person will be more strongly affected – less water content in the smaller body.

BODY CONDITION
A fat person will be more affected than a lean, muscular person – more muscle, less body fat.

THE SPEED YOU DRINK
If you drink quickly the build-up of alcohol in the body will produce a stronger immediate effect.

YOUR AGE
Young and old people tend to have a lower tolerance to alcohol.

DRINKING HABITS
People who don't drink regularly are more strongly affected by alcohol.

FOOD
If you eat before you go drinking then that fills up your stomach and slows down the passage of alcohol.

FIZZY DRINKS
Fizzy drinks affect you more quickly – the carbon dioxide forces the alcohol through your bloodstream.

- Alcohol does not solve our problems.
  It is not a good idea to use drugs, not prescribed by a doctor, to sort out our problems. Alcohol is never prescribed by doctors to solve a patient's problems. There are better ways to deal with such worries. Talking to trusted friends, phoning helplines, talking to our family or professional counsellors are much safer solutions.

- Mixing of alcohol with other drugs is dangerous.
  Some drugs make you high, others bring you down and some make you feel a bit out of your mind (trippy). Mixing uppers with uppers, uppers with downers or any other combination can have effects you did not plan for. Remember you cannot be sure of what is in any illicit drug nor its strength.

- Mixing alcohol (downer) and cocaine (upper) is particularly dangerous as the cocaine stops you from feeling drunk, and because of this you may drink more than you intended. Your body then generates a third and more dangerous drug (cocaethylene) that can cause fatal heart attacks.

- Some medicines prescribed by your doctor should not be mixed with alcohol. Cocktails of drugs, including alcohol, are often the cause of accidental deaths and suicides.

- For help with an alcohol problem contact:
  Drinkline Scotland
  Helpline 0800 7314 314
  Available 24 hours.
  Free from landlines and call boxes, but some mobile services may charge.
  Provides information on alcohol use and misuse, and where to find suitable sources of help in Scotland.

  Drinkline UK
  Helpline 0800 917 82 82 (Freephone).
  Available 24 hours

Main facts about illicit drugs

Having covered the main information you need on tobacco and alcohol we now look at illicit drugs. This is a much more complex story as the range of drugs covered are enormous and growing by the day. Fuller details of the most commonly used legal and illicit drugs are in chapter 8.

- The Law. [Laws on illicit drugs are very complex so are covered fully in the chapter 7] Unlike tobacco or alcohol the Dangerous Drugs Acts do not have any reference to children or the ages of anyone who might use them. The Dangerous Drugs Acts cover a range of drugs which are classified in three groupings, A, B and C. Group A is the most dangerous. The acts include a variety of penalties from fines to imprisonment, for possession or selling these drugs.

- Cannabis is now reclassified as a class 'B' drug. Cannabis was reclassified twice in recent times, causing great confusion. Its classification moved down to class 'C' and then two years later back up to its original class 'B' rating. This was because the quality and strength of cannabis changed quite considerably over a very short time. Serious concerns were raised about major mental health problems arising from the stronger and different types of cannabis now commonly available.

- Illicit drugs what are they?
  These are the hundreds of substances sold illegally by street dealers and on the internet. They can be prescribed medicines, or copies of them, and a whole variety of plant material and chemicals which have been turned into drugs that can alter our states of mind.

- Illicit drugs and brain damage.
  Misusing illicit drugs can cause damage to our bodies and the wiring up of our brains. We do not yet know enough about this to advise people well on how much damage they might do. Some drugs are known to trigger mental health problems or to make these problems worse. Anyone who has a diagnosed mental health problem is strongly advised not to dabble with illicit drugs, as they often make their condition worse.

Myth: Cannabis and acid cause schizophrenia.

Fact: Whilst it is true that people diagnosed with this form of mental illness can make their condition worse by using a range of illicit drugs, there is no definite proof that these drugs actually cause the condition. The confusion around this arises because schizophrenia is often diagnosed in the mid-to-late teens – a time when many young people are already experimenting with drugs.

- Using drugs not prescribed to you can damage your body and mind. Doctors only prescribe drugs that our medical condition requires. What they prescribe has been rigorously tested for side effects, especially if drugs are to be mixed with others. Using prescription drugs such as Valium, along with illicit drugs like cannabis, speed or ecstasy and alcohol, risks damage to mental and physical health.

- We can never be sure what is in illicit drugs.
  Illicit drugs can have good and bad effects on us. They may contain combinations of all sorts of things, including dangerous contaminants. Anthrax, an often deadly infection, was found in heroin in Scotland in 2010.

- Illicit drugs are about profit not a child's health.
  Illicit drug dealers are not qualified chemists, they are not licensed to dispense drugs. The dealers at street level are the last link in a very long supply line with people all along the line tampering with their supplies to maximise their profit. Often mixing in other drugs or cheap chemicals or waste from vegetation to increase the weight of the drugs to sell more. Their only interest is in making as much money as possible, not the user's safety.

- Deaths from illicit drugs in Scotland.
  There were 485 drug-related deaths in 2010. This is much less than many people think compared with the smoking- and alcohol-related deaths. Most of those who died were in the 25-54 age group and not children or young people.

- There are three main groups of illicit drugs.
  Uppers (stimulants)
  They increase blood pressure, speed up the heart, make it hard to sleep, make us hyper, we talk very fast, the pupils of our eyes open wide. When they wear off we feel depressed, down, agitated, you will want more of the drugs to get you going again. Tobacco, speed, cocaine and crack are four stimulants.

  Downers (depressants, opiates and pain killers)
  They slow down our hearts, make us sleepy, the pupils of our eyes get tiny, our breathing slows down, we may not care about things in our life such as studying or meeting our friends. Alcohol, heroin and methadone are depressants.

Hallucinogens (psychedelics, trippy drugs)
They alter how our mind understands things. We see, hear and feel things differently, we may be confused, it can be scary, we may feel paranoid or anxious and upset. You can get flashbacks months later without using the drug again. Cannabis, acid, LSD and ecstasy are hallucinogens.

- 'Legal Highs'.
  In 2009 new illicit substances called 'legal highs' arrived in the UK. They are often bought on the internet and the dealers give the impression that these are safe products for gardening or other purposes. They know only too well that the dangerous myths they have created about their great effects on the internet, Facebook, Twitter or to mobiles ensures their sales and profits. Very little is known about these substances, except that there have already been fatalities in Britain. One of the drugs, mephedrone has been included in the Dangerous Drugs Acts, but there are so many of these drugs around it will take years for legal restrictions to be enforced. The producers of these drugs just change the contents slightly as soon as they are made illegal. Using these drugs is foolhardy as nobody really knows what is in them. [If in doubt consult one of the recommended websites in chapter 10]

- How a drug affects us depends on three important factors.
  The drug.
  How it is used, e.g. smoked, injected, sniffed.
  The circumstances in which it is used, e.g. our mood, our experience of using it.

The following example explains this. If someone drinks large amounts of alcohol (the drug) when they are on their own (how it is used) and in a depressed state of mind (the circumstances), the alcohol will pick up their low mood and they may become even more seriously depressed. Perhaps even suicidal.

If on the other hand, someone chooses occasionally to use a small amount of cannabis (the drug) using a water pipe, with no tobacco (how it is used) with a group of experienced cannabis users who are in a calm happy state of mind (the circumstances), they will most probably come to little harm.

If someone is drinking large amounts of alcohol (the drug) and they also mix it with cocaine (how it is used) in a hot club dancing all night (the circumstances), the cocktail of drugs could cause heart failure.

- Tolerance, Dependence and Problem Drug Use (addiction)
Tolerance to drugs means that as your body gets used to using a drug, you need more of the drug to get the same effects as earlier use. Alcohol drinkers will be aware that when they first drank they got drunk on very little alcohol, but as they get older they can consume far larger quantities. That is what is meant by tolerance to a drug.

  Dependence on drugs means that as you develop a strong liking to a drug, from using it more often, you find that you are becoming dependent on the drug to feel good. You may feel that you could give up the drug if you wanted to, but using the drug has become a very strong psychological crutch.

  Problem Drug Use (addiction) means that you crave for the drugs you use every minute of the day and night. Your life is overwhelmed by a strong physical or psychological craving. Life is dominated by the drug use. You will feel miserable if you cannot have the drug regularly. People in such states may resort to criminal activities to get money for their drugs.

- How long do drugs stay in your body?
Different drugs remain in our body for different lengths of time, varying from a few hours to several days. So using drugs at the weekend can affect how we feel and behave during the following week. See chart with list of drugs and length of time to leave the body on page 222.

- Where to get help if your think you have a drug problem.
Your own doctor. If you feel able to, you should seek the advice of a doctor. Doctors are bound by a strict code of confidentiality and are there to support you to find the help you need.

  The following organisations all offer confidential help and advice. [See chapter 10 for more.]

  www.knowthescore.info or Tel: 0800 587 5879 (Scotland only)
This helpline will help you to find the help you need. It includes an A-Z of drugs. It is particularly important to consult them if you want to be sure that the advice includes Scottish law.

  www.talktofrank.com or Tel: 0800 77 66 00
This is the drugs helpline for England and Wales only. They can help find the help you need in your area. The site includes an A-Z of drugs.

6. Why do children take drugs?

KEY FACTS

- There are now more girls than boys starting to smoke.

- By age 15 the majority of children will have some experience of alcohol.

- By 18 years of age 90% of males and 86% of females drink alcohol.

- Cannabis is the most popular illicit drug used in Scotland and the UK.

- Two-thirds of children under the age of 16, in Scotland, do not use illicit drugs.

- In adolescence it is normal for children to experiment with a variety of substances as well as many other potentially dangerous activities.

- It is very rare for children under 18 to die from drug misuse.

- Ignorance about drugs is what can harm and kill children.

- The reasons that children take drugs are no different from why adults take them.

- Children, like adults, use drugs because they are available.

- Peer pressure is only one of many reasons for children using drugs.

- There is a demand for drugs, so there is an opportunity for big profits.

Drugs are common in our society

I am repeating here some of what I said earlier because I am aware that some readers may skip chapters and I consider these points are important to understanding why children take drugs.

For centuries drugs have been used in every society for healing; for fun, for religious ritual, to induce mental states such as fearlessness in fighting wars or to hunt animals for food, to have an out-of-the-normal mental experience or to ease the burden of everyday living.

Children today are living in a society where drug use is so common that it would be extraordinary if they did not at some point in their lives, from childhood through their adolescence into adulthood, use drugs for one reason or another.

All drugs are big, big business

If you add together the businesses across the world that make, market and sell chemical substances, drugs to you and me, they now amount to almost the biggest item of world trade. The legal drugs businesses include prescribed medicines, herbal remedies, homeopathic remedies, over-the-counter medicines, food supplements, health foods, power drinks, tobacco and alcohol.

If you then add to that list the illicit substances such as cannabis, heroin, cocaine and the more recent 'legal highs', the drugs available to children as well as adults number hundreds if not thousands. New ones are added constantly and are seldom removed from the list.

There are now more girls than boys starting to smoke.
Girls think it keeps them slim, is a cool adult thing to do and that it de-stresses them. They also believe that if they smoke in pregnancy they will have smaller babies so birth will not be so painful.

Some boys hate the smell of tobacco, think smoking is effeminate and have understood the message that you cannot train for activities such as football and be a smoker. The main reasons for boys smoking is that they too think it adult and cool, believe it calms them down and because they want to use tobacco along with cannabis.

To understand how illicit drugs can get to your children, you need to understand the scale of this industry across the world. The Scots are said to be amongst the highest users of illicit drugs in the world and the biggest consumers of cocaine. Scotland and the UK is an island. It has thousands of miles of coastline open to smugglers. The base materials and plants for illicit drugs are grown in places like Afghanistan, South America, and Columbia. They are often the subsistence crops of very poor farmers, who have no other crop to grow and sell to feed their families. The world's most important rain forests are being cut down and devastated to clear more land for the growing of coca, cannabis, and opium poppies for heroin. These source plants, for which the poorest of farmers get paid a few pence, earn millions of pounds as they pass on their way through the criminal drug cartels across the world. Moving through Africa, Central Europe and through well-established distribution routes such as Holland to arrive on our streets. Some other routes for these drugs include Russia and the Middle East.

As these drugs are all sold by weight, the easiest way to increase their profit is simply to adulterate the drugs with any substance you can lay your hands on. Chalk, dust, ground-down glass and many more substances are used in this process.

There is no quality control on illicit drugs; the buyer can never know what they are buying. Purity can range from 1-2% up to 8-10% or higher. Some illicit drugs contain nothing at all that could be called a drug, just waste vegetable matter.

myths & facts

Myth: Children say they take 5 or 10 ecstasy at once to get the best buzz.

Fact: If these drugs were ecstacy (MDMA), the real stuff, there would have been thousands of deaths from ecstasy. It averages less than 10 deaths a year in Scotland. The good news is that ecstasy is now going out of fashion because young people have at last started to realise that the dealers are ripping them off, selling them rubbish.

As fast as one illicit drug goes out of fashion others emerge to take their place. Even the best-trained drugs worker has a job keeping up with the latest trends. So parents will never be experts in the drugs that their children may take. Parents can however be vigilant and keep searching on reliable websites and read more of the reliable information on what is happening in the world of drugs that could affect their children.

myths & facts

Myth: I am not a smoker I only use cannabis.

Fact: Many children do not see themselves as smokers because they only smoke tobacco along with cannabis. Some do so very heavily. In time many become regular smokers of tobacco.

So why do children use drugs?

There are many theories about why we Scots and the UK are such heavy consumers of drugs of all kinds. One reason may be that we live high in the northern hemisphere where it is cold and dark for much of the year, we get less sunshine and less hot weather which would allow us to be outdoors in the light, than those in Australia or living nearer the Equator. There is some evidence that the further north you go in the world, the higher the number of people suffering from depression, committing suicide and abusing all substances. If you have ever been on holiday in a really hot country you will know that water and soft drinks are what you want to drink, not alcohol. Hence the lower consumption of that drug in most hot countries.

There is little we can do about living in the wrong place, unless we can afford to move to warmer climes. However we can look at ways of dealing with our climate and creating a culture that would be less dependent on drugs to keep us happy.

There is a demand for drugs, so there is a market opportunity

The fact is that those selling all drugs, legal or illicit, have a great market in Scotland and the UK because in our culture we seem to seek solace by getting out-of-our-faces on drink, or by retreating into heroin-induced sleep, instead of confronting our problems and anxieties. The demand is there, big profits are there to be made, so the business will continue until the demand is reduced. Capturing the supplies of illicit drugs has proved to be almost a waste of time as so few of them are ever found. At best 5% of illicit drugs are captured in police and customs activities.

Changing our culture through effective drugs education, finding ways to reduce the stress that people are under, and treating stress and mental ill-health quickly and effectively is likely to result in far fewer children or adults turning to drugs in the future.

Tobacco is coming under control

The damage that the tobacco industry has done in the past to our nation's health is now being addressed by more effective laws, strong implementation of these laws, public education, and a variety of programmes to help people quit this dangerous drug habit.

Alcohol is also starting to be controlled better

Using the same approaches as have been used against tobacco has led to new legislation to ensure that those who hold licences to sell alcohol are trained to know its dangers and to sell the product more responsibly. Public education about alcohol is very far from effective. The cost of alcohol needs to be increased to reduce demand. The laws on when children can use alcohol need to be radically revised to protect them from harm. Far more needs to be done to support those with an alcohol problem to find a cure to their problem drinking.

The illicit drugs trade is out of control

Unlike tobacco and alcohol there are no government licences issued to anyone to sell illicit drugs. The international illicit drugs trade ignores all attempts at law enforcement. **No government in the world has so far succeeded in substantially reducing the flow of**

illicit drugs into their country. At best they have managed to move the problem to some other country.

This out-of-control international business operates 24/7 with no quality controls, no health advice to users and no come-back to them, if they get hurt or killed. They pay no tax, they have no public liability insurance for you to claim against and certainly no annoying call centre to call customer services if you have a complaint about their products.

The dealers of illicit drugs in our communities are often problem drug users themselves, who are trying to pay for their own habit.

They do not know what they are buying, so they most certainly do not know what they are selling. The contaminated heroin in 2010 that spread Anthrax, caused 26 deaths and is an extreme example of this.

Even the so-called experts get it wrong
Police advice in England to the government that cannabis should be class 'C' instead of 'B' was based on their intelligence that suggested that the purity of the drug was very low. They then had to re-advise the government when new strains of cannabis, 'skunk' hit the streets. It seemed to be very much stronger, so the police then had to frantically campaign to get the government to further reclassify cannabis, within two years, back to class 'B'. As I write the word on the street is that 'skunk' is not what it was two years ago, that it is not very pure or strong. All of this illustrates the unreliability of all illicit drugs. Even the same local batch of what is sold as the same drug, from the same dealer, can vary enormously.

The BBC Scotland programme, *Avalanche: Scotland's Cocaine Epidemic* of 4/02/10 gave a graphic account of how Scots have become the biggest users of cocaine in the world. The country has been targeted by criminal gangs who have been driven out of America and seek new and more lucrative markets to sell this extremely dangerous drug.

When the trade is driven out of one community, or one country it soon finds new opportunities in others.

New and much more effective efforts by the customs, police and others are now targeting the sources of cash that funds these businesses. That strategy is likely to have much more success, as it will dry up the funds for criminals to use to cheaply bulk-buy their drugs.

Gordon Meldrum, the Director General of the Scottish Crime and Drugs Enforcement Agency (SCEDEA) featured in the BBC *Avalanche* programme. He made it clear that **'along with enforcement, public education was the other most important action that we could take against the illicit drugs trade'.**

The range of drugs on offer expands by the day. Twenty years ago there were about 20-30 commonly available illicit drugs in Scotland. Today there are hundreds of different substances on sale to children.

The new trend of buying the so-called 'legal highs' from the internet makes the whole drug scene even more difficult to control than it was.

What are 'legal highs'?
They can be herbal remedies, plant materials, gardening products, fungi and herbs. Although the buyers of these products are often advised that the substances are not for human consumption, the myths that have already been generated around these drugs drive people's curiosity to have a go. The marketing on these websites is very cool and often better understood by young people than adults. They are also brazen in their misinformation, giving the impression that herbs and plant products are safer than illicit drugs. They do not mention that heroin comes from the poppy plant and cannabis from another plant.

Because something is natural, coming from a plant does not make it safe. One website has adverts for 'Herbal Viagra, natural herb product based on Viagra'. Another for a 'Room Odoriser, it is "what we used to call poppers".' [Poppers are Amyl Nitrate a drug that can damage our immune system.]

Little is known about 'legal highs'. There are no laws in place to control them. Drugs workers and medical experts in the field of drug use have no idea what if any effect these substances may have if taken on their own. It may be good or bad! We know even less about what will happen if someone mixes these substances with other drugs, such as alcohol, tobacco, cannabis, heroin or cocaine. There is little reliable research to tell us about these new substances so that it is not possible to advise people confidently about them. They may even be harmless, who knows?

Drugs can kill or cure

All drugs have the potential to kill or cure. We can for instance easily overdose on aspirin or paracetamol, which is why they are now sold in much smaller quantities than they used to be.

Children under 18 seldom die from drug use. Some of the very few deaths in children under the age of 18, from drug use, are from solvents such as glues, petrol, cleaning materials and even gas lighter fuel. A very small number of deaths in children have happened when children used prescribed medicines, including methadone and strong sleeping pills. Some babies are born damaged by drugs because of their mothers' use of tobacco, alcohol or drugs. Very, very occasionally, drugs prescribed by doctors to children have adverse effects, which can be disabling or fatal. Thalidomide is one example. Mistakes in the doses of drugs given to children have also led to serious health problems or deaths.

Lies told through drugs education!

Too much of drugs education of the past has made a big play on the idea that drugs kill children. The facts tell a different story so we should not use that argument to con children out of using drugs. If you ask children how many deaths they think happen from taking ecstasy they will tell you it is hundreds or thousands. No, it is not even hundreds in a year in the UK. There has never been more than 10 ecstasy deaths in a year in Scotland. It has averaged around one death per year over the last two decades.

Of the 485 drug-related deaths recorded in Scotland in 2010 it was found that 33% were aged between 25-34. The fastest rise in deaths was of those aged 35-54. There was a fall in deaths under the age of 25.

Useless children's remedies, still on the shelves

Research has shown that many of the commonly used, over-the-counter remedies for children's illnesses, such as coughs, high fever, runny noses and the likes are useless and could in fact do harm to children.

In 2010, the UK government issued a statement about this and said that they were going to ask high street chemists to advise parents. The government later abandoned this idea. No surprise in that, as it was asking these businesses to cut some of their most profitable lines. Only a government ban on these products will resolve this if they are serious about it. Clearly they are not and the vested interests of the drugs industry has won the day and kept these useless but profitable lines.

Unless we are ill we don't need drugs

The human body and mind needs fuel to make it function and to keep it healthy. The fuel we need should come from our diet, from the air we breathe and even from the sun. These natural resources provide us with all the essential proteins, nutrients and vitamins that we need to keep us alive. In a sense our body is just like one big chemist shop, it uses the fuel that we put into it, to give us all the energy we need to function, as well as giving us the materials that we need to repair the damage we do to ourselves. A healthy diet and the right amount of exercise are what is needed to live a long and healthy life. We can survive for a long time without food but we will die very quickly if we do not have water.

Drugs such as alcohol and ecstasy can cause serious dehydration, which can be fatal if not treated fast enough.

A child is not an adult – so drugs can damage them as they grow. We are not fully grown, physically, until about the age of 19. Our brains are not fully wired-up until a bit later, about the age of 21. Some recent research from Australia suggest that male brains may not be fully mature until much later, perhaps around 25 years of age.

We should be particularly concerned about the possible damage that can happen to children under the age of 25, who are exposed to a whole range of drugs from an early age. We really do not know enough about how drugs used by children may retard and damage the final stages of the development of their brains. Nor has enough work been done yet on understanding human growth, but it is very likely that such early life drug use may prevent the final development of a growing child's brain.

Attention Deficit Disorder (ADD)
and Attention Deficit Hyperactivity Disorder (ADHD)
This a growing problem amongst children and adults. Some of the research into this very debilitating condition has found that the viewing of 2 hours or more of television or allowing children to view a computer screen for hours whilst playing games, can lead to very young children developing this disorder. Many over-stressed, tired, and busy parents think nothing of leaving their young children in front of a television or computer. This electronic baby sitting is clearly not something we should be doing now that there is evidence that it may be damaging the minds of children.

Babies born to mothers who continue to smoke and drink heavily during their pregnancy can be born with a variety of problems. Foetal Alcohol Syndrome is a well-known result of this. There are similar problems for babies born to illicit drug users. The damage can include reduced brain size, damaged mental function, reduced ability to learn as well as physical damage such as limb malformations.

Clearly putting large doses of chemicals into our bodies, which they don't need, can tip the chemical balance of our bodies and minds. This can cause us to have physical and mental imbalances that could lead to serious ill-health. These physical and mental health problems can mess up our relationships, affect our ability to sleep, to work, to concentrate on intellectual tasks, to control our emotions or to think clearly. They can also prevent us from performing what should be normal daily tasks such as playing, studying, working or generally enjoying our lives to the full.

Keeping children as drug free as possible has got to be a priority
So surely it makes sense for any parent to do all that they can to ensure that there are no chemicals, drugs, or other substances going into their children that are not necessary. This book has already covered a lot about this earlier in your role as parents. A parent's task is not an easy one as there is so much profit to make from food,

drinks, sweets and other products that are likely to be consumed by your children. Never forget that just because there are laws in place to control the sales of substances including food and drink, it does not mean that these products are free from harmful substances. These laws are constantly exploited and can become unfit for purpose.

Banning tonic wines and heavily caffeinated drinks!

There have been attempts by politicians to curb the sales or ban the sale of Buckfast, as it is so heavily consumed by young drinkers. This is a sweet sherry-type of wine, containing 15% of alcohol per volume. One bottle contains 11.3 units of alcohol. It is marketed as a 'Tonic Wine made by the Monks of Buckfast Abbey'. The fact is that after much anti-Buckfast campaigning, it is still the drink of choice for thousands of young drinkers, but the marketing now states on the label that it is 'high in caffeine'. Caffeine is a stimulant drug that in this case is mixed with the downer drug alcohol, all in the one bottle.

The mixture of cocaine (stimulant) and alcohol (downer) by adults is causing many deaths in Scotland. There are no laws yet in place to reduce the amount of caffeine that can be in drinks sold to adults let alone children.

I already mentioned the government concerns about over-the-counter children's medicines, also that the law on tobacco does not prevent a child from smoking, only from buying tobacco products. The law on alcohol allows the consumption of alcohol from the age of 5. Yet there is now new research which is suggesting that we should not give any alcohol at all to anyone under the age of 15. Energy drinks often contain high doses of caffeine, a stimulant drug, which can make children stay awake or be very hyper.

Why children use drugs, is not very different from why adults use them

For some children their parents or siblings use a particular drug like tobacco, alcohol or cannabis and then offer them some. Perhaps children are curious and want to try drugs for fun, to keep in with their friends, because they think they will make them more confident, less shy or less scared to do adventurous things. They may be having problems with sleep or with concentrating on study or reading. They may just enjoy the thrill of doing something illegal or a bit naughty or think that using drugs will make them a better dancer or driver. They may want to change their body to make it slimmer or fatter and believe that drugs are the easy solution. Some children even think that using drugs will make them sexier or better at sex. If you think hard enough about it you can probably add to this list your own reasons for using or for avoiding using drugs.

I've done sex and got the 'T' shirt!

In my health workshops with children I have heard it said many times by 16-18 year olds, 'I have done sex'. Meaning that it is old hat and not a big deal. They then go on to say 'drinking or drugs is better than sex'. How sad is that?

Sex education is not just about avoiding pregnancy or sexual diseases, it is about how having a better sex life would be a healthier social activity for young people than the drink and drugs that they throw down their throats. Unfortunately in our society we are so inhibited about sex that all attempts to improve sex education in the way I describe have so far been thwarted by campaigning parents and some of the churches.

So why is using drugs a big problem for children?

Ignorance of what drugs are and what they can do to our bodies and minds is the biggest danger to children. Even the best educated children will be very lucky to have enough knowledge about how their bodies and minds work to understand fully the consequences of allowing drugs into their bodies.

A child's development

As adults we may have forgotten all of this, so here is a reminder. Before puberty a child's social and emotional development is very basic, they need fed, played with, need to learn to communicate, need to sleep, be given rules to keep them out of harm and lots of love and affection.

In adolescence a lot of new things start to happen to a child, feelings and worries come along that they never had before. This may make children anxious, can affect their sleep and their energy levels. Their bodies start to grow upwards and outwards, some of that growth is embarrassing and some is very welcome.

Hormonal changes in girls start with their first periods, with mood swings for many of them. They become very conscious of their bodies and how they look as breasts develop and their body shape changes into that of a woman. Crushes on same sex, or opposite sex friends or adults can cause confusion.

For boys their hormonal changes may mean that their growth may be out of kilter with their peers, getting taller and wider, hair grows in places it never did before, wet dreams and erections can be fun, embarrassing, or scary. It gets harder to talk to parents about things in your life that were not a problem before like same sex or opposite sex attractions. The pressure grows to keep in with their peers by swearing, sharing dirty jokes, or doing daft or dangerous things.

The period between primary and secondary school is the most common time for boys and girls to experiment with smoking, alcohol, and usually a bit later with drugs and sex.
Pre-puberty, children are fairly compliant with the rules and values of their parents and other authority figures. Then they start making their own rules and want to make their own decisions about things. They can be very idealistic and often have very black and white views; this is good – that is bad, this is cool – that is not cool. A whole range of new possibilities comes into their lives. They will feel a very strong need to be part of the crowd, to be like their peers. They will start to fancy people, fall in love with people and perhaps start to feel that what their peers think and believe about life is far more important than the views that their parents or teachers have taught them, or expect them to live by. The influence of celebrities of all kinds, in the media, in music, films, or sports will also start to be as important to them as that of their families.

As a parent your memory of that whole period of your life, perhaps 20 years ago or more will have faded and it may have been a very happy or a very unhappy memory for you. One thing is for sure and that is that life today is very different to your adolescence and even more different from that of your parents, your children's grand-parents. What has changed in particular is the enormous variety of drugs that a child can experiment with today; when in your day it may only have been tobacco, alcohol, cannabis or a smoke of a cinnamon stick.

The range of drugs now in common circulation in every community in the land can affect a child's development in quite dramatic ways.

Getting drunk and finding themselves pregnant is a very common outcome of adolescence for too many young women in Scotland.

The aggression that can come with hormonal changes, mixed with using some drugs can lead many young males into uncharacteristic behaviour, from vandalism, to stealing and fighting or even knife crime. Later in this book the finer details of what different drugs are like and what they can do to those using them is there for you to study.

Children have a very limited amount of life experience to use and to learn from when making decisions about life. Hormonal imbalances during puberty can cause children to make some very bad decisions. We all know of teenage boys who are fearless and reckless, so end up in casualty with broken bones from riding bikes or skateboards in dangerous ways.

We will know of very young girls getting into relationships with males very much older than they are. Maturity comes from the constant practice of learning to deal with life's many hurdles. Disappointment in relationships, failure to get the grades they thought they should at school, rejection by what they thought were good friends or the failure to get picked for the team are just some of the hurdles a child must face.

For some living with debilitating illnesses like asthma, diabetes, attention deficit disorder (ADD) or obesity life will be a daily struggle.

I have already explained the many reasons that children use drugs, the most common ones are about thinking that they will make them more confident, less shy, improve their bad moods, boost their energy, or be more able to be part of the crowd. It could also be to make them look cool to their peers or to boost their courage to participate in things that they find difficult.

Natural, drug-free ways to build self-confidence and social skills
Children's play and involvement in team games or youth and children's groups are all useful in developing a happy and contented child. Learning to play a musical instrument is one good example. First a child has to learn to master the instrument and

then they need to learn to perform on their own or in a band or group. The intellectual, physical and social skills children learn from this is enormous. The Sistema children's orchestra of Venezuela have proved this point and the idea has been adopted by the community of Raploch in Stirling.

Likewise those who venture into the world of art, drama or dancing can achieve similar personal growth, to enhance the rest of their lives. The challenge of sports and outdoor adventure activities is renowned for building self discipline, self reliance, understanding how to assess risk and push children to higher levels than they dared think they could achieve.

Maturity does not come from drugs or pills. It has to come from learning from others wiser than ourselves and from accumulated life experience. All useful life-skills require practice, practice and more practice. We learn from our successes, but we can also learn from our mistakes. Parents spend their lives shielding children from making mistakes and from danger, but by doing that they may limit severely, a child's opportunity to make mistakes for themselves, mistakes that they can learn important lessons from.

Damage to children from drug use

Apart from death, the most serious damage that drug use in children can do is to retard their mental, emotional, and social development. Drugs can literally prevent some of the essential wiring up of the brain from happening. Children should be encouraged to use their minds to think for themselves. They should be helped to work out relationships, how to deal with feelings and moods and to make plans for their future. An active healthy mind helps children to widen their experience and to train them how to keep safe and improve their personal happiness.

Using substances to change moods, mask personal problems, or to anaesthetise children from the pain of growing up is not a quick-fix solution. It is a route to disaster. If the result is problem drug use, then this will be a very long and rocky road to a very dark place.

Drugs and mental health

Drug use can cause paranoia, anxiety states and may trigger latent mental health problems. We know for sure that those with serious mental health problems can make their condition much worse when self-medicating with drugs. Many of those who are diagnosed as problem drinkers (alcoholic) are suffering from years of depression which is only made worse by consuming alcohol.

Powerful stimulants like cocaine and crack cocaine can cause people to be very violent and aggressive. So clearly drugs and children do not mix. The only drugs they should be taking are those prescribed by their doctors.

If the drug laws are ever revised to protect children they will almost certainly put strict age limits on when children can use tobacco, alcohol and other substances.

Confusing messages from parents

Over the many years that I have worked with children and young people I have witnessed mixed and often contradictory messages being sent out from parents to their children.

I once was involved in rescuing a runaway 14 year old boy from such a situation. His father was a very authoritarian, ex-army man who had risen up the ranks to be the chief fire officer in his community. He neither smoked nor drank alcohol. The mother was a stay-at-home mum, a very nervous woman who smoked like a chimney. The boy ran away from home because his father was beating hell out of him when he caught him smoking. His mother was buying the boy cigarettes because she felt sorry for him being treated so badly by his father. She thought that smoking helped to calm the boy down!

In another family the mother believed that all drugs kill and the father had, since his youth, used cannabis. The father stopped using when he realised that his son had a problem with drugs. He was buying the cannabis for his son, believing he could control how much he used and that he would get 'good clean cannabis'. He also wanted to stop his son from getting involved with the 'criminal types' who sold cannabis. The son, at 17, was smoking cannabis, seven days a week and dabbling in other 'legal highs'. This boy had been using drugs since he was about twelve. When I met him he was in a very seriously paranoid state and close to mental breakdown. The knowledge that the father and son had about cannabis was well out-of-date and unreliable, as this was around the time that new strains of cannabis, 'skunk', were starting to be available. It was much more powerful and clearly causing serious mental confusion in the boy. Not a happy situation but it was resolved successfully.

What are the signs that a child is using drugs?
Drugs workers and others are often reluctant to provide a list of signs of drug use in children to parents. They are hesitant because such a list will include much of the normal behaviour of a normal child, going through adolescence and on into adulthood. This has already been described above. Mood swings, temper tantrums, secretive behaviour, being very withdrawn or excessively talkative, not sleeping or oversleeping or spending every penny they have, are all typical adolescent behaviours but could in some circumstances indicate that a child is experimenting with drugs or has a problem with drugs.

It is too easy to jump to the wrong conclusions about a child's behaviour unless you have some hard evidence. You may have observed a drunken youth in a violent tantrum which may be similar to another completely sober youth having a strop because he fell out with his girlfriend. We may observe moody teenagers withdrawing from family life for periods of time and think it is like someone under the influence of cannabis, when they are just being a teenager, day-dreaming and in a world of their own. For many recovery from a family bereavement can take its toll leading to some of the behaviour noted above, and nothing to do with drug use. Even the loss of a much loved pet can trigger serious moods and depression in children.

Clearly finding evidence of empty fag packets, empty wine bottles, injecting equipment or weird smoking pipes should alert us to things going on that could be a problem, but they may just be trophies of a fairly innocent party, a bit of adolescent parental wind-up, or innocent experimentation that may never become anything to worry about.

If a child is spending unusual amounts of money or stealing things to sell for cash, that may be a sign that should concern you. But remember that some of these signs of apparent drug misuse by children could just as easily be evidence that they are being bullied, are struggling to make and keep friends, are unhappy at school or work, are developing emotional or mental health problems which have absolutely nothing to do with them using drugs.

If you are seeing in your child really unusual, out of character disturbing mood swings or behaviour that is not easy to account for, do not immediately jump to the conclusion that your child is using drugs. Take time out and talk to your doctor, a trusted friend, to one of the many helplines or drugs projects that exist to support people who have drug use problems. Above all talk to your child – they may be desperate to hear what you can do to help them.

So my advice is don't panic.

Remember that children have rights too, including the right to privacy in their own home. Big confrontations between a child and parents based on hearsay could damage years of trust built up between them.

Please don't go rummaging through your teenager's diaries or their secret hiding places for a bit of porn, or a leaflet or tracts that makes you think your child is about to join the army, become a nun or monk or join a religious sect or protest group. If they find out you may take years to regain their trust.

Above all don't jump to hasty conclusions, on little real evidence, that you are living with a problem drug user, when in reality a child is just doing what you have long since forgotten you did at their age. They may just be exploring life in all its variety. Experimenting with drugs for many children today will be an inevitable and harmless part of exploring life as they find it.

The better informed a parent is about drugs the easier it will be for them to address this issue with their children. Parents who are ill-informed about drugs may be out of their depth and can easily be hoodwinked into thinking that their child does not have a problem when they do. There are now plenty of sources of help and advice available.

7. UK Drug Laws

Oxne important theme of this book is that existing drug laws do not protect children from coming to harm. They mainly protect business from falling foul of the law and protect adults from harm. This chapter explains the laws and highlights where the laws fail children and what we could do to remedy this.

How are drugs classified?
In the UK all drug laws are set by the Westminster Parliament

Some laws are in need of reform to protect children.

Some substances such as alcohol, tobacco, prescribed medicines and over-the-counter drugs are not covered by the same laws as illicit drugs.

The two main drug laws are The Medicines Act 1968 and The Misuse of Drugs Acts 1968 & 1971.

The Medicines Act governs the manufacture and supply of all kinds of medicinal products. Medicines are divided into three categories: Prescription Only is the most restricted, so can only be sold or supplied by a pharmacist if ordered to by a doctor or dentist; Pharmacy Medicines can be sold or supplied without a prescription but only by a Pharmacist; and drugs on the General Sales List, the least restricted, can be sold or supplied without a prescription by any shop. These are the Over-the-Counter drugs (OTCs).

The Misuse of Drugs Act 1968 & 1971 aim to prevent the non-medical use of certain drugs. Drugs subject to this legislation are known as 'controlled drugs'. The law defines a series of offences including unlawful supply, intent to supply, import and export (collectively known as trafficking offences), unlawful possession and unlawful production. Anyone convicted of the unlawful possession, supply or production of drugs controlled by the Misuse of Drugs Act could be imprisoned.

The Act lists the drugs which are subject to control and classifies them in three categories, Class A, B or C. Penalties for offences involving controlled drugs depend on the classification, with Class A drugs carrying the greatest penalties. It also distinguishes the penalties which can be imposed between the crimes of possession and drug trafficking, the latter attracting higher sanctions.

What's the difference between possession and supply (dealing or trafficking)?

Possession

This is where you get caught with drugs that you are going to use yourself. In Scotland, a report will be sent to the Procurator Fiscal to decide whether to prosecute you or not.

In England and Wales they operate under a different legal system. Their police have two different roles, not only to arrest offenders, they then decide if the offence is serious enough to merit being sent on to the court systems.

Supply (dealing or trafficking)

You do not have to be a big-time drug dealer to be charged with supplying drugs. If you are caught with drugs and it looks like you have bought them to sell on, or give to your friends, you could be charged with 'possession with intent to supply' or 'supplying drugs'.

Having a criminal record can make it difficult to get a job or visa to travel abroad.

Categories of drugs and the penalties that apply across the UK

Class A Drugs

Include heroin, ecstasy, LSD, cocaine, crack cocaine, methadone, morphine, more potent opioid painkillers, methamphetamine PMC, 2CB, magic mushrooms and amphetamines for injection.

Penalties for possession

Up to 7 years imprisonment or an unlimited fine or both.

Penalties for production/dealing

Up to life imprisonment or an unlimited fine or both.

Class B Drugs

Include cannabis, skunk, amphetamine, less potent opioid painkillers, dihydrocodeine, synthetic cannabinoids (such as 'spice'), pholcodine, methylphenidate (ritalin).

From 16/04/10 the 'legal high' methadrone has been added to this list.

Penalties for possession

Up to 5 years imprisonment or an unlimited fine or both.

Penalties for production/dealing

Up to 14 years imprisonment or an unlimited fine or both.

Class C Drugs

Include anabolic steroids, benzodiazepines, temazepam, diazepam, temgesic, tranquilisers, some painkillers, gamma hydroxybutyrate (GHB), GBL (gamma butyrolactone) BZP, ketamine, non-injectable preparations containing codeine.

Penalties for possession

Up to 2 years imprisonment or an unlimited fine or both.

Penalties for production/dealing

Up to 14 years imprisonment or an unlimited fine or both.

Any Class B drug in injectable form is treated as Class A.

Some Class C drugs are legal to possess – for example, some anabolic steroids are Class C, Schedule 4 Part 11 drugs, which means they may be possessed in medical form without a prescription.

Is the UK drug classification system still fit for purpose?

There have been problems with the UK drugs acts. They don't always help us to understand how dangerous any drug might be for us or our children. They take a long time to be brought up-to-date and they do not cover many substances regularly misused by people.

Because of the confusion in 2007 a group of UK drugs experts had a look at this and came up with what they believe to be a more useful way of classifying drugs. They hoped that describing drugs in a different way would help everyone to be clearer about how dangerous they really were. This idea was put to the UK Labour government but unfortunately it was rejected out of hand. This was mainly because the government is committed to supporting long established international treaties and agreements about classification of drugs and they did not want to be seen to disagree with other countries about this. The Americans in particular are big supporters of these now very out-of-date laws.

Regardless of the international politics involved in this, there is some merit in understanding the way that the UK panel of drug experts (all of whom were appointed by the government to serve on a national drugs advisory committee) described drugs differently from the existing legal classification system.

In my descriptions of the drugs that follow, the drugs have both their UK legal status noted, and a statement on the new rating allocated by this new system. I am grateful to the staff and volunteers of Crew 2000 in Edinburgh who described this new approach as 'The Nutt Scale' after Professor David Nutt of the University of Bristol, who led the team that created it.

The Nutt Scale lists how dangerous we should view twenty of the most commonly used drugs. The list runs from 1-20, one being the most dangerous and 20 the least dangerous substance, e.g. the Nutt Scale has alcohol rated as 5th most dangerous of the 20 commonest drugs used in the UK (previously it was not covered by the dangerous drugs act at all).

The Nutt Scale ratings of the 20 most common drugs

1 Heroin (most dangerous)

2 Cocaine (and Crack)

3 Barbiturates

4 Street Methadone

5 Alcohol

6 Ketamine

7 Benzodiazapines

8 Amphetamines

9 Tobacco

10 Buprenorphine

11 Cannabis

12 Solvents

13 4-MTA

14 LSD

15 Methylphenidate

16 Anabolic Steroids

17 GHB

18 Ecstasy

19 Poppers (Amyl and Butyl Nitrate)

20 Khat (least dangerous)

The Nutt Scale for drugs

The drugs experts scored drugs according to nine important factors, which should be taken into account when describing how dangerous a drug is. The scoring system then placed drugs according to how high they rate on the following three factors:

- The physical harm to the user, e.g. are its main effects good or bad?

- The tendency of the drug to induce dependence. (Remember that not all drugs are addictive)

- The effect of the drug on families, communities and society (as indicated by crime, number of deaths, serious health or mental health damage).

The Nutt Scale, includes illicit drugs along with legal substances like tobacco and alcohol, which were not listed in the Dangerous Drugs Act.

The Nutt Scale is not a foolproof system, but it has some merit. It still suffers from the same problem as the current system; it does not allow for the fact that many people mix a range of drugs together, which can seriously complicate the effects that these cocktails of drugs can have on the user. Cocktails of drugs are the main cause of drug deaths.

With illicit drugs you are never comparing like with like. With illicit drugs no batch of the substance is ever likely to be consistent with another batch, as they are produced in very crude ways, not in licensed factories. They are always adulterated as they travel across the world from their source country to the streets of the UK. This means that it is never possible to accurately describe what any illicit drug actually is, or what effects it will have on the user. So for instance cannabis could be of 15% purity or less than 3% in any one batch.

The Nutt Scale does not include 'legal highs' as they were not yet in common use when the list was compiled in 2007.

Police powers when dealing with drug offences.

The same drug laws apply in the whole of the UK but there is Scottish law and English law. There are also different police rules and regulations in Scotland, England and Wales. This means for instance that if someone in Scotland commits an offence the Police have to write a report, they then charge the person with an offence. Then they hand the case on to a completely independent organisation called the Procurator Fiscal's Office, whose job it is to determine if the offender is to go to court or not. They cannot just ignore the offence.

In England and Wales, the police regulations allow them to both charge a suspect with an offence and then decide if the case goes on to court or not.

Also in England and Wales the police have the powers to caution someone and then send them on their way without any further action. This cannot happen in Scotland.

What Happens to those Under 16 caught with drugs?

From 1 April 1997, the misuse of any drug, whether or not it's controlled drug, in terms of the Misuse of Drugs Act, can mean that a child has to go to a Children's Hearing if they are under 16 and up to the age of 18, if they are already attending a Children's Hearing (Scotland only). The police will refer these cases to the Reporter to the Children's Panel for a decision on what action should be taken. This unique Scottish children's justice system is there to try to provide the best care for a child and so prevent them from ending up in the adult justice system.

Existing laws do not protect children from coming to harm from drugs.

It is important that laws are fit for the purpose they were made for. Laws must also be enforceable and enforced if they are to be of any use. All laws also need to be revised from time to time to make sure that they are still doing what they are supposed to do.

I believe that UK drug laws need revised urgently so that they can be more effective in protecting children from harm.

Changes in the laws are reducing adult smoking and improving health. The banning of smoking in public places, along with increasing the age at which we can buy tobacco, is reducing adult smoking and should eventually reduce the number of smokers and deaths from smoking. The impact on children's smoking has not been dramatic.

If politicians dared to change the law on smoking to be one that made it 'illegal to buy or consume tobacco products before the age of 18', this would give a boost to the long-term aim of eliminating tobacco use in our society.

Far too many parents, carers and siblings condone smoking in young children by supplying them with cigarettes and even smoking with them. Even some youth workers think nothing of using cigarettess as a tool to control the behaviour of difficult young people they are working with.

The tobacco companies are desperate to protect their hugely lucrative business so they spend fortunes on opposing all the proposed changes in tobacco laws.

There is real confusion amongst young people about the laws on cannabis.

For the reasons that I mentioned earlier Cannabis was reclassified to a Class 'C' drug and then back again to a Class 'B' drug. Young people in Scotland read about this and believed that the police would no longer be arresting them for possession of cannabis. **What they did not understand was that only the English police can give someone a caution for possession of cannabis.** This did not apply in Scotland. Clearly when the UK Parliament is making changes to the law they need to be much more careful about understanding Scottish law and Scottish police regulations.

It is an offence to be in charge of a motor vehicle while 'unfit to drive through drink or drugs'. The drugs can include illicit drugs, prescribed medicines or solvents. **Thousands of young people have admitted to driving under the influence of cannabis** in particular, as they believe it to be a harmless drug. Clearly this is a law that needs more public exposure to protect young people from coming to harm.

Alcohol laws are a cocktail of confusion and contradiction.
A UK government health minister recently supported the idea that alcohol should not be given to anyone under 15 years of age at all. Nothing of course has followed this announcement – issued in an election year! What is clear though is that the existing laws cannot be used to enforce this proposal.

The current laws give a messy and confusing range of ages at which alcohol can be consumed by children. Different parts of the alcohol law apply at five, fourteen, sixteen, seventeen and eighteen and now ID is being required in some circumstances where anyone under 21 or 26 wants to buy alcohol.

There is also a growing body of evidence that suggests we should prevent people using alcohol under the age of 21. This is already the case in several countries.

The solution to this confusion would be to change the law on alcohol to protect children and young people. The law I propose would be similar to that for tobacco 'that a child under the age of 18 (or perhaps 21) should not be allowed to purchase or consume alcohol'. This would remove all confusion and would force adults to stop colluding with children in their drinking of alcohol.

I have been trying for a long time to get public debate and support for these law changes and have always been told that such changes would criminalise children. My answer to that is that there are many similar laws in place to stop children having guns, buying solvents, pornography, having sex before they are 16 or driving vehicles. I hear no one arguing that these laws should be scrapped because they criminalise children. They are there to protect children and to stop adults exploiting children. It would be the adults who were criminalised by breaking the laws I propose.

What well informed parents need to know about drugs

8.

KEY FACTS

- The many myths about drugs contain dangerous misinformation.

- There are no known health benefits from smoking tobacco.

- Tobacco is a gateway drug leading many children to other drugs.

- Changes in tobacco law will reduce most smoking and improve health.

- There are many hidden smokers – the cannabis smokers.

- Children do die of alcohol misuse, in road traffic accidents, from violence and suicide.

- Young men in Scotland's poorest communities are 32% more likely to die from being knifed. Alcohol is heavily associated with youth violence.

- Illicit drugs have only been common in the UK for about 50 years.

- Research into illicit drugs is limited. Very little is known about the new 'legal highs'.

- Drug deaths: 13,473 from smoking (2004); 1,282 from alcohol (2009); and 485 (2010) from illicit drugs.

For some parents the main facts in chapter 5 on tobacco, alcohol and illicit drugs is all that they think that they need. Such limited information will make parents as least as well-informed as most of their children. However if there is any possibility of drug misuse affecting any of your children then you will need a lot more information than the basics to form a balanced view of what damage drugs may do.

Tobacco and alcohol are two legally available drugs about which we already know a lot as they have been around for centuries and have been the focus of literally thousands of international research papers.

Illicit drugs are relatively new, only having been introduced to the UK widely in the 1960s when heroin, cannabis and acid (LSD) were the main substances being used. Since then the illicit drugs market has expanded and hundreds of substances are now in common use.

Illicit drugs are a very complex area of knowledge. There is some research into some of the substances and almost none into others. As a youth worker with a special interest in young people's health and in drug misuse since 1965, I could not accurately inform people about some of the newer drugs which are on sale. This book aims to make sure that any concerned parent is able to find the information they need on any drug that their child might be using or experimenting with.

The importance of keeping up-to-date
This book, like all written material will be out-of-date by the time it is printed, but it will still give readers a good understanding of the main things they need to know about the many substances in common use. Where it is not possible to provide detailed information readers are referred to the list of the most reliable information sources in chapter 10. There they will find reliable websites and help agencies who work in this field. These organisations have the resources to continually update and research the information that they offer, so

use them if you are looking for the best and most up-to-date information available.

Internet search dangers

The internet is a quite amazing knowledge base, but beware because it is an unregulated source of information. Anyone can set up a site on any topic. There are thousands of sites on health issues, including drugs. They range from those funded by governments, the BMA (British Medical Association) and similar professional organisations across the world.

There are also many websites run by particular interest groups, who have their own biased views on the substances that they are campaigning about. Some of these aim to increase the use of a particular substance such as cannabis, as they believe it is harmless or good for the world. Others are campaigning to have substances banned. Many sites are just a front for people selling drugs. Try searching for 'legal highs' if you want to see that for yourself.

In chapter 10 you will find some tips on how to search the internet successfully for information on drugs.

Myths about drugs can harm you and your children

From decades of delivering health education workshops for children I have collected dozens of myths on which children and adults base their understanding of drugs or sex. You are unlikely to find in other books or on the internet information on these dangerous myths about drugs. Such myths are passed on through families, amongst friends and peers. These myths are often the main source of information about drugs that you and your children have. If you explore these myths you will quickly realise that they are perhaps funny or even unbelievable, but they are believed by thousands of children which is why they can be so dangerous. If children believed and acted on some of these myths the consequences could be serious to their health. Here are examples to illustrate my point.

myths & facts

Myth: If you smoke when you are pregnant you have a smaller baby, so a less painful childbirth.

Fact: This is typical of old wives' tales that have passed from generation to generation. It is both dangerous to the unborn child and the mother. It is also difficult to resolve because there is no doubt that mothers who smoke and drink during pregnancy do usually have smaller babies. Such babies are often premature and are born with a range of health problems that a full term baby should not have. There are well established ways of easing the pain of childbirth that are no danger to an unborn child.

myths & facts

Myth: Cannabis relaxes you so you can drive better.

Fact: This is a comment I have heard so often from young people, that it really is a worry. Some really do believe it, even admitting they had cannabis before they did their driving tests. The myth flags up two problems of ignorance about drugs. First that using any illicit drug when driving is illegal and could invalidate the driver's insurance. Secondly these drivers are clearly not aware of the true nature of cannabis. It is a hallucinogen, a drug that alters our perception, playing tricks with our mind. We may think we are driving slowly when we are going fast. Our judgement of time will be distorted as are colours so we may not realise that traffic lights have changed. This myth highlights one of the best reasons for educating children and adults about the real facts on drugs.

myths & facts

Myth: You can get cancer from love bites.

Fact: I have heard this more times than I care to remember in sexual health workshops with adults and children. Cancer is the uncontrolled multiplying of cells in our body, caused by certain diseases, some of which may come from our use of tobacco or alcohol, or from the genes passed on from our parents. The superficial damage from love bites is just bruising of the tissue under the skin. Nothing to do with cancer. That children and adults should believe such a myth, when they ignore the fact that smoking has one of the highest cancer risks of any human activity, highlights why myths about health are something we should worry about.

fact

Fact: Brake, the road safety charity, reported in January 2012 that a survey had revealed that 1:9 drivers under the age of 25 admitted driving when they had used drugs.

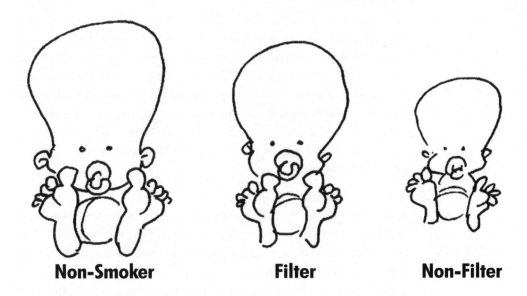

Non-Smoker   **Filter**   **Non-Filter**

A Channel 4 sex education programme in 2009 (*Sexperience*) reported that the majority of under-15s in the UK got most of their sex education from pornography, which they viewed on television, on videos or which had been sent to their mobile phones. Such porn is full of myths about male and female sexual parts and much more, e.g. that big penises equals better sex or that it is better to have sex with a woman who has shaved her genital area. Clearly myths are not a reliable source of information on sexual health or drugs.

Not addressing these common myths about drugs or sex or anything else leaves children vulnerable to the harm that ignorance can cause.

Before going into the fuller details of the thirteen most common drugs that children are likely to come across, I repeat again here the following information about how drugs affect us so that parents can understand the overall effects of drugs on a child or young person.

Tolerance, Dependence and Problem drug use (Addiction)

Tolerance
When we use some drugs our body adjusts to them and we build up a tolerance to them. We may then find that we need more of that drug to achieve the effect it had at smaller doses. Tobacco smokers and drinkers of alcohol should understand this problem well.

Dependence

As our use of drugs increases we get used to it, we start to like it a lot and may then find that it is hard to function without using that drug. This means that we have developed a dependence on that substance. We could give it up if we wanted to, or if we had to, perhaps because we could no longer afford it, or our doctor advised us to. If for instance you think that you drink too much alcohol, you will understand this point very well if you have ever tried to cut down your drinking for a while. Heavy dependence on drugs can for some people become problem drug use.

Problem Drug Use (Addiction)

I have tried in this book to use the term addiction as little as I can as it is loaded with moral overtones, as is the even worse word, Junkie. The problem is that because so many people see addictions as incurable, or something that they can do nothing about, this leads to a psychological acceptance of that problem, that allows them to feel comfortable with their condition. Such acceptance gives people the best excuse in the world for not addressing their Problem Drug Use.

Being a Problem Drug User means that your life is overwhelmed with the need to use your drug of choice. Every waking moment of your life is spent seeking more of the drug and trying to satisfy the extremely powerful need that the drug has created in you. You end up in a situation where the rest of your life will be on hold until you satisfy that desperate craving for the drug. The fallout from this is often broken relationships, lost jobs, no money, low self-esteem, the breakdown of mental and physical health, a life of crime to feed the drug habits and for some an early death.

The fear of most parents is that their child may get addicted to drugs. There is a commonly held view, that all drugs are addictive. This is not true. However, people can be addicted to many things apart from drugs, e.g. work, sex, gambling, exercise, shopping or eating.

What different types of drugs do to us

For simplicity I have chosen to describe drugs in three main categories – Stimulants (Uppers), Depressants (Downers) and Hallucinogens (Trippy drugs). It is not completely foolproof but most parents should find this a useful way of understanding the basic nature of the most common drugs.

A small number of drugs fit into more than one category because they are a mixture of different types of drug. Ecstasy for instance can be both a stimulant and a hallucinogen.

New, previously unknown drugs started to appear in 2009. These are the substances called 'legal highs. Methadrone is one of these substances. Very little is known about these, as most are not yet classified under any UK drug laws, so I will not be covering them in any depth in this book. Deaths have already being reported from these substances and the government is trying to find ways to control them. The effects of these drugs may fit into one or several of the three categories. See the resources list chapter 10 for reliable websites to visit or more details of any drug.

There is no quality control on illicit drugs so their effects can vary from one batch to another, or even within the same supplies being sold by the same dealer.

Stimulants (Uppers)

Tobacco, Nicotine, Solvents, Glue, Amphetamines, Speed, Sulph, Whizz, Crystal, Cocaine, Charlie, Coke, Crack Cocaine, Dexies, Poppers, Amyl Nitrate, Rush, Liquid Gold, pure Ecstasy (MDMA), GHB/GBH, Ketamine and Liquid Ecstasy and Khat.

Effects of Stimulants do vary but may include:

Speeding up of the central nervous system.

Decreased appetite.

They keep us awake and can cause sleep disturbance.

People talk a lot of high-speed nonsense.

They speed up our heart rate.

We may have very high levels of energy.

They dry up the mouth and dehydrate us (we pee a lot).

We may feel very confident or over confident.

The pupils of the eyes are opened up (dilated).

The user experiences a come-down, when the drug wears off, so they may feel very low and depressed.

The user may grind their teeth. They can damage the enamel of teeth.

Stiffness in the limbs and the jaw may occur.

Urinary tract problems in women such as Thrush.

Males may not be able to maintain an erection, or can, but cannot ejaculate

Heart failure can occur, even in young people.

Anxiety, paranoia and hallucinations occur in some users.

Arrogant, egotistical and sometimes violent behaviour is common.

Depressants (Downers)

Alcohol, Heroin, Valium, Diazepam, Methadone, Benzodiazepines.

Effects of downers do vary but can include the following:

They loosen our social controls (disinhibit us) so increase our risk-taking behaviour.

They carry greater risk of death from overdose than most drugs do.

The pupils of the eyes are pinned down into a tiny spot.

As these drugs depress the central nervous system, this can lead to physical dependence and Problem Drug Use.

Downers are used to ease the come-down from uppers – this can be dangerous.

Using downers when our judgement is already impaired from the effects of stimulants and psychedelic drugs is a dangerous cocktail, and not recommended.

Hallucinogens (Trippy drugs)

Cannabis, Skunk, Acid, LSD, Magic mushrooms, Ecstasy, MDA, MDMA, MDEA, 2CB (nexus) 4-MTA

Effects of Hallucinogens do vary but can include the following:

Our understanding of reality is altered.

Our understanding of time is distorted.

Our senses of vision; hearing, taste, smell, and touch appear to be heightened.

Auditory and visual hallucinations can happen.

Fears and nightmares can turn into mild or serious paranoia.

We may have a feeling of detachment from the world.

Music, art, what people are saying to us may take on different meanings from normal.

Flashbacks can occur. This is when the user re-experiences things that happened when using the drug in the past. We have no control over this so the experience may be a good one or a bad one.

It can be more difficult to see in the dark.

Mental dependency can occur.

Mental health can be affected, especially if we already suffer from such problems.

More detailed information of drugs most commonly used by children in Scotland and the UK is contained in the rest of this chapter.

The order of listing these drugs is deliberate, starting from those I believe to be used by the highest number of children and finishing with those that are less common. This should help parents to understand the scale and likely dangers. You may be surprised by what you read in this section.

Alcohol

(Depressant, downer type drug)

This is the drug that causes more problem for families in the UK than any other.

Street names: Booze, swally, drink, bevy, wine.

Legal Status: You can consume alcohol from the age of 5.

You can be in a bar at 14 but cannot drink alcohol there.

You can order cider, beer, perry (like Babycham) or table wine with a meal in a licensed restaurant at 16 and 17 years of age. Someone over 18 must buy the alcohol.

At 18 you can buy alcohol in a bar, supermarket or off-licence.

ID documentation can now be demanded by anyone selling alcohol to those under 26.

The Nutt Scale rating: 5th most dangerous of the 20 most common drugs used in the UK.

New alcohol laws

There were substantial changes to the Scottish licensing laws in 2010/11 which aim to make those who hold licences more aware of their rights and the responsibilities that come with holding a licence to sell the drug alcohol. The general public will have more say in who can have a licence. Those who hold alcohol licences will need to be fully aware of the law and make sure that all of their staff are trained to comply with the alcohol law when serving the public. This approach is part of the plan to educate the public to drink alcohol more safely.

Free tap water

Water now has to be provided free of charge in all licensed premises, but **you must ask for it**. Make sure that you do ask, so that this will encourage this healthy trend. It is common practice in parts of Europe,

Alcohol

America, Canada and Australia for free water always to be provided without asking for it. Drinking water along with alcohol dilutes the alcohol and so fills your stomach, making you less inclined to consume unhealthy amounts of alcohol. The water also combats dehydration and the associated hangover.

Liquor Licences

There are 17,021 liquor licences currently in force in Scotland. (554 fewer than in 1979). There is some evidence that as a result of the banning of smoking in public places many publicans are giving up their licences.

In Scotland 37% of alcohol is sold by off-sales licences, with supermarkets being the biggest outlets. Pubs hold 30% of all licences. The balance of licences – 33% – are held by private clubs, restaurants and places of entertainment.

Popularity

In the UK alcohol is the most socially acceptable and most used drug. In 2009 for those aged between 16 and 74 10% of men and 14% of women did not drink at all. **So 90% of men and 86% of women drink alcohol in Scotland.** [SOURCE: isd/scotland]

Alcohol consumption in Scotland

- Scotland is placed 8th in the world for alcohol consumption per head of population.

- The Scots drank 25% more alcohol per head of population than individuals in England and Wales.

- 1 in 3 men and 1 in 4 women in Scotland exceed recommended daily limits.

- Men's average weekly consumption is more than double that of women.

- In 2010 it was estimated that alcohol misuse costs Scotland around £3.56 billion per year – £900 for every taxpayer.

- There were 1,282 alcohol-related deaths in Scotland in 2009.

Alcohol

- Alcohol-related deaths among women have doubled in the last decade.

- 1 in 20 deaths are attributed to alcohol misuse.

- People living in the most deprived areas are 5 times more likely to die an alcohol-related death than those in least deprived areas.

- In 2006 there were approximately 720 drink-drive accidents, with 980 casualties.

- 1 in 3 adult pedestrians killed on the roads had been drinking alcohol.

- Alcohol is featured in over half of the deaths caused by fires in Scotland.

- 1 in 10 Accident & Emergency admissions in Scotland can be attributed to alcohol.

- There were 42,430 alcohol-related hospital discharges in 2007/08.

- An estimated 111,200 consultations with GPs and practice nurses for alcohol misuse took place in 2006/07.

- 1 in 5 patients discharged from psychiatric units have an alcohol-related diagnosis.

- Alcohol-related hospital discharges are most common in the 45-54 age group.

[SOURCE Scottish Executive]

Young People and alcohol

- Less than half of 15 year olds and a third of 13 year olds report drinking alcohol in the past week.

- The number of 13 year olds drinking in the past week has doubled since 1990.

[SOURCE: Alcohol Focus Scotland]

Alcohol

The nature of the drug alcohol

Alcohol is classified as a depressant (downer drug). This confuses many people because this does not mean that when alcohol is consumed, it will always make people depressed. It is perhaps easier to think of alcohol as being a disinhibitor, which means its effect is one of loosening off control of body and mind.

Think of it like this, if you are not normally someone who swears a lot you may find that when you are disinhibited by alcohol you may behave out of character and swear sometimes. If you are someone who is quite uptight, you may find that when you drink alcohol you tend to relax your body and emotions more, and so feel quite comfortable with this when you normally would not. It is these dis-inhibiting effects of alcohol that can on some occasions improve our good moods, but it can also increase the intensity of our bad moods, leading on to risk-taking and sometimes embarrassing behaviour reported back to us later.

Effects of the drug

Like most drugs alcohol's effect on us is dependent on our personality, our expectations and our mood at the time of using the drug. Many reading this will know from experience that if you are in a high, let's have-a-party sort of mood when you use alcohol, it can up to a point, make you less shy, more fun to be with, may make you feel very sociable, confident and perhaps even a bit outrageous. On the other hand, if you are someone who lacks confidence, are feeling very emotional, are already quite sad, full of anger, are already in a low or depressed mood, then alcohol picks up these moods and personality traits and will usually make things worse.

Some people find that alcohol causes them to express themselves much more emotionally or sexually, than they would normally choose to be. So clearly these are all effects of using alcohol that we may enjoy or worry about. If alcohol tends to make you violent, or suicidally depressed, then alcohol for you is not a good idea.

Many successful suicides involve alcohol use, sometimes along with other drugs. Alcohol increases the intensity of our negative feelings about ourselves so adds to the intensity of suicidal feelings.

Young drinkers need to learn the important lesson that alcohol picks up our deepest thoughts and our basic personality traits and

Alcohol

multiplies them up. Learning that early early in life may help some people realise that alcohol is not a suitable drug for them to be using.

Prisons and psychiatric hospitals are full of people who tried to solve their problems by using the drug alcohol.

All drugs alter the chemical balance of our bodies

The human body's source of energy is the fuel provided by the food we eat and the liquids that we drink. These natural products provide us with the complex mixture of vitamins, minerals, fibres, fats, proteins and carbohydrates that we need to keep our bodies in balance and healthy. The food and drink is providing the essential chemistry required by the human body. When we get it right we are in a balanced and healthy state. When we over-indulge on food and drink, we go out of balance and end up ill. This causes not just physical problems like lack of energy, tiredness or aching limbs. It also alters our mental states showing up in a lack of sleep, stress, anxiety, a compromised immune system, cancers and serious mental ill-health.

All alcoholic drinks are high in calories

As the sugar and calorie content of alcoholic drinks vary a lot between those that are dry (very little sugar) and those that are sweet, there is no easy method of calculating how many calories are in particular alcoholic drinks. It requires specialist equipment. There could be as few as 40 calories per unit of alcohol in a drink or as many as 150-200 calories. Drinks such as bacardi and coke or gin and tonic have additional calories because of the sugar in these mixers.

If you are watching your weight then think about how much you drink. A pint of lager has about 250 calories, a bottle of red or white wine has 510-555 calories, a pub measure of sprits about 126-140 calories and a bottle of Buckfast 980 calories.

A website like www.weightlossresources.co.uk lists the calories in a range of alcoholic drinks.

How the body deals with food, drink and drugs like alcohol

When we take anything into our stomachs, food, drink or drugs, the nerve sensors in our stomachs convey messages to our brains that there is something there that needs to be digested, or in the case of poisons, that something needs to be spewed out. Once there is something in our digestive systems, our brains send a signal out to pull extra blood supply towards our stomachs, to absorb what it needs from the stomach contents. These are usually vitamins, minerals, sugars, proteins and fats. All of these pass through our digestive system and straight into our bloodstream, from where they then go off around the body to do whatever they are supposed to do. The vitamins, minerals and sugars head for our muscles to energise them. Caffeine, stimulants, painkillers, alcohol and other drugs head for the brain to stimulate us, subdue our pain or make us sleep.

Shortly after we have had a heavy meal, with or without alcohol, our muscles are seriously deprived of blood and the energy it supplies, so we cannot perform high energy activities until the digestive process is complete. Our brain too is affected and slows down our reactions or makes us sleepy. Not a good state of mind to be in for studying at school, driving vehicles, working with machinery, looking after our children or participating in sporting activities. This explains why we feel like a snooze after a heavy meal taken with alcohol.

Things that we inhale through the mouth or nose, such as tobacco or cocaine are processed differently. They go through the lungs into the bloodstream. This happens faster than through the digestive system.

Short-term risks of alcohol

You can overdose on alcohol (alcohol poisoning). Accidents are a big risk due to impaired judgement – 'I'll just run across this road and hope no one hits me.' Even if you don't drink enough to kill you, it's easy to end up feeling like death, wrapped around the toilet bowl with the room spinning around.

Alcohol helps us to loosen up. Having a flirt with someone may leave us wanting to emigrate the next morning. Our fear of sexually transmitted diseases or pregnancy may decrease, so we just risk it and forget to use a condom.

Alcohol in moderation is not the problem.

Clearly putting large doses of unnecessary additional chemicals into the body, which the body does not need, can tip the chemical

Alcohol

balance of the body and the mind. This can also prevent us from performing what should be normal daily tasks such as driving, studying, looking after our children or generally enjoying our life to the full. We must never forget that alcohol is a very powerful drug.

Issues about children and alcohol

The majority of the Scottish population use the drug alcohol regularly.

Because alcohol is so common in our society, parents need to have a sensible approach to this drug. Children will almost certainly use it and some will inevitably come to harm, if they don't use it sensibly and that means in moderation. So it would seem that we should encourage moderate, sensible drinking within a family or amongst safe friends, but discourage drinking alcohol if it is going to badly affect the mood and behaviour of children.

BUT – a word of caution – there is a growing body of research that is saying that **the earlier children use alcohol the more likely they are to have problems with it later in life**. Many countries already have 21 as the earliest age for using alcohol. This may not be a priority for the UK government, and I am sure that the drinks industry would fight it all the way, but as the case for later use of alcohol builds we may all have to think again about introducing children to alcohol too soon.

There are recommended government guidelines for alcohol consumption by adults, but not for children. Legally children can consume alcohol from the age of 5 in the UK. Clearly our alcohol laws are not fit for purpose because they do not protect children.

Even allowing for our complex and confusing alcohol laws, parents may want to discourage their children from using alcohol until as late as possible in life.

Children are not adults.

As children's bodies and minds are not fully grown until around their twenties, so serious damage can be done to their physical and emotional development through consuming even quite small amounts of alcohol.

Scotland has one of the highest rates of teenage pregnancy in Europe.

Alcohol

First sexual experiences can be embarrassing and difficult to handle. Research shows that many of these child pregnancies happen when young people are drunk, or under the influence of other substances.

Many of the murders, rapes, violence and other sorts of sexual abuse have been committed by people who had been using alcohol. Alcohol can give us a false sense of courage by loosening off emotional controls so releasing aggression which in other circumstances would be kept well under control.

A large number of people who are diagnosed with depression, including children, have a problem with alcohol. Alcohol multiplies their feelings of self-hate, anger and depression and the other negative states of mind.

Does alcohol stunt the mental and emotional growth of children?
One of the biggest concerns that we should have about all drug misuse by children is that such drug use could literally stunt their emotional and social growth. When drinkers self-medicate to deal with the many troubles in their lives, it seems to prevent them from having to grow up. They shrink from having to take responsibility for themselves and others and this seems to leave them trapped in a sort of time warp, wrapped up in the cotton wool that the oblivion from alcohol or the major painkiller, heroin can provide.

The younger that children start to get into that sort of retreat from problem solving, by self-medicating with drugs, the more likely it is that permanent damage will be the result.

Babies born to mothers who continue to smoke and drink heavily during their pregnancy can be born with a variety of problems and disabilities.

Foetal Alcohol Syndrome (FAS) is a well known result of women drinking whilst pregnant. Children with FAS can be born with small heads and reduced brain size, abnormal facial features, malformations of the heart, kidneys, spine, limbs, palate and skin. They may also have poor co-ordination, learning and behavioural difficulties, attention deficit/hyperactive disorder (ADDH) and lifelong social and other problems. There are similar problems for babies born to other drug users.

Alcohol

Alcohol and violence

Alcohol use and misuse is heavily associated with domestic violence, youth violence and crowd violence after late night clubbing or major sports events.

Young Scottish men living in the most deprived areas have a 33 times higher chance of being killed in a stabbing incident than other young Scottish males. This is double the rate in any other European country. Alcohol and drugs are often a factor in these crimes of violence.

Why should this be? Part of the answer must be that deprivation is bad for us all. Living in areas with no work, few leisure facilities, poor transport and only expensive corner shops breeds discontent, anger and the ghetto mentality (including gangs) and the violence associated with it.

Alcohol, remember, is a disinhibitor – it loosens off our built-in social controls, such as our natural need to defend ourselves from threats. Alcohol can also increase our self confidence, including our belief that we can take on or fight off others. Alcohol also increases the need for young men in particular to show off and take what are often dangerous risks. It is known that teenage males' ability to assess risk is not fully developed. This is one reason why so many deaths and serious accidents happen to young male drivers. If we add into that mix deep-down hurt, anger and strong emotions that we may normally be able to keep well under control, then when we are drunk this all gets multiplied up into aggressive and violent behaviour. This is often what fuels the levels of violence that we see when alcohol is involved amongst young men and women.

The situation is then made worse when other drugs are also consumed along with alcohol. Strong stimulants like speed, cocaine and crack cocaine, taken on their own, are all associated with aggressive and violent behaviour. When they are mixed in a cocktail with alcohol it all just gets worse.

We should be aware that alcohol also picks up our personality traits and our underlying moods. So if we are by nature quite arrogant, short-tempered, have a short fuse, find it hard to express our anger or our emotions and happen to also be in a bad mood, then all of that is likely to kick off when drugs like alcohol and stimulants are in use together. The Young Offenders Institutions and the prisons are

Alcohol

populated with thousands of young men and women who have learned that lesson the hard way.

The price of alcohol

In the UK alcohol is about 70% cheaper than 30 years ago when compared to average wages. This is why the Scottish and UK Parliaments are determined to increase the price of alcohol to prevent harm to children, young people and adults. The price of alcohol is well within the spending power of most children and young people.

Using alcohol more safely

Understand units of alcohol – to drink more safely.

It takes one hour for one unit of alcohol to be processed through a fully grown, fit adult body.

If you had a heavy drinking session and drank a bottle of vodka, four large glasses of red wine and a couple of cans of beer. (not unusual for some binge drinkers) you could have consumed around 45 units of alcohol. It would take 45 hours for all of these units to leave your body. So it would not be safe to drive or operate machinery for almost 45 hours.

Examples or units of alcohol in common drinks.

- A 700 ml bottle of spirits like vodka, gin or whisky at 37.5% alcohol, has 26.3 units of alcohol.

- Pub measures of these spirits (25 ml) = 0.9 units of alcohol. (35 ml) = 1.3 units of alcohol.

- Alcopops vary from 4.7% to 5.4% alcohol, and have between 1.4 and 1.7 units of alcohol, so are not alcohol-free soft drinks.

- A large glass of red wine (250 ml) with an alcohol level of 14.5% has 3.6 units of alcohol.

- A large glass of a white wine (250 ml) with 11% alcohol has 2.8 units of alcohol.

- A 750 ml bottle of Buckfast at 15% alcohol, has 11.3 units of alcohol.

- Pint of beer (575 ml) at 4% alcohol = 2.3 units of alcohol.

- Bottle of Becks (330 ml) at 5.0% = 1.65 units of alcohol.

Alcohol

How many units of alcohol in drinks you like?

Multiply the volume of the drink (ml) X the % of alcohol and then divide by 1000.

e.g. a bottle of red wine 700 ml X 14.5% alcohol, divided by 1000 = 10.2 units of alcohol.

Safe drinking

Government advice used to recommend that women should drink no more than 14 units of alcohol per week with two days free of alcohol. Men should drink no more than 21 units per week again with two alcohol free days.

This advice has now changed to say 2-3 units per day for women and 4-5 units per day for men. This is confusing as many people who naturally go for the maximum figures allowed of 21 units for women and 28 for men, with two alcohol free days. Not what the government intended. But it suits the drinks industry as more is therefore sold.

myths & facts

Myth: A pub measure of vodka is stronger than a Bacardi Breezer.

Fact: WRONG. The pub measure of vodka at 35mls, 1.3 units of alcohol, the Bacardi Breezer is 1.5 units.

As we get used to alcohol, we develop a tolerance to it. That is not a good thing. As our personal tolerance to alcohol increases, so do all the side effects we don't want – getting fat, finding we need more alcohol to get the effects we had when we drank less, spending more of our cash on drink.

Women's bodies cannot process alcohol as well as a man can. Women's bodies have about 10% less water in them than men do, so they do not dilute the drug alcohol as well as men. They also have more fat in their bodies to absorb the extra calories that come from excessive drinking. This means they put on more fat as they drink more. The fat appears especially around their hips and backsides. This excessive fat brings with it particular problems for women who want to have children as it makes it difficult for them to get pregnant and causes serious complications in childbirth.

Drinking alcohol makes you pee a lot, so you get dehydrated. Being dehydrated means that your body is out of balance, it does not have enough water in it to keep you fit and healthy. Every cell in the body needs water to function as it should. Drinking free tap water, between alcoholic drinks will save you money and reduce your chances of getting dehydrated and having a hangover.

New Scottish licensing laws state: 'if you ask for free tap water in any licensed premises you must be provided with it'.

Useful Tip

Reduce the chance of a hangover by eating before going drinking, or do as the continentals do, eat and drink water whilst your are drinking, this slows down the rate of absorption of the alcohol and is kinder to your body.

myths & facts

Myth: Eating a fry-up when you are drunk will sober you up.

Fact: People mistakenly believe that a fry-up, or any food eaten when you are drunk will 'suck up the drink' and sober you up, as if the food acts like a great big sponge. Nice idea but the next question is – where does this sponge full of alcohol go to? Does it vanish mysteriously into fresh air or what? Perhaps it secretly drops out of our bottoms, unseen. But the alcohol will have left the stomach and will be in the bloodstream. So the fry-up will just lie in the stomach until it is digested in the usual way. It is worth remembering that the fat from the fry-up does not absorb the alcohol. It is just like any other excessive amounts of fat we eat, it gets laid down as fat around our body until it can be burnt off by exercise.

Hangovers

A hangover from alcohol is warning you that you are dehydrated and poisoned, so your body needs help. The hangover signs include a splitting headache caused by dehydration, nausea, sickness, depression and being short-tempered. The headache is due to the temporary shrinkage of the brain.

Alcohol

No – Irn Bru, hot sweet drinks, a fry-up or more alcohol will not help, nor does fresh air, a cold shower, or jogging round the block.

There are only two cures for a hangover. A pint of water before going to bed, to combat dehydration, and sleep. Your body goes into recovery mode whilst you sleep and uses all its energy to heal the damage you have done by drinking. If you have a headache, take care with painkillers. Alcohol and paracetamol together are common methods of self-poisoning and suicide. Stick to recommended doses.

Long-term risks of alcohol use

We should not under-estimate how dangerous alcohol can be. Alcohol kills many people and makes many others very ill. Heavy users can suffer a variety of problems from broken veins on their faces, cirrhosis of the liver, stomach and other cancers, psychosis, diabetes, obesity, brain damage to injuries from violence.

Alcohol the biggest drug problem facing Scotland and the UK. There are hundreds of thousands of families affected by alcohol misuse in Scotland and the UK. Without a doubt this situation is getting worse by the day with people in their early twenties having to be treated for liver damage, a problem that mainly used to affect only the over 50s.

Binge drinking

The government seems to be unsure about defining what binge drinking is, perhaps worried about being seen to either pitch it too high or too low. Or is government protecting the drinks industry from dropping sales or are they avoiding conflict with the medical profession about how harmful over-consumption of alcohol really is? They seem to think that it is better to say nothing. A big mistake in my view, as not advising people on what binge drinking is just leads to confusion, because the press and health experts continue to bang on about binge drinking students, drunken ladettes and the rest.

The common definition of binge drinking was 'consuming half or more of your weekly alcohol units in one drinking session', e.g. 7 units for a woman or 10.5 units for a man.

Binging at the weekend is the least safe way to drink alcohol. Spreading alcohol consumption over the week is a better idea, because it is kinder to the liver and other organs. Try to avoid drinking more than the safe limit too often, by spreading your drinking throughout the week. It is safer for adults to have a couple of small to medium glasses of wine a day than a whole bottle at the weekend.

According to an Audit Scotland study, it is estimated that damage from alcohol and drug misuse is around £5 billion per year in Scotland, £3.5 billion of that total is caused by alcohol misuse.

Mixing alcohol with other drugs is dangerous.
Mixing alcohol with downer type drugs, such as temazepam, valium and heroin, but also with stimulants like cocaine and crack cocaine, can result in an overdose and death.

Heavy drinking of alcohol does not improve the sex life..
Drinking small amounts of alcohol can make us more confident and relaxed, so may improve our chances of having sex with someone. Loading up on alcohol causes males to lose their sexual function (brewer's droop) and many young women get pregnant when they are drunk. Both sexes risk picking up sexually transmitted diseases.

Yer luck's in darlin' I'm tanked up and ready for action...

Using alcohol to try to solve problems in your life is bad news.
There are dangers when using drugs, not prescribed by a doctor, to sort out our problems. Alcohol is never prescribed by doctors to solve patients' problems. There are better ways to deal with our worries. Talking to trusted friends, phoning helplines, talking to your family or professional counsellors are much safer solutions.

Mixing of alcohol with legal or illegal drugs is not a good idea.
Some drugs make you high, others make you feel down or depressed and some make you feel a bit out of your mind (trippy). Mixing uppers

Alcohol

with uppers, uppers with downers or any other combination of drugs can have effects you did not plan for. They can even kill you. Deaths are now regularly being recorded in people who mixed cocaine and alcohol.

No one can be sure of what is in any illicit drug,
Street drug dealers buy their supplies from an international criminal network. This is hardly Boots the Chemist or a reliable legally controlled supplier.

Alcohol and cocaine don't mix.
Mixing alcohol and cocaine is particularly dangerous as you end up not feeling drunk, so you may then drink more alcohol than you intended. Your body then generates a third and more dangerous chemical (cocaethylene) which in some people causes fatal heart attacks.

Prescribed medicines for adults should never be taken by children along with alcohol.
A cocktail of drugs is often the cause of accidental deaths and suicides. Accidental poisonings from consuming alcohol along with methadone, paracetamol, sleeping pills or tranquillisers happen more often than people realise.

Some people cannot tolerate alcohol well.
Some people do not drink alcohol for economic, religious, moral or health reasons. Some only use alcohol occasionally. For some alcohol is not a drug that is good for them. It makes them sick and ill, or they find that it always causes them problems in their lives, they are better without it. There is some evidence that some of us are genetically unsuited to using the drug alcohol. Alcohol problems do sometimes seem to affect particular families. This may be because these families tend to use alcohol as their way of dealing with life.

myths & facts

Myth: Alcohol is not a drug.

Fact: I have spent many sad times with parents who have a child using illicit drugs, and I commonly hear parents saying 'see if it had been alcohol they were using, I would have known what to do about it'. These parents are badly misinformed, because they have not understood that alcohol is an extremely powerful drug.

Alcohol

Myth: You can drink yourself sober

myths & facts

Fact: Oh really! It takes one hour for one unit of alcohol to be eliminated from a fully grown adult's body. So how could the alcohol that is already in our bloodstream escape? Drinking more alcohol, to sober up will top up the alcohol that is already in your body. We may feel that we have sobered up, but a breath test, if you are driving, would drop you right in it. So don't go there, it is an old wives' tale and a dangerous myth.

Ok, I can't walk the line just now, but wait 'til I have a couple more wee swallows...

Myth: You can get drunk quicker by putting vodka in your eye.

myths & facts

Fact: No, no, no, that is a very bad idea unless you want to damage your eyes. This crazy myth came from a popular cult video passed around by young people.

Myth: Men's bodies can repair their livers but women cannot do that.

myths & facts

Fact: Absolutely not true. It is also not true that women all have smaller livers than men. The liver's function is to filter the blood. By doing this it gets rid of poisons and stuff that your body does not need. Excessive consumption of any drugs, and alcohol is a powerful drug, overloads the liver and damages it by not allowing enough time for it to recover and heal itself. Once your liver has processed the blood the waste is sent on to the kidneys and eliminated as urine. Excessive overloading of the kidneys can also lead to serious damage.

Alcohol

Myth: Drinking two or three bottles of Buckfast Tonic Wine is not binge drinking.

Fact: Oh yes, drinking that amount of Buckfast is definitely binge drinking as it involves consuming a massive 33.9 units of alcohol. That is almost a bottle and a half of spirits like vodka or whisky. That is serious drinking and a sure sign that someone is a problem drinker. This number of units of alcohol could kill a child.

The dodgy marketing of alcohol to children

Although the drinks industry denies it, they, like the tobacco industry spend millions on planning how to recruit new consumers to replace those that have stopped using their products or have died because of them. That is just a fact of life and of the drugs business.

In Scotland one of the routes into alcohol use for children is through Buckfast which is a very strong alcoholic drink with15% of alcohol by volume. It is a drink like sweet sherry that tastes very similar to the sort of drinks that children are used to. These facts make it easy for children to make the transition from Coke, Iron Bru and the likes into alcoholic drinks, which they may otherwise dislike.

The ironic thing about Buckfast is that it is produced and sold by the Benedictine monks of Buckfast Abbey. Benedictines are a teaching order of the Catholic church and are well-known for their education work with children. See the website www.buckfast.org.uk for full details. What you read will put the thoughts I have laid out below into context.

Over the last ten years there have been several unsuccessful attempts by MPs and MSPs to ban Buckfast. The problem with it is that it is sold in Scotland in vast quantities, mainly to children and young people living in our most deprived communities. A wander around the streets of our most deprived communities provides all the evidence needed – they are littered with broken Buckfast bottles. It is said, but I have not been able to confirm this, that 70% of the entire production of Buckfast is sold in the Coatbridge/Airdrie area of North Lanarkshire. That might be an exaggeration but it is a plausible figure and if the Scots did not drink so much Buckfast it would soon go out of production.

Strathclyde police in 2011 reported that 75% of all crimes of violence reported in their area involving young people had been committed whilst under the influence of Buckfast. Research into this in Young

Offenders Institutions and Scottish prisons also confirms this fact. A search through court reports in Scotland also confirms the level of this problem. Buckfast was mentioned in 5,638 crime reports in Strathclyde from 2006-2009, equating to three a day on average. One in 10 of those offences were violent and the Buckfast bottle was used as a weapon 114 times in that period.

Buckfast is a relatively cheap product so is easily afforded by people on limited budgets. It is an English drink, as is cider, and both of them have enjoyed especially low tax levels compared to other alcoholic drinks. The plan to introduce the minimum pricing of alcohol in Scotland is unlikely to affect its price as it generally sells for around £5.80 and £7 a bottle. It contains 11.3 units of alcohol so if the 45p minimum price per unit of alcohol figure was used for this drink it would not go up in price, as it is already well above the £5.80 minimum that the government wants to apply.

In the decades that I have delivered my alcohol workshops for young people in Scotland I found that twenty years ago youngsters regularly told me that they 'had a bottle of Buckie in the house before they went out drinking'. By 2010 when I last ran an alcohol workshop, young people were reporting consuming up to 3 bottles of Buckie before going out drinking. Three bottles of Buckfast is 33.9 units of alcohol, equivalent to almost a bottle and a half of strong spirits such as vodka. I have no reason to doubt these reports and when I hear what else young people are drinking along with the Buckfast the story is even more horrendous. It is no wonder that we now have people in their twenties with failed livers. Over a weekend of binge drinking many of these youngsters, some well under the age of 18, regularly consume 50 to 100 units of alcohol or more. Is it any wonder that the rates of alcoholism in these poor communities and in Scotland are so high?

The spokesperson from the Buckfast PR company, Chandler & Co. is regularly to be heard in the media denying that Buckfast is a problem or that there is any link between their 'Tonic Wine' and the health and crime reports that have been recorded over many decades.

The media pressure on Buckfast has had a couple of very interesting results. Firstly the monks of Buckfast Abbey have recently been offering charitable funding to projects for children and young people in these Scottish deprived areas. Secondly they have rebranded themselves to try to convince consumers that they are concerned

Alcohol

145

old Buckfast label

about their health. Unfortunately for them I have been studying Buckfast labels for many years, so I am able to reveal some facts that may surprise people. An analysis of the old and new Buckfast labels speaks for itself.

The old label says in very large print 'Buckfast' followed by much smaller text that says 'TONIC WINE'. The text below that states in very tiny print 'The name Tonic Wine does not imply health giving or medicinal properties'. This clearly immediately denies any possibility that Buckfast is in any way a tonic or a medicine. One of the common myths about this product is that people regularly say to me that doctors can prescribe Buckie to old people, because it is a tonic!

Even more interesting is that on the bottom right hand corner of this old label it lists what people imagine are the mysterious tonic ingredients, listed by their percentages. They include Vanillin 0.009%, Caffeine 0.05%, Potassium Phosphate 0.20%, Sodium Phosphate 0.05% and Sodiium Glycerophosphate BPC 0.65%. These turn out to be a flavouring, a stimulant drug and three preservatives to stop the colour or smell of the wine from going off. No magical health-giving tonic ingredients here. Yet the Buckfast website still gives the impression that it has tonic effects.

That label has for decades reinforced the common myth that Buckfast is good for you and plays down the information contained in the final piece of text which is in larger black type stating that this wine contains a lot of alcohol. 75cl e15% Vol. I have no idea what the 'e' refers to.

After years of bad press and many attempts by politicians to ban this drink the monks have now remarketed it with a new and even more confusing label.

The majority of the text on this new label (opposite, right) is unchanged but the text that has changed is very significant because it now states, not in bold print, that Buckfast is a 'Red Wine Based Aperitif 99.28% and that it contains Sulphites. I had no idea what the 99.28% figure meant. A Buckfast spokesman said it listed the amount of liquid in the bottle, which they had to state by law. Strange as no other alcohol containers list this information. The Sulphites are used in all wines to arrest the fermentation process.

There are two new additional statements. The first is that the drink is 'High Caffeine Content (37.5%/100mg)'. That is a very high level of caffeine, about ten times a standard cup of coffee, I believe. Caffeine is a stimulant drug which in this case is contained within an alcoholic drink which is a depressant drug. One is an

new Buckfast label

upper type drug and the other is a downer drug, not a good or healthy combination for an adult, let alone children. This mixture of two different drugs of such a high level is, it turns out, an example in very young people of a new trend in our society which can prove to be fatal. That sounds dramatic but in the last five years, the massive increase in cocaine use (the most powerful of the illegal stimulants), in combination with the binge drinking of alcohol, has caused deaths. Of the 574 deaths in Scotland from drugs in 2008 there were 79 from the cocktail of cocaine mixed with alcohol. There were no such deaths recorded 4-5 years earlier.

So the introduction of children and young people to Buckfast could eventually lead young people to a potentially lethal cocktail of drugs. This is clearly something that we must take seriously.

The new front label of Buckfast also tries to combat the criticism of the streets being littered with broken Buckie bottles by including the symbol for bottle banks. Attempts by MPs and MSPs to get Buckfast to change to plastic bottles has in the past been rejected by the makers.

Alcohol

147

new Buckfast back label

The back label on the bottle now lists some rather doubtful information which is likely to misinform the users of the product. Next to the large bar code there is a box with what looks like sensible government advice to 'Drink Responsibly'. But it misses some important details, such as that we should have two alcohol-free days a week.

This label has a logo about drinking in pregnancy. It also lists a website presumablly for further advice. Unfortunately the website as shown does not exist. It says in bold black print 'D-RINKAWARE.CO.UK'. A web search does not come up with anything. It may be that they just got it badly wrong and meant to print: www.drinkaware.co.uk. That is a website that does exist, but it is by no means an independent source of information on alcohol as it is one that is wholly funded by the alcohol industry.

Buckfast, the high caffeine, high alcohol drink, if consumed along with other high caffeine power drinks, is in my view a recipe for disaster for children and it should be modified and re-labelled with accurate information about its contents.

When MPs and MSPs have attempted in the past to ban Buckfast they have been threatened with court action by Chandlers & Co. I would hope that the Benedictine monks with their history of educational work would not want to undermine any efforts that are made to educate and protect children from the harm caused by heavy consumption of any strong alcoholic drink.

The Scottish Parliament is considering a ban on strongly caffeinated alcoholic drinks. There are other concerns about caffeine in drinks as Scottish school teachers are reporting having serious behaviour problems with children drinking cans of highly caffeinated energy drinks. The level of caffeine in some of these drinks is up to 300mg (a cup of coffee has between 80-130mg). They also contain very high levels of sugar. These energy drinks are making children extremely hyperactive and when the effects wear off they flop and have no concentration. All of this is typical of the effects of stimulant drugs.

Alcohol

Myth: Some bottles of Buckfast are stronger than others.

Fact: This is a myth I picked up from young people. They honestly believe that different bottles of Buckfast vary in strength and that you can tell by checking the bar codes, believing that a low last number in the code means it is has less alcohol in it. This, of course, is complete nonsense, as all alcohol must be labelled with exactly what it contains, including the percentage of alcohol. Other information like units of alcohol are not required legally as yet. At 15% alcohol per volume there are always 11.3 units of alcohol in a 75 cl. bottle of Buckfast.

myths & facts

Myth: Doctors used to prescribe Buckfast as a tonic for old people in hospitals.

Fact: Another of the myths passed down from generation to generation to justify the consumption of this powerful drink.

myths & facts

Myth: 'Aftershock' – it's so strong that pubs are only allowed to sell you one shot of it.

Fact: Aftershock is a liqueur with an alcoholic content of 30% (it was 40% until 2009). So it is sold just like any other spirit. No law exists to restrict the number of servings of a particular drink that bar staff can serve, although they must not sell alcohol to someone they believe to be drunk.

myths & facts

Myth: Women can hold their drink just as well as men can.

Fact: This statement is often made by women trying to imply that they can drink men under the table, as if that was a good, healthy, feminine activity. A comment that is made more often today than a couple of decades back, as many more young women now drink to excess frequently and are drinking just like young men have done in the past.

myths & facts

Alcohol

myths & facts

Myth: If you flick fag ash in your pint you get drunk faster.

Fact: Where such a myth as this comes from is a complete mystery. Common sense should tell us that this is complete nonsense but it is surprising how many people actually believe this. But it is not true. Fag ash is burnt tobacco, carbon probably, so has no known properties that would speed up our ability to get drunk. If it did we should be dumping great chunks of barbecue charcoal in our drinks. I don't think so.

Actions the government could take to reduce harm to children from alcohol:

- Change laws to protect minors from alcohol misuse;

- Simplify the advice on units of alcohol and safe consumption. Include advice for children if the laws are not revised;

- Carefully increase the price of alcohol through tax but be aware of negative consequences that would drive those who can no longer afford to drink alcohol to using black market suppliers or switching to illicit drugs.

Tobacco

(Stimulant/upper drug)

Tobacco is fast going out of fashion and parents should do everything they can to discourage children from using tobacco as it is often the gateway to other drug use for children.

Street names: Cigarettes, fags, cigs, snout, smokes.

Legal Status: Tobacco products can only be bought at 18 and older.

There is no law to stop those under 18 from smoking tobacco, so you can legally smoke at any age.

The Police and Park Keepers in uniform have a duty to confiscate tobacco or cigarettes from persons aged under 16 found smoking in a public place.

In Europe the age for buying tobacco is between 16-18 and in Asia between 15-21.

Time will tell if the levels of smoking in children decrease after the law on buying tobacco was changed in March 2006 making it illegal to buy tobacco until 18 years of age. It had been 16 years of age. **The law does not prohibit children from smoking – only from buying tobacco.**

The Nutt Scale rating for tobacco – 9th most dangerous of the 20 commonest drugs used in the UK.

There are no known health benefits to be had from smoking tobacco products.

The drug that kills most people in Scotland and the UK is tobacco.

In 2004 there were 13,473 deaths from smoking in Scotland. That was 24% of all deaths.

Tobacco

151

About 100,000 people in the UK die from smoking each year.

In 2007 UK households spent £16.6 billion on smoking.

There are about 10 million smokers and 10 million ex-smokers in the UK. (SOURCE: ASH fact sheet 2011)

In Scotland in 2005/6, more than a million adults smoked tobacco.

Smoking in Scotland

• Adult smoking has gradually reduced from 37.7% in 1999 to 25.2% in 2008.

• There are now fewer children starting to smoke. One theory is that children are now preferring to spend their pocket money on topping up their mobiles or to pay for downloading music onto their music players.

• More girls than boys smoke.

• 14% of 15 year old boys smoke regularly.

• 16% of 15 year old girls smoke regularly.

• 41% of 15 year old regular smokers said they would like to give up smoking altogether.

• 1% of 15 year old regular smokers had tried to give up smoking.

• 65% of 15 year old regular smokers had been smoking for more than one year.

• 6% of 15 year old regular smokers reported that at least one of their parents was a daily smoker.

• 64% of 15 year old non-smokers reported that none or almost none of their friends smoked.

[SOURCE: ASH Scotland]

Tobacco

The nature of the drug tobacco

Tobacco is a stimulant drug

Tobacco smoke contains nicotine, carbon monoxide, cyanide, droplets of tar, and about 4,000 other chemicals are added across the product range, including many poisonous gasses.

When tobacco smoke enters the lungs it is passed quickly into the blood stream and almost immediately into the brain.

Nicotine speeds up the pulse rate and our blood pressure, it reduces appetite and lowers skin temperature.

Smoking tobacco psychologically stimulates and arouses us, but this wears off after a very few seconds, so the smoker seeks further stimulation by inhaling more tobacco smoke. **This circle of stimulation followed by the come-down is what makes tobacco use so highly addictive.**

Smokers falsely believe that tobacco is a relaxant – it is not, no stimulant drug can relax you.

Nicotine is eliminated from the body quickly so if someone gives up smoking it is out of their system within 3 weeks on average.

The behavioural aspects of smoking
The Social Smokers

Some people start out as social smokers. They don't particularly like the taste or smell of cigarettes but feel they ought to smoke in order to be one of the crowd. If they don't inhale – and many don't – they are unlikely to become addicted and when they decide to quit can do so relatively easily. Or they may only smoke the occasional cigarette – often given to them by someone else – when out with the crowd and do not smoke when on their own. The ban on indoor smoking has made it a lot easier for social smokers to quit.

Real Smokers

Social smokers who inhale can become addicted and become 'real' smokers, with the result that quitting becomes more difficult. The people who have most difficulty in quitting are those who find real behavioural benefits. These people often smoke more when they are at home alone, than they do in company. They are also likely to be the heaviest smokers of all. These people fall into two categories.

Tobacco

Comfort smokers

Those who smoke in order to comfort themselves because of poverty, anxiety, poor environment, lack of friends, not wanting to get fat, etc. They may start out as social smokers but find that the act of smoking gives them a respite from worrying, or it acts as a substitute for food, or it is simply a bit like a baby's comforter, something to hang on to when things are not going well in their lives. In fact, smoking may be making them more anxious as nicotine is a stimulant. It may also be contributing to poor nutrition and poverty as cigarettes are by no means cheap. Nevertheless, if people believe they need to smoke, they are likely to become addicted to nicotine and also to the comfort that the ritual of smoking offers them. Such people are unlikely to want to quit unless or until the other aspects of their lives start to improve or they have a really bad health scare – like bronchitis which goes into pneumonia – and they realise they must do something. Interestingly when these people decide to quit they are often surprisingly successful because they are used to having to deal with difficulties in their lives and may have developed a strong character as a result.

The Nervous Smokers

These are people who find it hard to sit still or who, if they weren't smoking, would need to find something else to calm them and occupy their hands. The whole ritual of taking out a cigarette, lighting it, waving it about or repeatedly tapping it on the ashtray acts a bit like 'worry beads' and allows these people to concentrate on work or study, or to calm down and be more relaxed. Just a minute, I hear you saying. You've said that nicotine is a stimulant so how can it be relaxing? The answer is in the word 'ritual' or, to put it another way, familiar habits. Familiar habits are soothing simply because they are familiar, and predictable, and so a cigarette which contains the stimulant nicotine can still be soothing and relaxing for people who need a prop to occupy their hands and their mouths. Psychologists would call such people 'oral' types and for them the joy of smoking is not to be sociable or one of the crowd but for personal psychological satisfaction. If such people don't inhale deeply – and many don't – the trick to stopping or cutting down is to find something else to do with their hands or to use gum as a help to quitting. For those who have inhaled deeply and are therefore heavily addicted, stopping can be very hard work. Joining a support group is often the best way forward as oral types also like to talk and joining a support group

Tobacco

encourages people to talk about how they are getting on in the company of others with similar problems.

[SOURCE: Ann McClintock, Psychologist]

Damage to health

Smoking damages almost every part of our body, the skin, heart, lungs, hair, eyes, teeth. Tobacco smoke dumps tiny droplets of hot tar into the lungs, as this builds up over the years of smoking it gets very hard to breathe making it hard to dance, walk or play energetically.

Smoking and preventable cancers

It is almost entirely smokers who get mouth, tongue, throat, larynx, and lung cancer. Smokers have a 1 in 2 chance of suffering from these cancers. Other cancers associated with smoking include bladder, kidney, stomach, pancreas, cervix, oesophagus, bones and brain. Non-smokers are much less likely to be afflicted by any of these cancers, unless they are affected by passive smoking in their work environment or from living with a heavy smoker. Acute bronchitis, emphysema, non-insulin dependent diabetes, vitamin and mineral deficiencies are all made worse by smoking tobacco, as are skin wrinkles, facial ageing, skin complaints such as psoriasis and the healing of all wounds. Allergies made worse by smoking include rhinitis, sinusitis and various other immune system damage and infections.

Smokers in their 30s and 40s suffer five times as many heart attacks as non-smokers.

Is it too easy for children to buy tobacco?

Even with the age for buying tobacco moving up from 16 to 18 there has been little difference because children still find no difficulty in buying tobacco.

For decades, the police and other authorities had little interest in enforcing tobacco purchasing laws in the UK. This has been a very big mistake and has led to hundreds of thousands, if not millions, of children starting to smoke. There are now serious efforts underway to address this.

Moves to ban cigarette machines and to hide from view tobacco

Tobacco

155

products in shops is being considered, but the tobacco companies are trying to prevent this change by spurious court cases slowing down the introduction of these law changes.

The use of ID cards which is already the common practice in places like the USA,Canada and Australia has reduced access to tobacco for children, but only when the retailers are punished sufficiently for not checking ages. Why has introducing these child protection measures been avoided for so long in the UK? Perhaps it is the power of the vested interests in the tobacco industry?

Tobacco the gateway drug enticing children into using other drugs
It is very unusual to find someone with a serious drug problem such as heroin use, who does not also drink alcohol and smoke tobacco. Although things are improving it is still true that for many children their first contact with drugs will be through passive smoking and then experimenting with tobacco. This makes tobacco a common gateway drug. It is the route that gets many children started on a journey into using other substances later. The most common scenario is that children start smoking, then drinking alcohol, then for some cannabis. For a much smaller number other illicit drugs are used. Listening to the drug use histories of clients with serious drug problems too often reveals exactly that route through drugs, to a serious addiction problem.

We must discourage children from smoking
Any action that parents can take to discourage children from smoking will at the very least delay by a few years the age at which they start to experiment with other more dangerous illicit drugs. Most cannabis users mix it with tobacco. Learning the rituals around smoking ordinary cigarettes may give children new status with their peers. Learning to roll a joint of cannabis requires even more social skills. For many children, this gives them the acceptance amongst their peers that they want or crave. Not a useful social skill nor a healthy one.

Changes in the laws are reducing adult smoking and improving health. The banning of smoking in public places, along with increasing the age at which we can buy tobacco, is reducing adult smoking and should eventually reduce the number of smokers and deaths from smoking.

Tobacco

Smoking laws are ineffective in protecting children

This is true because existing laws only prohibit the purchase not the smoking of tobacco or tobacco products. You can smoke at any age, but you cannot buy tobacco products until you are 18 years of age.

Adults condoning smoking in children!

Far too many parents and siblings condone smoking in children by supplying them with fags and even smoking with them. Even some youth workers think nothing of using fags as a tool to control the behaviour of difficult young people.

The tobacco companies are desperate to protect their hugely lucrative business so they have spent fortunes on opposing all the proposed changes in tobacco laws.

Even organisations like ASH (the Scottish anti-smoking charity) argue that proposals on changing tobacco laws to protect more children, would criminalise children. They are right, but why do they have no qualms about laws which may criminalise children, but certainly protect them from harm, e.g. that you cannot have sex until you are 16 nor drive a car or motorcycle or own a gun. Such laws are there to protect children from harm. But of course they only work if they are adequately enforced.

If politicians dared to change the law on smoking to be one that **made it 'illegal to buy or consume tobacco products before the age of 18'**, this would give a boost to the long-term aim of eliminating tobacco use in our society. If the public got behind supporting such changes in the law we would see a substantial drop in smoking amongst children in a generation.

Tobacco is a stimulant drug, not a relaxant

What I call the **'circle of addiction'** is demonstrated in the sequence of events that follow from puffing on a cigarette. First we get the stimulation from inhaling tobacco, followed by the come-down that happens as the stimulation wears off in a few seconds, then more stimulation is sought by the smoker. This is what makes tobacco, like all the stimulant drugs, so addictive. We all prefer psychological highs to the come downs and depressive lows. Smokers quickly seek added stimulation after the come-down, and as tolerance to the drug

Tobacco

develops rapidly, the inexperienced, virgin smoker soon needs to increase his or her dose of nicotine to achieve the satisfaction they had from beginners' smaller doses.

myths & facts

Myth: Smoking calms you down.

Fact: No it does not calm you down. It only calms down your craving for the drug nicotine in tobacco. If you are a non-smoker your body is not stressed up by nicotine, so you have no need to use tobacco to calm down the stress that tobacco induces in your body and mind in the first place.

What the smoker is doing is relieving, temporarily, their addiction to the drug tobacco. That is no different to the false relaxation that the injecting heroin user feels when they take another hit of their drug of choice.

Passive smoking is particularly bad for children's health
Children living in homes where they are exposed to passive smoking from adults get more health problems such as glue ear, chest infections, asthma and sore throats. They are also 90% more likely to become smokers than those living in smoke-free homes. Research suggests that up to 40 cot deaths were attributed to passive smoking in the UK in one year.

Smoking in cars is a particularly bad idea
Smoking in cars traps children and other passengers in an enclosed space where the concentration of the damaging chemicals and gasses is much more intense than in open spaces. The Scottish Parliament is considering a bill to outlaw smoking in cars when children are present.

On March 24th 2010 a letter appeared in *The Times* newspaper signed by 21 doctors and professors from the main Colleges of Physicians in the UK. The letter stated the following:

Sir, A new report launched today by the Royal College of Physicians, Passive Smoking and Children, confirms that passive smoking is a leading cause of death and disease in children. About two million children (in the UK) are currently exposed to cigarette smoke at home, and many

Tobacco

more outside the home. In addition to the serious health risks of passive smoking, however, the report also points out the additional health risk to children posed by family smoking, which makes children about twice as likely to become smokers themselves.

These health hazards to children can be avoided entirely by acting to reduce the number of adults who smoke, particularly parents and care-givers, and to reduce still further the exposure of children to smoke and smoking, both in and outside the home. This will require a comprehensive strategy including tobacco prices rises, mass media campaigns, more effective health warning, prohibition of point of sale display, generic packaging and better provision of smoking cessation services.

Smoke-free legislation also needs to be extended much more widely, to include public places visited by children and young people, and including prohibition of all smoking in cars and other vehicles. The Chief Medical Officer (of England) in his foreword to the report, says that we must keep up the momentum to continue to reduce the harm of tobacco use in our communities, and create a truly smoke-free future. As doctors, we agree, and call on governments to take the necessary actions to protect children's future.

myths & facts

Myth: It takes years for children to become addicted to tobacco.

Fact: There is evidence that children get addicted to tobacco very quickly, becoming addicted to nicotine very soon after starting to smoke. Around 3-4 cigarettes is now thought to be enough to hook children into this highly addictive behaviour.

Children are a soft-target, they give the tobacco industry the recruits to smoking that they need to replace the thousands of adults who are giving up smoking. There have in the past been reports of tobacco company sponsorship of school sports and other educational activities in some of the poorest countries in the world. Clearly tobacco company research has shown poor children to be a lucrative new market. In the 1990s it was estimated that for every 10 primary aged school children recruited to smoking, around $500,000 in profit is generated for that industry in the lifetime of these smokers. Clearly that estimate is well out of date now but it is still scandalous.

Tobacco

I believe that China is currently the most profitable target for recruiting new smokers as they have no legislation to ban smoking in public places.

myths & facts

Myth: Smoking cures boredom!

Fact: Many children say that they only smoke because they are bored. I know of no drug or medicine that cures boredom. If anyone does, please let me know, as I would love to be proved wrong on that one. Nicotine has no magical ingredients to cure boredom, although this is one of the most persistent myths that children use to justify their smoking. A discussion of the many things that they could do to overcome boredom, usually brings out some really positive suggestions. Listen to music, going for a walk, taking some exercise, having a laugh, reading, cooking, shopping, playing games, watching a movie or television and of course sex are all great cures for boredom.

myths & facts

Myth: Smoking is a very sociable activity.

Fact: It is interesting that the ban on smoking in public places has to some extent increased the need for those who continue to smoke to socialise more by grouping together in huddles outside pubs and other public buildings. This serves to reinforce even more, the association between smoking as a habit being a sociable thing to do, especially as it is too often seen as having an amazing ability to cure boredom. Suffice to say that there are better, cheaper and much safer ways to cure boredom than smoking ourselves to ill-health and an early death. If you are a non-smoker, just think for a moment about what it is that you do to cure your boring moments in life, and share your thoughts with friends who fear they cannot live without tobacco.

Smoking is a learned behaviour

We were not born to smoke. If we had been, we would have had a chimney or vent in our heads to let out the dangerous gasses. We can unlearn any bad habit, such as biting our fingernails, spitting, having too much sugar or salt, or smoking. Habits and other learned behaviour can have a social aspect which endears us to our peer group. Smoking is seen by some children as a thing that they have to learn to do to keep friends. There is some evidence that we can

Tobacco

unlearn annoying habits in less than two weeks, if we are motivated to do so.

Many children see smoking as a cool activity

Research into smoking amongst young people, and especially young women, tell us that one of the strongest reasons for them smoking is that it is seen as a 'cool' adult behaviour. That belief used to be driven by the insidious advertising of tobacco showing glamorous film stars and fashion models smoking. The equivalent male targeted advertising made an association with car racing, cricket and other sports. Now that smoking advertising is banned, the same messages are still being delivered through the story lines and characters in soap operas that are popular with young and old. Dot Cotton in *East Enders* is but one example. The many reruns of old films are littered with smoking portrayed as cool and adult.

myths & facts

Myth: Smoking keeps you slim.

Fact: There seems to be a grain of truth in this myth, because many people find that if they quit smoking they may put on some weight. This is not entirely true. To understand why smoking keeps you slim is a myth, you need to know that there are three human body types (shapes):

Ectomorphs – a person with a lean build of a body, (tall slim).

Mesomorphs – a person who is of a compact muscular build (pear shaped).

Endomorphs – a person of a soft round build (round apple or barrel shaped).

We all fit into one of these body types, which come from our genes, so if we look at our parents and grandparents we will see where our shape came from.

Take a moment to read and understand this fact of life. It is important not just to clear up the myth that smoking keeps us slim but also to help the serial dieters of this world to stop trying to be an Ectomorph (tall & slim) when they clearly are not and never will be.

If you are an ectopmorph (tall & slim) then your metabolism is such that you can eat and drink for the rest of us, so when ectomorphs

Tobacco

quit smoking, unlike other body types, they will not put on any weight.

Mesomorphs and endomorphs have metabolisms that do not burn up food and drink as fast, so if they over-indulge they just become bigger mesomorphs and endomorphs, bigger pear- and apple-shaped people. This is just one of these cruel facts of life, but one worth knowing about if we are worried about our weight or body shape, as many children are.

To understand this myth further we need to know that when we smoke tobacco, our taste buds are sort of sent off to sleep, they are dampened down, so we do not get the full taste of the food or drink we consume. When we quit using tobacco, our taste buds waken up again, so food and drink tastes so much better again. The person who is quitting smoking then often over indulges in eating and drinking, a sort of comfort eating, to compensate for depriving themselves of tobacco, but also because food and drink starts to taste so much nicer.

Regardless of being told this, many young women in particular, continue to believe that tobacco keeps them slim. Although the advertising of tobacco is no longer allowed, it is known that young women do pick up the very subtle messages that associate smoking with keeping slim from celebrity role models. Again, these myths are perpetuated in the story lines in soaps, films and the media. The fact that so many models and female film stars are chosen is because they fit the right image of the tall slim ectomorph shape. This is neither well understood or accepted by many young women.

Subconscious beliefs determine our behaviour
Challenges to our subconscious personal beliefs about tobacco can make it easier for us to quit. This is about understanding the massive power of the mind and ability of the subconscious mind, to alter our personal codes of behaviour, making it possible for us to change or modify our beliefs. Change can then happen, because it is our subconscious personal beliefs that drive our addictive smoking behaviour.

A Psychologist view on the smoking and keeping slim myth
Nicotine is a stimulant so it does speed up the metabolism a bit, and when you stop smoking the metabolism drops. It tends to drop further in those whose metabolism is naturally slower – i.e. the endomorphs (apple-shaped). The slower the metabolism the more likely you are to put on weight. In terms of obesity, therefore, the endomorphs may successfully use smoking to keep their weight down and are likely to put on more weight when they stop. However, the endomorphs run a higher risk from smoking as they will often use a cigarette with a coffee to replace one or more meals in order to stay even more slim. They therefore run all the health risks that apply to smoking but also have less well-nourished bodies to resist the illnesses that smoking can cause.

Mesomorphs (pear-shaped) being naturally muscular and athletic are less likely to be smokers as they tend to become addicted to sport or exercise rather than substances – except for alcohol which appeals to the social and outgoing nature of the mesomorph. As the mesomorph ages there is a real danger that muscle will turn to fat as a result of less exercise and that alcohol will contribute to higher blood sugar levels with resultant obesity and possible risk of diabetes. Mesomorphs who do smoke are less likely to lose weight as their metabolism is already high. Quitting smoking will lead to weight gain only if the mesomorph increases food intake to compensate for stopping smoking and does not up the level of exercise taken.

The ectomorph (tall slim) who smokes is likely to be very thin indeed, as ectomophs also have a naturally high metabolism and, like the endomorphs, are likely to be poorly nourished if they substitute fags for food. Ectomorphs who quit are likely to experience a weight gain of a few pounds but are unlikely to retain that weight gain for very long as their body will naturally adjust unless they absolutely gorge themselves. This is unlikely to happen with ectomorphs as they have a very good regulatory mechanism in their brains which tells them when to eat and when to stop. We all have this mechanism but some of us have it less strongly developed or have developed the ability to ignore bodily signals that tell us when we need to eat or that we are full up.

[SOURCE: Ann McClintock, Psychologist]

Tobacco

The tobacco industry has told lies or not clarified the truth about smoking and weight. When the tobacco industry was able to advertise their products they encouraged the idea that smoking keeps you slim. They used images of slim, tall female models, or even slim ballet dancers with fags in their hands. Public advertising of tobacco is now banned, but the myth still persists. Perhaps this is because smokers want to believe this.

One of the cigarettes on the market is called 'Slims'. It is not difficult to work out who that brand of cigarettes were marketed at. Young women perhaps!

Why do some children not become smokers?

We do not know enough about why some children choose not to smoke. The most common reasons I hear from young males is that it would stop them from participating in sports like football. Some young men say they do not smoke because they think it is effeminate, like homosexuals. This makes some sense, as boys must be able to observe for themselves that more young girls than young boys are starting to smoke. So smoking could be seen as a feminine activity. There is also quite a strong anti-gay feeling amongst adolescent males who may be struggling to establish their sexuality and see any behaviour that makes them different, or non-heterosexual, as being threatening. It is also true that some very effeminate gays do seem to smoke in ways that are quite flamboyant and over the top – feminine. There may be another explanation but I have not found it yet.

Females most often say it's just bad for your health, they hate the smell or cannot afford it.

Smoking makes you smell

Many young men report that they hate the smell of smoke and especially the smell of smoke on girls and women. Sexist, but that is what they say. This view of smoking does have a positive side to it, giving some young males the excuse not to start smoking.

Many adults are now saying how much they enjoy being able to go back to pubs again, because they don't come home with their hair and clothes stinking of smoke. Many families now do not allow anyone to smoke within their home. It is commendable to see how many adults stand outside their homes to smoke, away from the children.

Tobacco

There is a campaign on creating 'smoke-free homes'. [see the ASH website: www.ash.org.uk for details]

myths & facts

Myth: I only smoke when I am drinking – so I am not really a smoker.

Fact: Many people say that they only smoke when they drink alcohol. Clearly they associate smoking with the relaxing, sociable activity of drinking alcohol. The tobacco, a stimulant upper drug, takes them up and the alcohol, a downer drug, brings them back down again, they see this as relaxing them. Once people understand that tobacco is a stimulant and cannot relax or calm them, then they can start to address this problem. The ban on smoking in public places should have an impact on this particular group of smokers, eventually.

Helpful Tip

Smoking roll-ups reduces the amount of tobacco that someone uses, because the ritualistic, behaviour associated with the building of the roll-up cigarette takes up some of the time a person might normally be inhaling the tobacco smoke. Cannabis roll-ups do not count, they are a different sort of problem addressed later.

myths & facts

Myth: Smoking does not really cost me all that much.

Fact: Each cigarette now costs 35p. The average costs of smoking 10 standard cigarettes a day, including 6% inflation is:

£3.50 per day

£24.50 per week

£106.46 per month

£1,277.50 per year

£7,201.38 over 5 years

£16,838.42 over 10 years

To make these calculations I checked at three supermarkets for the average cost of the three most popular cigarettes. In 2009 for a change I checked the cost of cigarettes in three small local corner shops, in poorer areas. To my astonishment, I found that the most popular cigarettes

Tobacco

165

myths & facts

being sold were the most expensive ones. Clearly the tobacco companies, even without public advertising, have managed to convince the poorest people, who can least afford to smoke, that the higher the cost of the cigarettes the higher the quality of the smoke? Another shocking and dangerous myth.

myths & facts

Myth: The most expensive fags must be the best and strongest.

Fact: That the more expensive cigarettes are the best is a very costly myth, which badly affects those that can least afford to be smokers.

myths & facts

Myth: The tobacco companies make the biggest profit from fags.

Fact: Four pounds out of every £5 spent on cigarettes goes straight to the UK government in tax and only £1 to the tobacco companies. The tax on cigarettes is almost 80% of the cost, so who are the real profiteers from tobacco? The taxman collected £11.1 billion in 2010/11. Perhaps this is the reason that our government has been so slow to tackle the scandal of health damage from smoking. Today about 50% of tobacco bought in the UK is imported illegally by criminal gangs losing the UK Government around half of the annual tax income from tobacco.

Poisonous cheap fags

As the price of tobacco increases, criminal gangs have swung into action to deliver cheap fags and rolling tobacco. The source is often China and other countries where there is little control on dodgy manufacturing of all sorts of food, drink and medicines. Checks show that these cheap forms of tobacco are highly contaminated with poisonous materials, including lead, cyanide and worse. Smokers are literally taking their lives in their hands by supporting the criminals who flood the market with their dangerous products. Sadly those hit most by poverty will be an easy target for this criminal activity and the government is losing billions in tax revenue.

The hidden smokers

There is a hidden group of smokers that we know virtually nothing about, many of whom are children. The hidden smokers are either those who only use tobacco when they are smoking cannabis, or,

Tobacco

they may already be regular smokers who also mix tobacco along with their cannabis. Most UK cannabis users do this.

It is not known how many people smoke cannabis with or without using tobacco. There are many areas of public health for which the government does not have any reliable statistics. The real number of cannabis users is one of these. As most cannabis in the UK is smoked along with tobacco, these users should be recorded in figures for national smoking rates.

myths & facts

Myth: If I gave up smoking tobacco I could not use cannabis.

Fact: In the UK most cannabis users consume cannabis along with tobacco. I know from working with children that the reason that many of them are resistant to quitting smoking tobacco is that they do not want to give up using cannabis. It is much safer to consume cannabis in a special water pipe or a vaporiser, without using tobacco, but this is not all that popular or common in the UK. The internet is full of offers for vaporisers.

Smoking tobacco along with cannabis increases the risks of getting a range of cancers. One roll-up of cannabis and tobacco (joint) is thought to be equivalent to 4-5 standard cigarettes. This is because of the way that people smoke cannabis with tobacco. Cannabis users usually draw the smoke deeper into their lungs than when just smoking tobacco on its own. They hold the smoke in their lungs for longer, to get the maximum buzz from the drug. The combination of the cancer-inducing elements in both tobacco and in the cannabis, can result in this cocktail of drugs being four or five times higher in carcinogenic elements than the tobacco smoke alone.

There are now young people, under the age of 30, who after regularly using cannabis for ten years or more, are getting mouth, gullet and throat cancers.

Home-grown cannabis has its dangers
Thousands of mini factories growing cannabis have been found by the police across the UK. This new trend of using home-grown forms

Tobacco

167

of cannabis (often called skunk), may increase the health damage even more. Although the skunk may be less contaminated with other substances it is reported to be much higher in THC, (purity & strength) so giving the user the buzz they want. We do not know yet what effect that will have. As always the illicit drug traders will in time reduce the purity levels as more contaminants are added to bulk up the weight of the drug for street dealing. Illicit drugs are sold by weight and dealers always get greedy.

Lack of government harm reduction advice leaves children at risk
Government policy on cannabis is that it is an illicit drug, so the government is not prepared to offer harm reduction advice on using cannabis safely. This is peculiar as the government have funded needle exchange schemes for heroin users and happily provide free condoms, even to children under 16 and anyone at risk of catching sexual diseases such as HIV and Aids, or Hepatitis C. They also advise adults about sensible levels of drinking alcohol, so why the hypocrisy on how to use cannabis more safely?

The smoking, alcohol and cannabis link to mental ill-health
Some research is showing that children under the age of 15 who smoke tobacco, use cannabis and alcohol regularly, develop mental health problems at a much higher rates than children who are non-smokers, non-cannabis users and non-drinkers. This growing evidence should alert us to the possibility that drug use in children is endangering their brain development and therefore their mental health.

Quote about smoking from children – 'You have got to die of something'
This is a sad statement repeated across generations which has very little meaning as most children have little or no experience of death or the prolonged and often painful end that those who develop smoking-related illnesses have to suffer. Even the graphic horror pictures now printed on tobacco packets quickly lose their effect when seen every day by smokers. Children today are desensitised about death and violence from the constant watching of television, films and electronic games.

Tobacco

Children do not die from smoking

This is true because the health damage from smoking takes a very long time to kick in.

Because most children have little experience of death they need to be able to understand that nobody would volunteer for the cancers associated with regular smoking. Who would want to lose their tongue or their voice box to cancer, leaving them unable to eat, taste food or talk to their friends? Who would want to be so short of breath from lung cancer that they could no longer play sport, talk, dance or even walk upstairs? If parents are to have a discussion with children about why they should not smoke it is useful to discuss these life and death facts. It is also important to explore with children the many other health problems associated with smoking already mentioned. Especially ageing skin, damaged hair and teeth and that they can become dependent on nicotine. Also that for many children this opens the door to them moving on to other, sometimes even more dangerous drugs to satisfy their needs.

Subtle media messages reinforcing smoking myths

We only need to watch some of the soap operas on television to see the actors like Dot Cotton in *East Enders* appearing to overcome her stress by her Bible reading and calming herself down with cigarettes. She portrays the nervous type who needs her cigarettes to calm her down as she deals with the many problems that life throws at her. This is a very subtle way of getting over a false message that cigarettes calm you down. It is fascinating that it is the smoking behaviour that is picked up by children but not the Bible reading anymore. It is rumoured that tobacco companies pay scriptwriters to keep such story lines going. The government is being urged to legislate to prevent this form of product placement on television from spreading myths about smoking and drinking.

If you feel strongly about this remember that laws can be changed. Parents in Scandinavia have managed to get their governments to ban television advertising of unhealthy and unnecessary products to their children. So why can we not follow this example?

Tobacco companies have been very successful in convincing smokers that smoking is cool, smoking is relaxing and calms you down. These are lies. Once smokers get their heads round the lie,

Tobacco

169

then it is relatively easy to stop smoking, as long as smokers can find other ways to deal with the stresses in their lives.

Helpful Tip

In Alan Carr's book on quitting smoking, he says that one of the biggest barriers to quitting is the fear of stopping. Fear of not being able to do it. Fear of not knowing how to cope with other smokers, fear of losing smoking friends, fear of putting on weight. Once a smoker can identify and face their fears then stopping smoking he says is not so difficult. See resources list in chapter 10.

Cigarettes contain thousands of chemicals and dangerous gasses. It is almost unbelievable that any substance can be sold legally to the public today in which the manufacturers are not required to declare exactly what is in their product. How the tobacco companies have got away with this one for so long is unbelievable. It is time for the governments of the world to take this one on. We should be asking ourselves would we happily allow our children to consume sweets, drinks or food that were loaded with a vast range of unknown chemicals? Not likely is it?

The French government, who used to own the tobacco companies, sold them off a few years ago for fear of litigation.

The tobacco lobby, especially in the USA, is one of the most powerful campaigning groups in the world. They have heavily funded many presidential elections.

myths & facts

Myth: My granddad smoked heavily for 40 years. He only got cancer when he stopped.

Fact: This is another common myth that smokers cling on to. It is, I must admit, hard to argue against this myth, but the best explanation I have heard is that genetically, some of us are just programmed to be less likely to get all cancers. In some families most of the women get cancer; in others the males are more prone to this disease. It is never a good idea to depend on an extreme example as an excuse for not quitting smoking. The fact that a grandfather was diagnosed with cancer after giving up smoking is just a coincidence because many cancers develop, unseen, and

Tobacco

very slowly over many decades in some people. This is why it is so important to do all we can to dissuade children from ever starting to use tobacco in any form. Smoking-related cancers are avoidable by not smoking.

This myth illustrates how ignorance about the nature of tobacco, and not understanding how our body and mind works, can trap children, into using tobacco. As with any substance, once the user understands the basics of the effects of tobacco, they can then make progress towards quitting smoking if they really want to.

Smoking in pregnancy is dangerous for the baby
It is not advisable for women to continue smoking when they are pregnant as anything that goes into their mouths, ends up in the baby's body. Babies born to smoking mums are usually born underweight. If the mother smokes and drinks these problems are made worse. As the motivation to quit is known to be a very important factor in smokers quitting, it should not surprise us that many young women today do take seriously the potential harm to their growing baby, as a highly motivating reason for them to quit smoking.

There are pilot projects running in Scotland to pay pregnant women in food vouchers to give up smoking during pregnancy. Although this sounds controversial, if it even gets 5%-10% of young mums to stop smoking this preventive health measure is well worth supporting. At the very least it will save on NHS budgets as the women and their children should be healthier.

Myth: Smoking is so addictive I could never give it up.

myths & facts

Fact: This is a myth that the tobacco companies certainly do nothing to dispel. It is true that tobacco is as addictive as heroin or methadone, but that does not mean that smokers cannot give it up, if they really want to.

Nicotine is one of the most powerful drugs which gets its users addicted very speedily. However 99% of the nicotine will have left the body within three weeks. The withdrawal from tobacco is not as painful as people imagine. Even before the introduction of the

Tobacco

smoking in public places ban in Scotland in 2006, tens of thousands of smokers had already given up smoking. The most successful method of quitting, used by 90% of quitters, is said to be just stopping, all by themselves – cold turkey. Ask around amongst friends who have quit and you may be surprised how often you can confirm this.

The vast majority of smokers, 75 – 80%, say that they want to quit, and that they wished they had never started to smoke tobacco.

Nicotine Patches are not effective

Nicotine Replacement Therapy (NRT) also called Patches, seems to be the treatment most often offered by the NHS in the UK. However according to research from the US government and the NHS the success rate from NRT Patches is only 2%.

Smoking cessation programmes for children have very limited success

They are too often modelled on what works for adults. New approaches need further development. One of the reason for this lack of success is that children are in a sense 'virgin smokers', and have not yet arrived at the stage where health damage is obvious to them. Many children just do not believe the health warnings on smoking, especially if they have smoking parents or siblings around them. There have been pilot schemes around the UK to support children to quit but much more needs to be done to find more effective solutions. Some of the children I have worked with live in homes where five or more adults are smokers, so it is almost impossible for them to be in a smoke-free environment.

Actions the government could take to reduce harm to children from tobacco:

- **Change tobacco laws to do more to protect children;**

- **Advise the public how to use cannabis safely without tobacco.**

The best health decision anyone can make is to quit smoking. We should all be doing everything we can to encourage children and adults to quit smoking. There is a variety of help available for those who want it.

See the recommended books, helplines, websites for help with quitting smoking in chapter 10.

It is far easier to stop smoking than most smokers believe. It has been found across the world that the most important factor in successfully quitting smoking is how highly motivated we are to quit.

SMOKELINE Tel: 0800 84 84 84 (12 noon to 12pm). For information, advice, counselling and support to quit smoking.

Tobacco

Cannabis

(Hallucinogenic drug)

Street names: Joint, Spiff, Smokes, Blow, Dope, Draw, Hash, Marijuana, Grass, Pot, Weed, Skunk, Northern Lights and many more.

The quality of cannabis like other illicit drugs can vary enormously so many users find it hard to believe that it is a hallucinogenic / psychedelic drug.

The level of (THC) Tetrahydrocannabinols, the trippy bit, is what varies enormously from 1-3% upwards. Skunk which is a more recent form of cannabis can sometimes be much stronger.

Cannabis is still the most commonly used illegal drug. However, it isn't as popular as it used to be: just 1 in 6 people aged 16-24 had tried it in 2010/11. [SOURCE: talktofrank website]

Legal Status: Classified as class 'B' in 2009 after a couple of years when it was temporarily re-classified as class 'C'. This was at a time when cannabis was believed to be less dangerous than had been thought, so it was argued by police in England that they could save lots of police time if it was downgraded to a less serious drug category.

The Nutt Scale rating for cannabis – 11th most dangerous of the 20 most common drugs used in the UK.

After alcohol and tobacco cannabis has been the most popular drug for decades in Scotland and the UK. Many parents reading this book will themselves have experience of using this drug. Parents' knowledge may be flawed because the cannabis that they may have used in the 1980s and 1990s or earlier was very different from what is on the streets today and it is changing all the time.

Cannabis

Effects of cannabis

Cannabis is a bushy plant that can be grown almost anywhere in the world. Until very recently most cannabis came into this country from Afghanistan and the Far East. Since around the year 2000 home-grown cannabis has become more common in the UK. This is mainly produced in illegal 'cannabis farms', often in isolated properties using illegal Chinese immigrants to farm these crops. The police and customs officers are very active around the country closing down these businesses. New cannabis farms are being found and closed down almost every day in the UK.

The main variety is cannabis sativa. The main psychoactive element in cannabis are the tetrahydrocannabinols (THC) which is concentrated in the tops of the plants.

Before skunk was available, hashish or hash was the commonest form of cannabis in Scotland and the UK. This is the resin scraped or rubbed from the plants, which is then compressed into brown blocks. Other materials are often added to increase the weight of the cannabis as it is sold by weight.

myths & facts

Myth: The gunge left at the bottom of a pipe or bong is pure cannabis oil.

Fact: Oh no, it's not, it is highly contaminated residue of the plant material. Pure cannabis oil is almost never seen in the UK as it is too expensive to produce, because an enormous amount of the source plant is required to extract the cannabis oil.

The types of cannabis are changing all the time but the common resins are Moroccan (dark, greeny brown, also known as soapbar, rocky, or Eurobar), black (brown-black, oily and soft) and slate (dry and yellowish). The effects of each type is different and some people have their own particular preferences.

Grass comes in a wide variety of forms, the strongest being specially bred for strength (such as skunk and northern lights). The stronger the variety, the higher the content of THC (the active chemical that gets users stoned) and gives them the trippy effects.

As hemp, cannabis had a very long history of being used for the making of clothes, paper, rope and sails and for burning in oil for lamps. Cannabis cultivation can be traced back to the fourth

Cannabis

millennium BC in China. There are still companies across the world producing hemp fibre for clothing, health products and ironically, in the manufacture of cigarette papers.

myths & facts

Myth: Cannabis is much stronger today than it was in the past.

Fact: The home-grown cannabis produced in the UK varies just as much in its quality and strength as any that was sold in the past. The reason for this is that dealers are always looking for ways of boosting their profit, the only easy way to do that is to increase the weight of any deal by adulterating the source material with something that costs next to nothing, but weighs heavy – usually any free plant material they can find. The so called 'gritweed' cannabis has had powdered glass added to it to try to fool people into thinking that they are getting the really pure crystal-like beads of cannabis that are found in nature. All just another big 'rip-off' to make money. Samples of the UK home-grown cannabis have been tested and are regularly found to contain only 2% of THC, no better than the previously imported supplies. Apparently the reason that the UK grown cannabis is so low strength is that the cannabis farmers have been harvesting their crops too early, to get a faster profit rather than waiting a few weeks longer.

Because the market for cannabis is now getting a bad name again, as did the ecstasy market a few years back when people realised they were being ripped off, cannabis dealers are starting to raise the THC levels to around 6-8% again. This will not last long before greed overcomes the dealers' concern for losing buyers. In the 1960s the average THC level would have been much higher, perhaps up to 15%.

Illicit drugs is big business looking for bigger and bigger profits, from less and less outlay. So short of growing your own, which is illegal, you can never be sure of the quality and strength of any batch of cannabis that is bought from illegal traders. **One of the arguments for legalising cannabis is that it would ensure the quality of the drugs sold and a tax revenue to the government.**

Old cannabis equals poor cannabis
The minute any plant is removed from the earth or picked it starts to die and wither. If you cut a lettuce from the garden it is lovely and

Cannabis

sweet and fresh. Leave it around for a few days, even in a fridge and it loses its taste and strength. The same is true of the source plant for cannabis. Much of what is sold in the streets of the UK is months if not years old, so even if it started off as strong stuff it will have lost much of its potency by the time it is bought.

How many people use cannabis?

Surveys have revealed that around 10 million of the 61.8 million UK citizens admit to having tried cannabis and that around 2 million use it regularly. This is probably now well out of date as there is little government interest in updating this information.

Why do people use cannabis?

People use cannabis for a variety of reasons. To relax, to get a trippy out-of-mind sort of experience, to make them laugh or to feel sociable. It can enhance the senses – sounds, colours, taste and smell – and has muscle relaxant and appetite-stimulating properties.

Short-term risks

Most users experience paranoia or anxiety from time to time, making them feel anxious and uneasy (the door bell rings and you just know it's the police). These feelings can also be associated with mild withdrawal symptoms. The effects depend on your mood before using it, and what happens to you when you're stoned. Dealing with your landlord, your mum or any unexpected drama while on cannabis can be a nightmare.

The 'whitie' (too much, taken too quickly) – particularly associated with mixing cannabis and alcohol – is a common bad effect. It causes light-headedness, fainting and sometimes nausea. Although this experience can be intense and unpleasant, it usually ends relatively quickly.

The other 'risk' in the short term – the munchies – is wanting to eat everything in the house before starting on the furniture! This is particularly true of growing teenagers who by their very nature get the munchies regularly, especially late at night.

Cannabis

Long-term risks

Cannabis is usually smoked with tobacco and as we all know, tobacco is filled with tar and thousands of chemicals and gasses including poisons like cyanide. Although 'joints' are a social way to take cannabis, cutting out the tobacco is one way to reduce the health risks. Smoking without the tobacco is safer, but even smoking cannabis on its own (whether resin or grass) can cause lung damage. Problems with short-term memory are common for many users.

It is safer to consume cannabis in a special pipe without the need to use tobacco, but this is not all that popular or common in the UK.

Government policy on cannabis is that it is an illicit drug, so the government is not prepared to offer advice on using it safely. Giving such helpful advice would be the harm reduction approach to using this drug. I find this peculiar as governments have funded setting up the needle exchange schemes for heroin users and happily provide free condoms to children under 16 and for anyone at risk of catching sexual diseases such as HIV and Aids or Hepatitis C. So why the hypocrisy with using cannabis more safely?

Cannabis and mental health

Government statisticians have noted that children under the age of 15 who smoke tobacco, cannabis and use alcohol regularly develop mental health problems at a much higher rate than their non-smoking, non-cannabis using and non-drinking peers. There is a growing body of evidence that drug use by children is endangering their brain development and their mental health.

Cannabis is particularly bad for people who suffer from serious mental health problems.

The evidence on whether cannabis causes serious mental health problems is conflicting as some mental illness, like schizophrenia, tends to be diagnosed in adolescence or late teens, when many young people are experimenting with drugs like cannabis. That does not prove that these drugs cause the mental ill-health. However there is no doubt that if people do suffer from serious mental health problems then using cannabis is a very bad idea, as it will almost always make their condition worse.

People using cannabis tend to inhale the smoke deeper into their lungs and to hold the smoke in their lungs for longer. This increases

Cannabis

the deposits of dangerous chemicals from the cannabis and the tobacco in the lungs. One cannabis joint can be equivalent to smoking 5 cigarettes.

Problems with Cannabis Use

Many more cannabis users are now turning to drug agencies for help having become problem users. They find that cannabis takes over and becomes everything in their lives and they're too stoned to do anything. This is the manana, manana (I'll do it later) effect, when you find it too easy to tell yourself that things that need doing today can be done tomorrow – but tomorrow never comes.

myths & facts

Myth: Doctors in the UK can now prescribe cannabis for you, especially if you have MS.

Fact: Not generally true, but before 1928 it was used for medical purposes in the UK.

However, in 1995 a very small number of doctors were licensed to prescribe the use of dronabinol, which is a tiny part of the THC in cannabis, to a very small number of cancer patients.

A pharmaceutical company in the UK has been granted a UK licence to grow cannabis with a low THC content for medicinal cannabis-based products. A second company has registered a patent on cannabis 'aerosols'. At present, prescribing of cannabis by doctors is very, very limited.

myths & facts

Myth: Cannabis is an effective painkiller.

Fact: Official UK government sponsored research has still not agreed on this. Only a tiny part of the THC in the purest cannabis relieves pain, but only in some people. Many street samples may not have these painkilling properties. So believing that it is safe to use cannabis as a painkiller is not sensible. There are many other, very safe drugs such as aspirin, codeine or paracetemol that will do the job far cheaper and safely, as long as we follow the advice on the packaging.

There is growing evidence though, that some parts of the cannabis plant may be useful in alleviating pain for MS sufferers and for relieving the nausea associated with chemotherapy in cancer patients as well as relieving the pressure in the eyes of glaucoma patients.

Cannabis

It is illegal to use street cannabis for what you may believe are medicinal purposes. There have been many court cases in the UK and Scotland, but the courts seldom impose serious sanctions on those found guilty of this offence.

Sleeping Problems

Sleeping after using cannabis may for some users be better, but evidence shows that the depth and quality of sleep is affected in heavy users. Sleep deprivation is becoming a major health problem for children. Sleep deprivation leads to lack of concentration so it can cause school children and students to drop out of education when their exam marks are affected.

Reducing the risks

Skunk is a different variety of cannabis and can sometimes be stronger than the average street cannabis. First-time users are very surprised by its powerful hallucinogenic properties. Users need to go easy on it! Heavy use can mash the brain and can cause anxiety, paranoia and introversion (when we 'go into ourselves' and find it hard to talk to people). These symptoms usually disappear after a break from the drug.

Hot Knifing

Some cannabis users do 'hot-knifing' (when a small piece of cannabis is burned between two red hot knives and the smoke is inhaled). Although tobacco is not involved in this method of use the hot smoke from this is particularly damaging to the throat and lungs. **So hot-knifing is best avoided.**

Cannabis stays in your body for longer than most drugs. Regular or daily users may never be clear of the drug. As use builds up the user's tolerance to cannabis increases. This is not a good thing as we still do not know enough about the long-term effects of this on humans.

The risk of becoming a problem cannabis smoker can be reduced by a cannabis user making themselves a set of rules for its use, such as only smoking at weekends, or only after 6pm if they are a daily smoker. It is not a good idea to be a daily user of this drug. Remember the manana, manana effect mentioned earlier.

Myth: Cannabis is a downer, it relaxes you and helps you to sleep.

Fact:This not true as cannabis in all of its forms, is classified as a Hallucinogen. This means that it is neither an upper nor a downer. It is a hallucinogen which alters your perception of what is going on. You may experience time lapsing, where you seem to lose track of time or cannot estimate time well. Small things that might irritate you can make you more anxious than they should. You might have nightmares or be paranoid when you are not normally. Some people do have a sort of out-of-body experience when they can feel music, smell food better or sense emotions differently.

myths & facts

Myth: Cannabis is a natural drug, made from a plant, so it is harmless.

Fact: Oh really! So what is heroin made from? – poppies, a natural drug! Cocaine is made from the coca plant, so because a drug is produced from a natural source such as plants does not make these drugs safe or harmless.

myths & facts

Myth: Eating street cannabis is safer than smoking it.

Fact: Sorry, but this is not true because the average deal of cannabis is produced in very unhygienic conditions and contains loads of muck, sometimes including the shit of animals, debris from food processing, decaying vegetation or soil. Avoid mixing cannabis with yogurt because it too is full of bacteria so will multiply up any contamination problems.

Eating pure home-grown high quality hash on its own, or in food and drink, such as cake or soup or in a coffee, would avoid the risk of lung damage from smoking cannabis, but there are other issues to consider.

myths & facts

When cannabis is inhaled through smoking or from a pipe, it gets into your bloodstream in seconds. When eaten, cannabis can take

Cannabis

around an hour to kick in and gives a totally different effect from smoking. People get impatient and think that they did not take it properly or that the strength of the cannabis was low. Then impatiently, they eat more and as it is absorbed slowly through the guts and time passes, the first lot of cannabis consumed kicks in, followed later by the second dose. Eating cannabis makes it much harder to control the effects of the drug. Effects tend to come on suddenly and like a sledgehammer, so go steady and eat less than you think you should (first timers should not try eating more than a joint's worth).

It is much safer to consume cannabis in a special water pipe or a vaporiser, without using tobacco.

Although it is legal to buy cannabis seeds and equipment to grow it at home, it is illegal to grow it in the UK.

The one advantage that would come from allowing people to grow their own is that it would ensure that they can grow the strength of the drug that suits them and be sure that there is nothing added into it by dealers. In California people are allowed to grow their own for home use, with certain limitations, including the quantity. They can also be licensed to grow larger amounts to supply dispensaries that are allowed to sell medicinal prescriptions which have been supplied by some specially licensed doctors. This is currently under review again because of political concerns.

myths & facts

Myth: If you use cannabis you will then go on to harder drugs.

Fact: Many parents are convinced that if their children use cannabis it is inevitable that this will lead them on into other more dangerous drug use. There is some logic to this thinking as it is certainly true that you would be hard pressed to find a heroin user that has not used cannabis. However, it is not quite that simple. In 2012 there were 59,600 heroin users officially listed as in treatment in Scotland. This is an underestimate because people who have not yet sought treatment are not included in the statistics. So there could be around a million people in Scotland who have used cannabis and perhaps half of that number are still using it occasionally or regularly. There is a problem though because for a child or young person to use cannabis they

Cannabis

need to visit an illegal dealer and so they may meet up with other people who are using a variety of other drugs. The facts do seem to confirm that only a small number of cannabis users do move on to more serious drug use. The exception being alcohol which as you will have seen earlier in this book is the number one problem drug used in Scotland and the UK. There is evidence that cannabis use amongst young people is starting to go down now.

Moving on to the hard stuff is not inevitable if you think about people you know who are alcohol drinkers. Some of them only drink spirits, others only drink beer and some just wine. Only a minority of the drinkers use the whole variety of products that are on offer. It is all about taste and our need for the effects that any drug offers us. So it is not inevitable that children who try cannabis will move on to other illicit drug use.

Price of cannabis
Across the country cannabis varies in price, with affluent areas paying more than others. It also depends on supply. When the police are particularly active and successful at capturing big hauls of cannabis the price will shoot up as the supplies diminish.

One of the reasons that young people use drugs is that they are generally cheaper than alcohol or tobacco. **So government plans to hike the prices of tobacco or alcohol could misfire badly and drive users towards illicit drugs, such as cannabis.**

Is cannabis a harmless drug?
No drug is harmless, all drugs have the potential to harm some or all of us, depending how we use it, its purity and other things such as how healthy our mental state is.

Although cannabis itself is not considered to be an addictive substance, the way it is used along with tobacco changes that. Tobacco is highly addictive, so the combination of heavy cannabis and tobacco use together, is most certainly not harmless.

Cannabis

Cannabis deaths

There have been virtually no deaths from cannabis but for some chaotic users it will add to the deteriorating health to such an extent that it will certainly contribute towards their eventual early deaths. This situation could change in the future as young people in their 30s who have used cannabis very regularly start to get mouth and other cancers that were not common decades before.

Cannabis and alcohol – a good or bad mix?

Cannabis is very commonly used before drinking alcohol, especially during the sociable, hang-out, chill-out and have a wee-smoke type sessions. This may be a fairly harmless activity for many young people. However it has its dangers as well, especially if done in binges.

Because cannabis is a hallucinogen, it alters our perception of what is going on in our minds. Alcohol on the other hand is a downer, depressant drug which picks up our underlying moods and personality traits.

So the possible good effects of the cannabis / alcohol cocktail might be because you are a cool sort of person who is in a happy mood, very relaxed and enjoying the company you are in. If the cannabis is giving you good sorts of feelings then this may be enhanced by using small amounts of alcohol. However, if you are quite a nervous, paranoid sort of person and you are in low spirits, or a bad mood, then using cannabis with alcohol might multiply up your paranoia, adversely affect your low spirits and your low mood. This is because alcohol will take the range of negative feelings that you have and will multiply them up, leaving you in a not very nice place.

All of this illustrates that fact that depending on what the strength or quantity of the drug is, and what we expect to get from using the drug, added to the circumstances in which we are using drug, can all affect the outcome. Anyone who drinks alcohol will be well aware of what I am saying here. If you are feeling low or depressed do not expect alcohol to buck you up.

Cannabis the sociable drug

Young people and many adults see cannabis as a fairly harmless, sociable sort of drug. Although the quality and strength of any batch of cannabis will always vary, the way people tend to use it, in social groups, is fairly well controlled. This is especially true when smoking cannabis or when using it in a pipe, or water pipe, the user can stop and start as the effects kick in, and hold back if it gets too heavy. If cannabis is used in a group setting then the sharing of knowledge about what is happening as you use the drug is shared, giving people feelings of safety in numbers. In that sense, it would be true to see cannabis as a reasonably sociable drug, compared with group use of alcohol which often gets well out of hand resulting in fall-outs, violence and unwanted sexual behaviour.

Using cannabis on your own is much more problematic
Most of the people I have known who have had problems with cannabis have been loners, or people who tend to use it most often on their own. The reason for that might be that their mental states are not stable, so retreating into a cannabis haze increases the dangers. In individuals who are by nature fairly paranoid this can really multiply up that mental state into one that is dangerous for their mental health and their own safety.

Is cannabis addictive?

Cannabis on its own is not considered to be addictive, but heavy, daily users of this drug do develop a high tolerance to it and a very, very strong dependency on the drug.

I have met and worked with many school children and unemployed young people who are daily, 24/7 users of cannabis, from a very early age, perhaps as young as 8-10 years old. Many of them would say that they are addicted to the drug, but as many of them are also heavy tobacco smokers it is likely that this combination of drugs is what they are addicted to, rather than cannabis alone.

Are there addictive personalities?
I think that this is a factor that needs to be considered. The debate on this has gone on for years, with strong arguments on both sides. I tend towards believing that there are people who seem to have the

Cannabis

sort of compulsive addictive personalities which draw them towards fanatically doing all sorts of things that could be described as addictive. It may be playing computer games, watching porn, smoking, glue sniffing, drinking alcohol, gambling, sex, extreme sports or collecting things. In my experience such people are at high risk when they get involved in using drugs, including cannabis, when they are very young and vulnerable. Some of this behaviour in young children can be fuelled by the problem I raised earlier in the book, the parental fear of children being out in the big bad dangerous community, which causes many children to spend far too much time, mainly on their own, in their bedrooms, doing compulsive things which often includes their daily use of cannabis. Hidden away from sight and parental observation it does not take very long for unhelpful behaviour to turn into habits that are very difficult to stop.

Because children are not adults, and their emotional development is not complete and their brains are not yet fully developed, there are serious concerns about them using cannabis at all, let alone on a daily or several times daily basis. Remember that I have tried in this book not to use the words addict or addicted, as it implies an incurable condition, which then brings the user to believe that they cannot escape their problem drug use. They can always be helped to reduce their use and to give it up altogether if they are motivated to do so.

Heavy use of cannabis and tobacco is a bad cocktail of drugs which over even as little as 10 years can cause cancers of the mouth, tongue, throat, larynx and lungs, as well as mental health problems.

There are now many adults in Scotland and the UK whose cannabis use is so regular that they end up as problem users. This is especially true of people who may have underlying, unresolved mental health problems. It is true that cannabis is likely to make most mental health problems worse, not better. The numbers of cannabis users who are seeking help to deal with their problems is escalating year on year. The expertise required to address this sort of drug problem in the UK is very limited.

Should Cannabis be decriminalised or legalised?
As this issue is very complex I will not attempt to cover it in depth in this edition of the book. If the debate on this is to have any real opportunity of being driven by public opinion then it is essential that such public opinion is based on the latest facts, figures and

research. This book aims to encourage as many parents to gain the knowledge they need to join in a full and well-informed public debate on the use of all drugs in society. See appendix for basic arguments for and against decriminalising or legalising illicit drugs.

All this business about hallucinating when you're doing hash is rubbish, Mum.

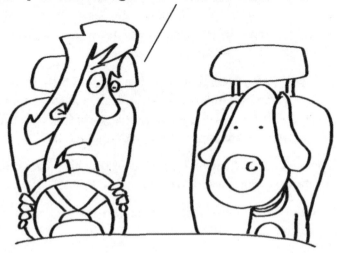

Myth: Cannabis relaxes you so you can drive better.

myths & facts

Fact: This is a comment I have heard so often from young people, that it really is a worry, because they really do believe it, some even admitting they had cannabis before they did their driving tests. The myth flags up two problems of ignorance about drugs. First that using any illicit drug when driving is illegal and could invalidate the driver's insurance. Secondly these drivers are clearly not aware of the true nature of cannabis. It is a hallucinogen, a drug that alters our perception, playing tricks with our mind. We may think we are driving slowly when we are going fast. Our judgement of time will be distorted so our understanding of stopping distances is distorted. Our perception of colours too are affected so we may not realise that traffic lights have changed. This myth highlights one of the best reasons for educating children and adults about the real facts on drugs.

Cannabis

Ecstasy
(Stimulant & Hallucinogen)

Street Names: The names for drugs vary around the country but some of the most popular names are; 'E', Eccy, XTC, pills, MDMA (its chemical name), brownies, sweeties, X Rolex's, Jabs, Mitsubishis and Dolphins.

Legal Status: Class 'A' so it is illegal to possess it, to give it away or to sell it. Possession can lead to a jail sentence up to 7 years. Supplying someone else including your friends can get you life in prison and an unlimited fine.

The Nutt Scale rating for ecstasy is 18th most dangerous of the 20 commonest drugs used in the UK.

Looks like: Pure ecstasy is a white crystalline powder known to chemists as MDMA.

The ecstasy sold in the UK may or may not contain MDMA. Tablets come in a whole variety of shapes and colours, with many different logos and symbols stamped on them.

Purity: Police forces across the UK have found over 90 different tablets being sold as 'E', some of which contain nothing more than inert powders. Ketamine and PMA are sometimes sold as 'E'. Ecstasy is sometimes cut with speed or amphetamines, caffeine and other substances, making it cheaper to produce, so increasing profit.

myths & facts

Myth: You can tell a good 'E' when you see it.

Fact: Hmm! So how come the police have found over 90 different 'E' tablets in circulation? The colour, shape and logos stamped on 'Es' tell you nothing, except its marketing image. Only a proper chemical analysis can reveal the actual chemical content.

Ecstacy

Night clubs in Holland sometimes offer a service to analyse the drugs in use by dancers, so they can then advise the users of the possible dangers. This has given the Dutch useful intelligence on new drugs circulating in their area, so alerting them faster to new and dangerous trends. The UK government has not been supportive of this harm reduction approach.

Effects of the drug

Ecstasy is a drug that has been heavily associated with the rave, dance and club scene, where people seek the extra energy from it to stay up all night socialising.

Ecstasy is usually swallowed although it can be smoked and snorted. This is less common. The effects usually take about half an hour to kick in and reach a peak after about two hours and can last up to six hours. This is followed by a gradual comedown.

The general effects of ecstasy are described as partly speedy (stimulating) and partly trippy (hallucinogenic). Users experience euphoria, feel more energetic, are able to dance for a long time, and they say that it enhances their enjoyment of music. They often experience sensual rushes through the body, have feelings of empathy ('loved up'). Users are very talkative, chatty and sociable on 'E'. It is not a drug associated with aggression or violence.

Myth: Ecstasy is an aphrodisiac, makes having sex just amazing.

Fact: As ecstasy is in part an hallucinogenic drug which alters our perception of reality, we may imagine things that are not actually happening. There is no conclusive proof that ecstasy is an aphrodisiac. Pure ecstasy (MDMA) inhibits orgasm in men and women and may inhibit male erections. One of the concerns about 'E' users feeling 'all loved up' is that this can lead to unsafe sexual activity and the spreading of sexual infections, including HIV or Aids.

myths & facts

The fact that there is such a range of substances found in 'E' means that the user can never be sure what if any effects it is likely to have on them. Even when two apparently identical tablets are bought.

By the end of the 1990s users were starting to accept that what

Ecstasy

they were buying were of unreliable quality, so there has been a drop off in the use of 'Es'. Users are thought to be switching to cocaine instead and to the 'legal highs' mentioned earlier. This is not likely to be a good move.

Short-term use

As there is no way of knowing what is contained in anything sold as 'E' there is a danger that if the user does not get the effect they are looking for within about 30 minutes, they will take more, only to discover later that they then do not feel well. The macho culture of young males in particular, sometimes leads to them showing off and taking anything up to 5 – 10 or more pills. This is a highly dangerous thing to do.

Side effects include a tingling feeling or stiffness in the limbs and the jaw, increased heart rate, sweating and dilated (enlarged) pupils. As the drug kicks in, users can sometimes feel a bit uneasy, sick and 'spaced'. These intense sensations usually subside once the drug has taken full effect.

Users can get anxious, confused or can have panic attacks or paranoid psychotic states.

Failure to sweat, a side effect of using ecstasy, is not a good sign – when we stop sweating, the body cannot cool itself.

Cramps can occur in the legs, arms and back.

Users can faint or lose consciousness.

Some users find that they can't piss and that their urine is highly coloured (dark yellow/brownish), a sign of dehydration. Some users experience vomiting. Others get suddenly tired and irritable. If any of these things happen, the user needs to chill out and sip some water immediately! **Large amounts of water should not be taken as this leads to other complications.** We need the right balance of water in our bodies, too much or too little is dangerous to our health. We can live far longer without food than without water. Serious dehydration, a loss of more than 10% of our water content can be fatal.

If someone collapses while dancing after using 'E' they need immediate medical attention.

Ecstacy

Taking speed, alcohol or very sugary drinks with 'E' make dehydration worse, so heat stroke is more likely to occur.

Long-term use

Heat stroke has been the cause of many deaths from ecstasy. Heat stroke can occur when the body gets too hot from dancing all night. This amount of physical effort can be equivalent to running a half-marathon. No one would try to do that without training and pacing themselves or without drinking enough fluid. Heat stroke can kill. It is recommended that users slowly sip about a pint of water, or a non alcoholic drink, every hour to prevent dehydration. Taking the water too fast can interfere with the salt balance in our bodies. Drinking too much water can also be dangerous. Research suggests that because women retain fluid more readily than men, they may be more at risk.

myths & facts

Myth: There have been thousands of deaths from ecstasy in the UK.

Fact: There have been just over 200 ecstasy-related fatalities since 1996 in the UK.

Although users do develop a tolerance to 'E', so may take more to get the effects they got from lower doses, there is no physical dependence on it, which would cause heroin-like withdrawal symptoms.

myths & facts

Myth: Regular use of ecstasy causes irreversible 'brain damage'.

Fact: Researchers have found that pure MDMA (ecstasy) depletes the levels of serotonin in the brain. Serotonin is the chemical which helps regulate our moods. Reducing the levels of serotonin in the brain would account for the midweek downer or blues, reported by many ecstasy users. However, there is growing evidence that these effects result in irreversible 'brain damage' but the evidence is still not conclusive. Since much of what is sold as 'E' is not pure MDMA it is difficult to establish if brains of regular users of so called ecstasy are being damaged.

Ecstasy

191

Regular use of ecstacy may harm our heart and liver

Using too much 'E', too often, can cause depression, anxiety and paranoia. In some users latent (underlying) mental illness has been triggered by ecstasy.

Some people have been killed or injured in vehicle crashes on the way from clubs, raves and music events where 'E' had been used.

Long-term users report that they are more susceptible to colds, flu and sore throats.

Some women report increased genito-urinary tract infections.

Reducing the risks

Users need to avoid mixing ecstasy with alcohol or other drugs. Apart from anything else, it puts extra strain on the heart, liver and kidneys.

The ingredients in ecstacy tablets vary a lot so it is advisable to test out a half first (and give it time to kick in, up to an hour).

Stay away from ecstasy capsules (they are easier for dealers to adulterate).

Tolerance to 'E' builds up quickly. So users find that they need an increasing dosage to get the same effect. If this happens they should really take a break from using 'E'.

Do not use ecstasy when you are on your own. If others are around assistance can be found if you have bad reactions.

Ecstasy and Asthma

Little is known on how 'E' affects asthma, but the hot, damp, smoky atmosphere of a nightclub or dance event is unlikely to help someone with asthma. Dry ice appears to be particularly bad for asthma, so it's a good idea to keep well clear of smoke machines. Deaths associated with 'E' raves or dances and asthma have been reported, but it is unclear if they are directly related to drug taking, to the environment of the event, or to a combination of both.

Ecstacy

Myth: You can easily take 5-10 ecstasy in a night and not come to any harm.

Fact: I have heard this said more often than any other myths about 'E'. It is of course nonsense. If the user had taken pure MDMA (the real stuff) they would be dead. If they did take 5–10 'E' in one night, then what they consumed was certainly not 'E'. They have been ripped off buying virtually nothing, or very low quality, low strength and impure tablets. A lot of the 'E' captured in police raids contains no MDMA.

Taking more of a drug never ensures that you get the good effects only. You are just as likely to get the bad effects hitting you like a ton of bricks. Ask yourself would you take 5–10 paracetamol at once to try to get rid of a headache faster – I don't think so.

Ecstasy

Amphetamines
(Stimulants)

Amphetamines have been very popular with young people since the 1950s or 60s at a time when they were commonly used by doctors to treat nasal congestion, weight loss and depression. They were also used to energise troops in World War II. Amphetamines such as Ritalin and Dexedrine are still prescribed by doctors to treat attention deficit disorder (ADT) in children and for other conditions.

In the 1950s, some of the amphetamines leaked into the youth drug culture from excessive prescribing by doctors and thefts from chemist shops. Doctors agreed to a voluntary ban on prescribing to try to reduce the problem. Then in the early 1970s the illicit versions of the drug were manufactured and so speed became one of the most popular illicit drugs.

Newer versions of the illicit forms of amphetamine, called methamphetamines, are now causing major problems in the USA and are starting to become popular in the UK where police have started to uncover the so called 'meth labs'.

Amphetamines

Speed
(Stimulant)

Street names: Whiz, Amphetamine, Base and Sulph.

Legal Status: Class 'B' and class 'A' if prepared for injecting.

All the Amphetamines are prescription-only drugs under the Medicines Act and are also controlled under the Misuse of Drugs Act.

The Nutt Scale rating for amphetamines including speed is 8th of the most dangerous of the 20 commonest drugs used in the UK.

Looks Like: It usually comes as a white or grey powder and can be snorted up the nose, smoked, dabbed on soft tissue like the mouth, dissolved in water or soft drinks and injected. In tablet form it is swallowed. Speed is sometimes called a 'dirty' drug because of its high level of impurity. It is sometimes mixed with caffeine, glucose powder or chalk.

Effects of the drug

Over the 3-4 hours after taking speed, the user feels full of energy, wide-awake, talkative, confident and 'invincible'. However, this false energy is only borrowed from the drug and lasts about 3 hours. Then the user comes back down and over the next couple of days you will feel tired, depressed, lethargic and hungry. The pupils of the eyes become dilated (open wide).

Users experience a loss of appetite and they find it hard to sleep, they may feel anxious, get in a panic and experience hallucinations.

Speed is addictive, users do build up a tolerance to it and then desire more to sustain the effects that they are enjoying.

Speed

myths & facts

Myth: Speed makes you go at it, like a rabbit.

Fact: A 'speedy willie' (floppy) is more likely to be the result. Some males report that speed makes them very erect but then they cannot ejaculate (come). In some women urinary tract infections like thrush seem to be one problem experienced in regular users of speed.

Short-term use

Nasty effects include dry mouth, dehydration (you pee away too much body fluid – this is made worse if you are sweating as well), tense jaw, jitters and talking absolute rubbish.

Users can experience mood swings and become agitated and irritable.

Speed can trigger latent (hidden) mental illness, so people who think that they might be at risk should avoid it.

Long-term use

Amphetamines like speed are addictive so users can quickly become problem users.

Regular use causes high blood pressure and puts a serious strain on our hearts.

Speed is an appetite suppressant, so regular users may lose weight and have health problems such as malnutrition and vitamin deficiencies.

Prolonged use and 'binges' on speed can lead to paranoid delusions and hallucinations. These symptoms can become extreme and can require treatment. Such problems usually disappear when they stop using, but it can take a long time.

Speed has been responsible for causing a small number of deaths from overdose (causing a heart attack or a stroke).

Reducing the risks

Avoid mixing speed with alcohol and other drugs. The alcohol increases the chances of suffering not only a monster hangover (too much booze combined with a speed come down) and it also puts

Speed

extra strain on the liver. Remember that you only have one liver and transplants are not easy to come by.

Speed can have a powerful effect that lasts a long time and taking too much will only increase the chances of coming to harm. Users should avoid using speed too often.

To ease the come down some people spread their use over the week. This makes the eventual come down far worse and increases their chances of suffering the worst of the side effects such as paranoia and hallucinations. If it is used on weekdays as well as the weekend this can be a sign of someone having lost control.

Speed is particularly bad for the teeth – it damages the enamel leaving cavities.

If you suffer from heart problems, high blood pressure, mental illness, anxiety and panic attacks, or are on prescribed drugs such as monoamine oxidase inhibitors (MAOIs), beta blockers or antidepressants you should avoid taking speed.

Speed

Cocaine
(Stimulant)

Street Names: Street names for drugs vary around the country. For powder cocaine the street names include coke, Charlie, C, white, Percy, chico, snow, toot, white stuff, fairy dust, chong and snow. More details about crack cocaine are covered later but the names for crack include rocks, wash, stones, pebbles, base and freebase.

Legal Status: Cocaine is a Class 'A' drug – illegal to have, give away or sell. Possession can get you up to 7 years in jail. Supplying someone else, including your friends, can get you life in jail and an unlimited fine.

The Nutt Scale rating for cocaine is 2nd most dangerous of the 20 most common drugs used in the UK.

Looks like: Cocaine is a white or creamy/yellowish powder and is derived from the leaves of the coca shrub which is commonly found in the Andean region of South America, Bolivia and Peru. It is then trafficked through Panama, Argentina and Brazil across to the West Indies and Africa and finally on into Europe and the UK.

The white cocaine powder is usually laid out on a flat surface and divided into lines which are then snorted up the nose using a straw or rolled up bank notes. It is difficult to smoke it in this form. Powdered cocaine can be prepared for injecting.

Purity: When cocaine leaves its country of origin it is around 90% pure. By the time it reaches the UK its purity will have reduced to between 20-50%. It will then have been cut further, to bulk it up and increase its selling weight, with other materials such as glucose power. By the time it hits the streets its purity can be 15-25% or very much less. You

Cocaine

198

cannot tell the purity of this drug by testing it with your tongue.

It is true that before 1904 Coca-Cola did contain small quantities of cocaine.

The cocaine wars

The supply of cocaine world wide has been in the hands of criminal drugs cartels since the 1980s. The American CIA along with other international law enforcement agencies have tried for decades to curb this trade with little success. The main result has been that many different routes across the world have been created, to transport the cocaine to users. **Literally thousands of people have been killed in the wars against cocaine traders** – around 30,000 in the five years between 2006-2011.

It was recently reported in Columbia that nearly 300 bodies of people killed by the drug lords had been found in a disused mineshaft. These bodies of men, women and children had been tied up, blindfolded and usually shot in the back of the head. These people were the human drug mules who carried the drugs for the suppliers and were no use to the criminal drug barons when their task was finished. Life it seems is cheap when there are billions of dollars to be made from drugs. That is the price that we pay for satisfying our desire for the thrills of using cheap cocaine in the UK.

By using cocaine we are supporting criminals and thugs who have no respect for anyone's life and certainly not yours.

In the early part of the twenty first century, the Americans have been very successful at stopping cocaine entering the USA. The downside of this is that the UK and Scotland in particular have become the most lucrative dumping ground for the cocaine. **The UK now has the highest use of cocaine anywhere in the world.**

The Scottish Drug Enforcement and Serious Crime Agency have established that in 2010 the top Scottish drug dealers are now buying their supplies of cocaine and crack directly from the suppliers in Columbia to cut costs and increase their profits. The source materials bought for £1,500 are then sold in Scotland for around £50,000.

Cocaine

Effects of the drug

Cocaine is usually sniffed-snorted and can enter the bloodstream through any soft membrane such as the gums.

myths & facts

Myth: Putting cocaine on your private parts makes you really horny and you go like a raging bull.

Fact: More likely you will have very itchy, sore parts to live with.

Ahm oan the pull tonight, give me 5 grams of the good stuff on my love rocket

Cocaine powder is a stimulant with powerful, but short-lived, effects which temporarily speed up our thinking, making the user feel on high energy, alert, very confident, agitated and irrational. It also raises body temperature and heart rate, it makes us indifferent to pain and reduces feelings of hunger.

When cocaine is smoked it reaches the brain very rapidly. Snorted powder cocaine is absorbed more slowly. All forms of cocaine prepared for injection reach the brain very rapidly and in high doses, so can be very addictive.

Cocaine

200

The stronger the stimulant the shorter the high!
When the stimulant drugs such as speed and other amphetamines are used, their effects can last for up to 3-4 hours before the effects drop off and the depressive 'come-down' kicks in. With cocaine the effects last only from 15–30 minutes. **With crack the effects can last for as little as 10 minutes.**

So the more powerful the stimulant the less time on a high you get for your money. This not only means that users can spend a fortune but also that loading the brain with heavy doses of this drug is not a wise move.

Short-term use
When cocaine is sniffed the effects peak after 15-30 minutes and the downer that follows leaves the user wanting more very quickly. The effects of cocaine are like a much more high powered amphetamine such as speed. Users are aroused psychologically, they can feel less pain, have high energy so may not want to sleep. Sometimes they feel great surges of physical strength and a loss of appetite. If the use is excessive over several hours the users can get very anxious, agitated and paranoid, some may even hallucinate. The effects will usually wear off given time.

Many of the effects and some of the side effects of cocaine are similar to those of using speed, but some users describe the effects as being 'smoother'. Cocaine is renowned for making people behave in arrogant, egotistical and sometimes violent or highly sexual ways.

The risk of psychological dependency is higher with cocaine than with speed. Because the effects of cocaine don't last as long, so the strong desire to keep taking more can be hard to resist, especially if the party is in full swing and there's a long night ahead. This is the addictive circle mentioned earlier. You get high, then low, so you want to be high again, so you keep loading up on such addictive drugs.

Mixing cocaine with alcohol is not advisable as it can cause heart failure, even in very young people.

Long-term use
Regular sniffing of cocaine can damage the membranes of the nose,

Cocaine

in severe cases holes are left in the nose. Frequent users develop a strong psychological dependence on this drug. They find that the euphoria that they used to feel is replaced by mental states such as feeling very restless, anxious, depressed or very hyper. They find it hard to sleep and get exhausted and mentally confused. Some heavy users develop paranoid psychoses. In most cases this will wear off if the user takes a break from using the drug.

Those with serious mental health problems, such as those who are bi-polar or manic depressives, should avoid these drugs as they can make their conditions much worse.

Using cocaine in any form when pregnant can cause harm to the baby, including miscarriage, premature labour and low birth weights. Cocaine also causes some users to lose weight. Smoking cocaine can cause pains in the chest and breathing problems.

myths & facts

Myth: You get addicted to cocaine and crack almost instantly.

Fact: It is because of these short-lived extreme highs, followed by quick and then sometimes severe downer effects, that these two drugs get a reputation for instant addiction. Nobody likes dealing with the depressive come downs, so if users have the financial means and enough of the substance available, they tend to greedily keep going, until they have run out of supplies or cash. They do not get addicted instantly, but heavy use certainly leads very quickly to problem use. There have been reports of users blowing literally thousands of pounds in a few days on cocaine or crack.

Overdoses and deaths

Cocaine overdoses can cause a heart attack or the user can stop breathing. How much needs to be taken to cause an overdose will differ from person to person. Those with high blood pressure or undiagnosed heart problems are at particular risk.

It is not scare-mongering to say that mixing cocaine with alcohol can be fatal.

As cocaine has become cheaper, fatalities have started to show up in the statistics. In Scotland there were 4 deaths in 2000, by 2002 it was 31, in 2007/8 there were 79 deaths. In 2008/9 the deaths came back down to 57, and down to 33 in 2012, but that may be only a temporary drop.

So why should that be? The answer is simple. Many cocaine users are people who also like being in pubs with their pals, drinking

Cocaine

alcohol. Alcohol is a depressant (downer) drug, which dampens down our behaviour. Cocaine is a massive stimulant (upper) drug, which makes us high and very hyper. When we mix these drugs together we no longer feel drunk. In the social setting of a pub, this usually leads to even more alcohol consumption, often to excessively high and dangerous levels. When this mixture of drugs kicks in a third drug is generated in our bodies – it is called cocaethylene. This increases our dopamine release, which can lead to sudden cardiac arrest and death, even in quite young people.

What is unique about these drug-related deaths is that the victims range from across society, from registered problem drug users, to people who would not see themselves as drug users at all. They may be business people, people holding down full time jobs, musicians, actors, students and other professionals, as well as the ordinary law-abiding citizen that any of us might meet in a pub or club. People out for a good laugh and a good night out. Such deaths are both very sudden and unexpected, making them an even bigger shock and tragedy for the families involved.

The Bank of England reports that **the residue of cocaine is found on millions of bank notes,** as people use the rolled-up notes like a straw, to snort the cocaine.

It is reported that 2 million UK citizens have now used cocaine
So its use is starting to be seen as normal as using cannabis or alcohol. This normalisation of cocaine involves many people who would certainly not see themselves as 'problem drug users'. Many users have ended up in court or in prison for using or supplying these drugs to friends socially, mistakenly thinking that they were just being good to their friends. Cocaine is a class 'A' drug, so supplying friends or using it socially are both illegal with stiff penalties. A Scottish policeman who had worked in the drug squad was one of those sent to prison for this offence.

Physical damage to health
Smoking cocaine can cause damage to the respiratory system. Users get very wheezy breathing and can lose their voice temporarily. Those who inject cocaine risk major abscessing and other serious infections, especially if they are sharing needles with others.

Cocaine

Crack Cocaine
(Stimulant)

> **Street Names**: For crack cocaine the names include rocks, wash, stones, pebbles, base and freebase.

> **Legal Status**: Crack cocaine is a Class 'A' drug – illegal to have, give away or sell. Possession can get you up to seven years in jail. Supplying someone else, including your friends, can get you life imprisonment and an unlimited fine.

> **The Nutt Scale rating** for crack is also 2nd most dangerous of the 20 most common drugs used in the UK.

> **Looks Like**: Crack is made by a process of reversing the last stages of the method used to produce cocaine. A baking process is used to make the crack crystals or rocks. It comes in small white or creamy/yellowish rocks or lumps about the size of a small pea or raisin. Crack cocaine can be prepared for injecting.

> **Purity**: Crack is produced close to the market it is sold in, often by drug dealers in their own kitchens. As always the purity of the street versions of this drug will vary enormously, making it an unreliable drug to use. Thought to be on average around 40% pure across the UK, it can and often is very much less pure.

> Crack is sometimes sold in a two-for-one deal called 'brown and white' by dealers along with heroin. Some heroin users use crack along with their heroin.

Effects of the drug
Crack is a more powerful, faster acting form of cocaine. The stimulant effects happen almost immediately and peak after about 2 minutes and are then gone within 10 minutes.

Crack Cocaine

Crack is usually smoked in a special pipe, or chased (heated on foil) so it reaches the brain very rapidly. It can also be flaked into a joint or injected. Smoked crack tends to be much stronger and more addictive than the snorted powder cocaine.

Crack is a stimulant which has the powerful, but short-lived effect of temporarily speeding up the processes of the mind. It makes us feel high-energy, super-alert, very confident, agitated and sometimes irrational. It increases body temperature and heart rate and reduces feelings of hunger.

myths & facts

Myth: You get addicted to crack the first time you use it.

Fact: Not true but it is extremely addictive. The high from crack is even more powerful than cocaine so people get greedy for more of it. This can quickly turn some people into problem users.

Crack makes users extremely arrogant, aggressive, highly sexual, overconfident, imagining that they are untouchable, so nobody can see them. Police have reported situations where they have raided the premises where crack is being produced and found those producing the crack unaware of their presence. They are so high, they did not hear the police arrive or notice them coming to arrest them.

There have been many rapes, shootings and murders associated with the crack trade across the world.

Short-term use
Crack kicks in almost immediately and takes the user higher than snorted or injected cocaine. The high however, only lasts about 5-10 minutes and the inevitable come down is very intense, leaving the user with feelings of anxiety, irritability, depression and paranoia. Users may also be unable to sleep.

Long-term use
Crack like so many illicit drugs is a very crudely produced and unreliable substance, varying enormously in its purity and strength. Using crack is a particularly high-risk activity. It can be really hard to

Crack Cocaine

control crack use as the desire for it can increase very rapidly and can so easily lead the user into being a problem user. Users take downers such as heroin to help deal with the crack-crash and this can lead to another drug dependency on heroin.

There are very few treatment options currently available to crack users, e.g. nothing like the methadone used to help heroin users. So getting a serious crack habit is not a good idea.

Cocaine and crack used to be the rich man's drugs, but with the success of the Americans in stopping imports, a massive stockpile of cocaine has been built up. This has left the dealers with the problem of establishing new markets, so they have done what any business would do – sell it off cheap as a loss leader to establish the market. Once the market is established and users are well and truly hooked into this drug, the price goes up and up, creating a very large group of people dependent on the drug. As with previous drug fashions, this will continue until the public get fed up with being ripped off – or another drug becomes the latest craze.

'Legal Highs'
(Stimulants and Hallucinogens)

This new range of substances first appeared early in the 2000s. To begin with they were mainly sold on the internet rather than being sold by street dealers. They started to appear in the head shops selling drugs paraphernalia.

I have included only limited information about this new drug trend, because even very experienced drugs workers know little or nothing about them.

Readers are strongly advised to consult with the reliable websites listed later for the most up-to-date information.

Street Names: The names of drugs vary across the country. Some of the common names for 'legal highs' are herbal ecstasy, ephedrine, dimethocaine, herbal viagra, salvia, benzo-fury, 5-IAI, silver bullet and ivory wave.

Legal Status: These new substances are not yet under the control of the Misuse of Drugs acts but some are covered by the Medicines Act. The government has announced that it intends to introduce temporary bans on 'legal highs' to allow time for experts to consider their legal status.

The producers of these substances are attempting to stay ahead of international drugs laws by constantly altering, just slightly, the chemical characteristics of the drugs. By doing this they are hoping to make a fast profit, before drug laws are amended to ban them. Like all illicit drugs they are produced and sold for vast profits by international criminal gangs.

Legal highs are not listed in the Nutt Scale rating as they are too new.

Legal Highs

myths & facts

Myth: 'Legal highs' are not a problem – because they are sold on the internet and are legal.

Fact: Even if a drug is legal to possess does not mean that it is therefore safe to use.

What are these drugs?

We know almost nothing about these substances. The 'legal highs' are being produced all over the world, including China, Russia and the Far East. They are designed to fool people into believing that they are buying drugs that are similar to the illicit drugs that people are already familiar with. They are marketed as if they are safe and legal products. Website information tries to give the products credibility with ambiguous wording and although they may state that they are not for human consumption, they are still misleading people by calling them research chemicals, plant foods, bath crystals or even fish pond cleaners. Such clever website marketing spreads the myths about the wonderful power of these products, giving hints to the buyers on how to use them and hoping that naive young people will be persuaded. Unfortunately they have been successful in finding a new market for drugs, with in some cases, fatal results. A quick web search using 'legal highs' will reveal how they are marketed.

Effects of the drug

Because it is very difficult to know what is in these drugs the knowledge of the effects is limited but growing all the time.

Reported effects include reduced inhibitions, drowsiness, over-excited paranoid states, coma, seizures and death.

Ivory wave is reported to cause psychosis, paranoia and hallucinations.

Long-term risks

Why we should be particularly concerned about children using these unknown substances is that too many have believed the myths that as they are 'legal highs', so they think that they must be safe – 'or the government would have stopped their sales'.

Because these substances are so new, we know almost nothing

Legal Highs

about what is in them, or what short- or long-term problems they may cause. They have been around for such a short time, not enough data on them has been collected to indicate the likely consequences of mixing these new substances with existing illicit drugs or with tobacco or alcohol. We only learn more about these drugs every time someone is hospitalised or another death is recorded from using them. Below is a description of one of the first of the 'legal highs'.

Mephedrone
(Stimulant)

Street names: Meow Meow, 4MMC, Meph, M-Cat, White Magic or plant food. Also known as Bounce, Charge, Drone, Methylone, Methedrone and Bubbles.

Legal Status: Class 'B' from April 16th 2010. This drug is one of the 'legal highs' it is now illegal to possess, give away or sell to another person. Penalties for possession are 5 years in prison and/or a fine. Supplying the drug can mean serving up to 14 years in jail and an unlimited fine. Mephedrone is already banned in Ireland, Denmark, Norway and Sweden.

Nutt Scale Rating: Mephedrone is not included on the list of the 20 most dangerous drugs used in the UK, as it did not exist when that list was compiled. It would most likely be placed very high on the danger list.

Looks Like: It is a fine white or off-white or yellowish powder. Also comes in capsules and pills. It was usually snorted like cocaine or swallowed 'bombed' in wraps of paper. It could also be smoked and in rare cases has been injected. It is produced in China before shipping to the UK. It is sometimes mixed with other substances including caffeine.

Mephedrone

myths & facts

Myth: It must be safe as it is a legal drug, so the police cannot arrest you for having it.

Fact: Not true. Mephedrone was considered for listing by the Advisory Council on the Misuse of Drugs (ACDM), after a public outcry because of 25 reported deaths of young people in the UK. It was given a fast-track classification as a class 'B' drug. This is one of a family of drugs known as cathinones similar to amphetamines such as speed, methamphetamines and ecstasy (MDMA).

Effects of the drug

Mephedrone is a stimulant type of drug, which makes the user high. Users feels alert, confident, euphoric and talkative, and empathy to those around them. Effects last about an hour.

Short-term use

Include nosebleeds, headache, nausea, insomnia, anxiety states, paranoia, palpitations, loss of short-term memory, vertigo, grinding of teeth, sweating and uncomfortable changes in body temperature. Can over-stimulate the heart, some users report blue or cold fingers. Can also over-stimulate the nervous system causing fits, agitation and hallucinations.

Long-term use

There were 25 deaths associated with this drug in the UK in 2009/10. As with other stimulants such as cocaine, when mephedrone is mixed with alcohol there are the added dangers of sudden heart attacks and death.

It is reported that once users start a session of using mephedrone it becomes quite compulsive, so leading to a psychological state of dependence. Users find it hard to stop until they have finished their supplies.

Although mephedrone is now banned it has not stopped variations of it quickly being made available.

Mephedrone

Benzodiazepines
(Depressant)

Street Names: Drug names vary around the country but here are some of the common ones: benzos, tranquillisers, vallie's, jellies, eggs, norries, rohyphnol, rugby balls, roofies, downers, and moggies.

Legal Status: Class 'C' drug. Tranquillisers can only be prescribed by a pharmacist. It is illegal to possess benzodiazepines, including temazepam without a prescription.
Possession could get you 2 years in prison and an unlimited fine. Supplying, including to your friends, could mean up to 14 years in prison and an unlimited fine.

Nutt Scale Rating for Benzodiazepines is 7th most dangerous of the 20 most common drugs used in the UK.

Looks Like: They come in tablets, capsules, prepared for injection or in suppositories (for insertion in the anus).

Effects of the drug

As these minor tranquilisers are normally prescribed for relief of daytime anxiety or sleeping problems, many parents and grandparents and other adults may have been prescribed them so children can very easily get them from their own homes. There was in the past quite a problem with over-prescribing of these drugs by GPs but this is now well monitored.

These drugs have a sedative effect. They work by depressing the nervous system and slowing down the body. They are used to relieve tension and anxiety, so they make the user feel calm and relaxed. In large dozes the user may get forgetful and may fall asleep.

Children and young people use them to calm down if they have

211

got too high using stimulant drugs such as ecstasy, cocaine or speed, or for sleeping and anxiety problems.

Short term use

This range of drugs is addictive. As tranquillisers are depressants it is dangerous to mix them with other depressant drugs like alcohol, because of the high risk of fatal overdosing.

Some of the tranquillisers cause short-term memory loss.

Long Term Use

The injecting of melted down gel tablets is extremely dangerous and sometimes fatal. The chalk in the tablets and the gel itself can cause serious damage to blood vessels and veins. This practice of using jellies was common in the 1980s and 90s but has now gone out of fashion.

Withdrawals from these drugs can cause bad headaches, nausea, anxiety and mental confusion. It should only be done under medical supervision as sudden withdrawal can cause panic attacks and fitting.

Spiked drinks

There have been many press reports of sex crime involving tranquillisers such as Rohyponol, when the victim's drinks have been spiked with the drug. They end up in a paralysed stupor and are either unaware of or unable to prevent being sexually assaulted. Research into this is inconclusive and suggests that many victims have heavily overdosed on alcohol and then blamed spiked drinks for their dilemma. Both women and men have had this experience.

Benzodiazepines

Volatile Substance Abuse (VSA)
(Depressant)

Street Names: Gas, glue and aerosols, sniffing.

Legal Status: Since 1999, it is illegal for retailers to sell butane gas refills to anyone under the age of 18. It is also illegal for solvents to be supplied to people of any age in the knowledge that they are to be abused.

Nutt Scale Raring: Volatile Substances were not listed in the most dangerous of the 20 commonest drugs used in the UK.

Looks like: The range of volatile substances that can be used is enormous but the most common ones include Butane gas for cigarette lighters, disposable cigarette lighters, aerosol sprays such as hairsprays or air fresheners, whipped cream cans and glues in cans or tubes.

Effects of the drug

These substances have been mostly used by young adolescent males, although others are known to use them. Deaths from VSA in Scotland has been as high as 10 per year.

In the UK since 1992 there has been a decline in deaths from VSAs. Between 2000 and 2007 the average number of deaths have been 56 per year. Between 1993 and 1999 the average was 76 per year. [source: Drugscope]

The effects of inhaling these volatile substances is similar to being very drunk. The users feel dizzy, giggly and light-headed. Some users do hallucinate. The effects last from a few minutes to 30-45 minutes. Because the effects last a short time, users tend to return for more fairly quickly. The substances are usually poured into a plastic bag and inhaled through the top of the bag. They can be sniffed from rags.

Volatile Substance Abuse

Short-term use

The user has a hangover type of feeling for a day or two. Nausea, vomiting, blackouts, a bad cough, spots and sores appear around the mouth. May have a bad headache or be very tired. They can have persistent colds and may develop heart problems. Inhaling from the plastic bag can lead to suffocation. It is extremely dangerous to squirt gas of any kind into the mouth as this can cause sudden death. Sometimes the users heart stops beating when they have been sniffing solvents.

Long-term use

Regular use of VSAs can cause damage to the brain, liver, kidneys, nervous system, lungs and the reproductive organs. Deaths from VSAs often happen when the user is sick and then swallows their vomit. Also from accidents falling off buildings or walls and into outdoor water such as canals or lakes.

For fuller information on the use of VSAs visit www.re-solv.org

Volatile Substance Abuse

Nitrates & Poppers
(Stimulant)

Street Names: Street names for drugs vary around the country. Nitrates & Poppers are know by some of the following names: ram, thrust, rock hard, hardware, kix, TNT, liquid gold, rush, locker room, poppers, amyl nitrate, butyl nitrate and alkyl nitrate.

Legal Status: Amyl nitrite is very rarely used in medicine these days but is controlled under the Medicines Act. Possession is not illegal but supply can be an offence. There have been cases where the Medicines Act was used to fine shops for selling them, but they are still sold as room aromas or deodorisers in sex shops and some clubs.

Nutt Scale rating for nitrates is 19th most dangerous of the 20 commonest drugs used in the UK.

Looks Like: Nitrites originally came as small glass capsules that were popped open, hence the name poppers. Now they are usually sold in small bottles with brand names like Ram, Thrust and Rock Hard. Usually bought in sex shops, head shops and some clubs.

myths & facts

Myth: Only gays use poppers.

Fact: The original use of poppers was for cleaning vinyl records. It was then taken up by the gay community of San Francisco, where users claimed it improved sexual pleasure. It relaxes the anal passage. It then crossed over into the dance scene and is used by young people regardless of their sexuality to supplement the use of dance drugs.

Effects of the drug
An initial head rush that lasts a couple of minutes.

Nitrates & Poppers

Sniffing poppers during sex is said to make orgasms feel like they last longer, and some males say sniffing poppers enhances their erections, others report that they cannot get erections after using them. Not surprising as many of the stimulant drugs cause erection loss like 'speedy willy' in males.

The effects of poppers do not last very long and sometimes leave people feeling sick, faint or weak, especially if used when dancing.

Some people get very bad headaches using them.

Purity
This is not an issue with Poppers.

Short-term use
They can cause rashes around the mouth. They can also burn the skin. May relax the sphincter muscles in the anus.

Long-term use
Heavy use of amyl nitrates like poppers can damage the immune system and was thought to be one of the reasons that the gay community in California were hit more severely by the spread of HIV and AIDS.

Sniffing Poppers can damage the nasal membranes if used heavily.

Poppers are not considered to be addictive, but regular users can develop a tolerance to them so need more to achieve the effects they want.

Poppers are toxic so can kill if swallowed.

It is dangerous for users who have chest or heart problems, anaemia or glaucoma, an eye disease, to use poppers.

Poppers are highly inflammable so should not be used near lighted cigarettes, lighters or barbecues. People have been known to burn off their eyebrows.

If you are taking medication for high blood pressure or are using Viagra you should not use poppers as it can cause a sudden and dangerous drop in blood pressure.

Nitrates & Poppers

Heroin
(Depressant)

Street Names: Junk, H, skag, kit and smack.

Legal Status: Class 'A'

Nutt Scale rating for heroin is 1 in the most dangerous of the 20 most common drugs used in the UK.

Looks like: A brownish-white powder, sometimes it is a brown/black colour. It is produced from scraping resin from poppy heads. Over 85% of heroin used in the UK is grown in Afghanistan.

Purity: The opium paste from which heroin is initially produced can be around 95% pure but by the time it is cut with a variety of materials for sale on the streets, the purity can be between 20%–50% or very much lower. The wide variation in purity can result in users overdosing and some batches of heroin have been contaminated with dangerous bacteria or viruses. Anthrax spores found in a batch of heroin caused 13 deaths in Scotland in 2010, and many other users were infected with this very serious disease.

Effects of the drug

Heroin is an opiate (derived from opium) and is an extremely powerful painkiller. As it slows down the central nervous system and our breathing, the biggest danger with heroin is death from overdose (you can stop breathing), especially if it is injected. It is usually injected although it can be smoked from heated tinfoil (chasing the dragon). There are around 59,600 heroin users in Scotland and the estimate for the UK is 270,000.

Heroin

myths & facts

Myth: If you smoke heroin it's not as addictive.

Fact: This is not true, because it is the same drug regardless of how it is used. I worked with young people who saw the film 'Trainspotting' and discovered that you could smoke heroin which was not a common practice in the UK before that. After this some of them started to use heroin.

The risks of overdose is increased if heroin is mixed with alcohol or other drugs.

Short-term use

Many heroin users are forced into criminal activity to fund their drug use. This brings many of them into the justice and prison systems where opportunities for treatment are still very limited, especially if they are on a prison sentence of less than three months.

Most of the heroin users in Scotland are adults but there are still unfortunately young people being drawn into using this very dangerous drug. Especially by smoking it.

Smoking of heroin did start to increase when young people wrongly believed that it was safer to smoke it than to inject it. Drugs education has had some success in reducing this problem. Smoking heroin can lead to injecting because after a while the user learns that they get a faster and stronger hit by injecting. Not everyone who tries heroin ends up dependent, but many people who think they can use it as an occasional 'treat', then find themselves using it more often than they thought they would.

Tolerance to the drug increases very fast, so using only at weekends can easily get out of hand, as the weekend can start then on Wednesday and last until Tuesday. Some of these users end up being problem drug users.

Heroin can make users vomit and being sick when they are totally out of it can cause them to choke or suffocate.

Long-term use

There has been an increase of about 4,500 heroin users between 2006-2011. The majority of the 59,600 users of heroin in Scotland

Heroin

are still living in our most deprived communities.

There are very high levels of undiagnosed and untreated mental health problems affecting heroin users. By self-medicating on this powerful painkiller users try to escape from the many painful problems in their lives.

Those who do seek treatment for heroin addiction are often prescribed methadone, a drug similar to heroin, which takes away the craving for the drug. For many people this stabilises their lives enough for them to be able to start to solve their problems. However as too often their mental health issues are not resolved they quickly return to chaotic lifestyles associated with heroin use and drop out of rehabilitation.

Anyone who has gone through withdrawal from heroin (cold turkey) will tell you it is very unpleasant. Symptoms include muscle cramps, vomiting, diarrhoea, runny nose, insomnia, hot and cold flushes and sweating. Cold turkey lasts for about a week but the powerful craving for heroin and the inability to sleep can last a lot longer.

Heroin

Prescribed and Over-the-Counter drugs

Prescribed and Over-The-Counter (OTC) drugs

When most parents think about the drug problem that might affect their children they are usually thinking about illicit drugs, like heroin, cocaine, cannabis and ecstasy, rather than tobacco or alcohol.

Surprisingly there is a well-hidden but growing problem of misuse of common, everyday drugs available in corner shops, supermarkets or chemist shops. Some are also bought on the internet, often by people desperate to find a solution to health problems a doctor has not been able to treat successfully. Cough mixtures, painkillers, anti-inflammatory pills, herbal remedies, diet products, multi-vitamins, Viagra, slimming pills and many more substances are the hidden drug problem few are aware of.

There are many over-the-counter drugs that are mixed and matched with prescribed drugs and illicit drugs. There can be dangerous side effects. There is also a growing problem of the over-prescribing of pharmaceutical drugs by general practitioners. **It is reported that in America around 40% of children are addicted to drugs prescribed by their own doctors.**

Common children's remedies

In March 2009 a group advising the UK government on over-the-counter medicines, released a report on the suitability of these drugs for children. The report said that most of the common remedies, available over-the-counter from chemist, supermarket and corner shops, for treating childhood illnesses such as the common cold, fever, headaches or coughs have no effect at all. They went on to say that in some circumstances they may be harmful to children under 6 years old. Pharmacists were to be sent guidance about this and were to be asked to advise parents on what is safe, what works and what is not suitable for young children.

The government has since abandoned this expert advice, presumably because it could lead to a massive loss of revenue for pharmacies and others who sell these ineffective substances. **So much for governments being trusted to create laws and set policies on drugs to protect our children.** The profits from vested interests win the day again.

It is very important that parents understand that buying medicines not prescribed by a qualified doctor can be a very dangerous thing to do.

Actions the government could take to reduce harm to children from illicit drugs:

- **Adopt the Nutt Scale for describing illicit drugs more accurately;**

- **Publicise more regularly the harm to the environment caused by growing illicit drugs;**

- **Create laws to prohibit drug driving;**

- **Do more to educate parents about the dangers of illicit drugs and children;**

- **Make it illegal for children to purchase or consume illicit drugs.**

Over-the-counter Drugs Agency
This Scottish charity is the only professional organisation in the world of its kind. Providing advice for anyone concerned about addiction caused by the misuse of over-the-counter drugs and medication. Their website has an extensive list of articles and papers on this topic and useful links to many other organisations working in this field. They have advice on their website about buying medicines online.

For further information visit: www.over-count.org.uk

FOR DETAILED INFORMATION ON THE MANY DRUGS THAT HAVE NOT BEEN EXPLAINED ABOVE GO TO CHAPTER 10 WHERE THE RELIABLE SOURCES OF INFORMATION ARE LISTED.

Prescribed and Over-the-Counter drugs

Drug detection periods

One question that should concern us about any drug we use is, could it impair our ability to drive, operate machinery or to concentrate on important tasks such as child rearing or studying? How long a drug remains in our bodies varies. Some employers now undertake unannounced drug testing of their workforce and the police have the right, under certain circumstances to require us to submit to drug testing, especially when driving vehicles of any sort. If we are caught driving under the influence of alcohol or drugs we can invalidate our insurance cover, as well as other legal penalties.

The following is a rough guide to how long common illicit drugs can be detected in urine after use, at dose levels typically taken by drug users:

Amphetamines: 2–3 days

Cannabis: (casual use) 2–7 days; (heavy use) up to 30 days

Cocaine: 12 hours–3 days

Diazepam: 1–2 days

Ecstasy: 2–4 days

Heroin: 1–2 days

LSD: 2–3 days

Temazepam: 1–2 days (longer if injected)

Methadone: 2 days

Alcohol: 1 unit of alcohol takes about 1 hour to be eliminated from the body of a fully grown healthy adult.

These detection times can vary with food and fluid intake, our metabolic rate, our kidney function, the amount of drugs used and for how long, what other drugs have also been taken, as well as the sensitivity of the test used. Times may change as drug testing methods improve.

Recovery from Drug Problems

9.

The emphasis of this book has been about educating parents to prevent children from having their lives damaged by the use or misuse of drugs of any kind.

I have tried to explain what drugs are, why people use them, how they use them, the many reasons why people enjoy using drugs, as well as the problems of misusing drugs. Before adolescence very few children have drug problems, but a growing number of teenagers and young people do, and they are still our children. There are of course many safer things for children to do to have fun in life, that do not involve drugs, but even these activities may carry risks of accidents and even death in a small minority of cases.

Unless we are ill and in need of medication from a doctor, a healthy well-fed human body does not need drugs to function properly. There are many things that children can do as an alternative to using drugs to change their moods, to help them socialise or to solve the problems in their lives. However, these alternatives may not always be easily available to them in their communities; some may not be aware of their existence, or the activities are outside their experience or culture, so are not taken up. Unfortunately some of the healthy activities may be far too expensive for some to afford, compared to the relatively cheap cost of using drugs. There is also the relentless pressure on children today to only enjoy the must-have, social activities that the commercial world of entertainment provides.

When a child goes off the rails and develops a drug problem we need to pull the stops out to prevent escalation. Even armed with the knowledge from a book like this some parents will need to face the problem of finding help for a child with a drug problem. What follows are some ideas of what help is available.

People do not choose to become a Problem Drug User
Contrary to what many people think, almost nobody chooses to become a problem drug user. Some people experiment with drugs, start to like them and may be able to use them occasionally, without

apparently coming to any serious harm. Others try drugs and decide very quickly that they are not for them.

Some people find that drugs appear to be an easy solution to their emotional, mental or social problems, so they continue to use them even if they do not like them. Almost every problem drug user that I have ever worked with can tell me of things in their upbringing and family background that nudged them towards their drug use. Often bereavements early in life of one or often several family members is such a trigger to drug use. Bullying, all forms of abuse, family break-up, moving house or disruption to their schooling are just some of the many reasons that I have heard related over and again as the starting point for drug use in children.

Many of the problem drug users start from very occasional use, only to find that it can very easily escalate. Before they know it they have built up a tolerance to using a drug, and then such a strong dependency on it, that they soon find that their drug use is out of control.

The route to recovery

It is important that parents understand that nothing at all can be done about finding a solution for a drug problem, until the person with the problem is able to accept that they have a problem. This can be a very long, difficult and painful process. Parents can play a signific-ant role in helping a child to find a route to recovery, but they may have to accept that other people are better placed than the immediate family to be the main supporter of a young person through this process.

Knowledge is power

Parents are often at a loss as to where to turn to for help, when they realise that their child has a drug problem. They find it difficult to know where to start or to understand what is going to be involved. The range of help they may need is confusing and not something they have any personal experience of.

Parents have needs too

The problem can be made worse if parents feel that it must have been their fault that a child of theirs has a drug problem. They may feel ashamed and worry about others knowing about their imagined failure. They find it difficult to know who to trust or even who could talk them through what they should do next. Be assured that drug problems within families in Scotland and UK are now extremely common, so you are not on your own.

There is help available if you know where to look. Family support groups do exist and are willing to meet with others facing the same problems. The most common drug problem in Scotland and the UK is alcohol misuse. The highest number of deaths from drugs is from tobacco causing the death of adults.

Deaths from illicit drugs alone are far lower than the general public realise, but that is slowly creeping upwards.

Drug problems can be very complex

By now you will know that the reasons for people having a drug problem can be very complicated, because human beings are complex, and so very different from each other. Because of this, those with a drug problem need a wide range of treatments to be available to them. We know that what will work for one person will not necessarily suit another. The reality for many parents will be that the ideal service they seek for their child is not readily available in their area.

For too long governments have thrown money at one quick-fix solution for addictions after another, only to learn the hard way – that there are no quick-fixes or instant solutions to complex medical and social problems. All the media and public concern about using methadone to help heroin users is just one example of this. Believe me, it does work very well for many who are trapped in heroin use, but it does not work for all and is most certainly not a quick-fix solution. Many users get trapped on methadone so never recover completely. Likewise smoking patches can help some smokers to quit but across the world its success rate is only about 2%.

Does recovery mean total abstinence from all drug use?

Many people may think that becoming completely drug free, or abstinent, is the ideal solution and the only really successful recovery.

The reality is that for many problem drug users that may not be the final outcome. For some, just to get their drug problem of many decades, under some control, so that they are no longer involved in criminality to feed their habit, is accepted as a major step forward towards an eventual recovery. Being able to work or study again, or hold down even a part-time job, is like climbing Mount Everest for someone trapped in serious drug misuse. Support will be needed every small step of the way towards achieving a suitable and successful route to recovery. **Insisting on total abstinence from drugs for some people, especially young people, will drive them away from the sources of help they need.**

Some people never give up their drug use completely and are able to organise their lives well enough to function without causing undue concern to their families and friends. Many famous political leaders, artists, musicians, actors, sports people and other highly creative people in history have functioned for decades whilst using large amounts of drugs every day of their adult lives. Children are not daft. They know that many celebrities appear to function best under the influence of substances. So we should be wary of insisting that they join an abstinence-driven rehabilitation as is the norm in America.

There are many hurdles to be overcome

As already mentioned, the road to recovery can only start with the person who has the problem being able to accept that they have a problem and being seriously interested in finding a solution. For many people this is the hardest part of the recovery journey. They may spend years avoiding addressing their problem and endure decades of misery and pain before finally coming to terms with the reality – their life is out of control, they are overwhelmed by their drug use – that they are a problem drug user.

Those who have successfully been through this often talk about having to hit the bottom of the pit, before they can even face digging themselves out. But, that is not an inevitable route for everyone.

For most problem drug users, by the time they accept that they have a serious drug problem they will have had decades, when they only managed to cope with life by turning to one drug or another to ease their pain or even just to make them feel normal. Using drugs is as normal to them, as not using drugs may be normal to a non-user. Turning to drugs is how they have dealt with their lives. It may have been a painful experience but it has been one that they understood and have learned to put up with. The thought of living without the crutch of drugs is a terrifying idea and one that is easily dismissed from their minds as more drugs are consumed. Powerful drugs like heroin, used by 59,600 Scots, is a major painkiller and is used successfully in everyday medicine. Alcohol was for centuries the main anaesthetic used by surgeons in their operations. So it should not surprise us that so many people find heroin and alcohol a good way to ease their pain.

Who can offer what help?

There is a constant debate about whether problem drug use is a medical problem, a mental health problem, a behaviour problem or a social problem. In my experience it is usually a mixture of all four for most people. So the sources of help required are not only from the medical profession. Too many current approaches to supporting problem drug users are under the control of doctors. They most certainly do not have all the answers. Below is a brief description of what different experts can offer.

Doctors

The first and most important link in the long chain of help should be your GP (family doctor). They are important because in the UK's National Health Service, it is family doctors who have the birth to death records and notes of an individual's health history. That medical history may hold important information which is particularly relevant to understanding why someone has developed a drug problem, e.g. years of back pain, mild or severe depression, nervous conditions, diabetes or alcohol and smoking issues, or a spate of deaths in the same family and mental health issues. GPs are well trained to analyse health problems and know how to refer people to the most appropriate specialist help that they need and that is available.

If for any reason you are not comfortable with talking to a GP then there are other options. Whatever way you deal with this, at some point your GP will become involved in your ongoing healthcare, because the record of your treatment will eventually be sent to your doctor. It is well known that many professionals like doctors, dentists and vets do themselves have serious drug misuse problems, so know only too well what is involved.

Community drug and alcohol services

A wide network of these services have been developed across the land. They are provided free and many of them allow people to refer themselves to their service, but most will want a GP to assist in assessing the person's suitability for the service, before signing them up for treatment. Such treatments are expensive so it is important that this scarce resource is offered to the right people.

Psychiatrists

Unless you can afford to pay for one yourself, you would normally be referred to an NHS psychiatrist through your GP. A psychiatrist is a medical doctor, who has additional training to diagnose if someone is suffering from a mental illness, or from a personality disorder. Once they make their diagnosis they prescribe the appropriate treatment in conjunction with your GP. Some psychiatrists are also addiction or problem drug use specialists. Others specialise in child psychiatry. Some of the work of psychiatrists is about analysing a person's background to unearth the experiences they have had in their lives, which may have lead to them becoming mentally ill. Mental, physical, emotional and sexual abuse is often found in people with serious drug problems. So this may be something that needs to be addressed along with the physical dependency on a particular substance.

Psychologists

Their training and experience is different from psychiatrists, so they offer different forms of help. They are experts in understanding human behaviour, how and why we behave as we do. They are able to discuss with people what sort of person they are, how they deal with different aspects of their lives, what stresses them up, what makes them angry or sad, how they cope with relationships and much more. Psychological testing is used to establish what problems exist and a wide range of counselling techniques are used to help the patient to find solutions to their problems that will work for them. Some psychologists specialise in working with children or families or on addictions and phobias.

Counsellors

Both the NHS and private medicine can provide a wide variety of counselling services. There are many types of counsellors, with different approaches. It is best to seek advice from a GP, a drugs service or some other knowledgeable adviser to find out what might be most useful for a particular individual. Some counsellors specialise in alcohol, smoking, illicit drugs, gambling, sexual disorders and the problems of children or young people.

One counselling technique for working with problem drug users is called **motivational interviewing**. It involves the counsellor helping the client to prepare themselves for dealing with the changes they need to make to overcome an addiction. This approach accepts that drug misuse is a relapsing condition and that drug misusers may want to change their behaviour but be reluctant to do so. This form of counselling is particularly useful early on in the treatment of a problem drug user as it can strengthen their motivation to stick with the treatment they need, talk through what they think their problem is and what solutions they think would work for them. This is done in such a way that the client works it all out for themselves so when they decide to deal with the problem it is entirely their choice and not one imposed by someone else.

Likewise **cognitive behavioural therapy** is another counselling technique which is being found to be useful in helping people who are problem drug users. It helps people to analyse how they behave and how their emotional states affect their behaviour. The therapist works with the patient on how to solve their problems by setting goals for themselves, also through learning skills that help them to change their thinking and their behaviour.

Support groups

There are specialist support groups for individuals or families who are dealing with dependencies on alcohol, tobacco, cocaine, cannabis and some of the prescribed drugs.

The longest established is Alcoholics Anonymous (AA) who are established all over the world, as are Gamblers Anonymous and Cocaine Anonymous. These groups are fellowships of like-minded people, supporting each other in their local communities to deal with the daily cravings for their particular drug or addiction. Most of these groups are for adults rather than children, but there is Alanon for families and Alateen for teenagers.

All of these support groups require that people commit themselves to a life of abstinence from their addiction. This is the main approach to drug and alcohol problems in the USA and it has its critics as it leaves no room for anyone who would prefer a programme of help that would allow them to control their drinking or drug use. In my experience this approach is seldom one of choice for children or young people. The meetings are often dominated by older adults.

Specialist Youth Projects

There is now a small network of special youth projects who are working with some success with young people with drug problems. Crew 2000 in Edinburgh, West Lothian Drug and Alcohol Service are two examples in Scotland, others can be found by an internet search.

There are similar projects for children and young people with mental health problems. Penumbra in the Scottish Borders and in Edinburgh is one of these. Any of these organisations can also help parents to find similar projects around the UK. They are usually happy to talk to a parent or a child on the telephone to assist them towards the help they need.

Tobacco Cessation Clinics

The drive by our government to encourage people to quit smoking has led to the setting up of special Smoking Cessation Clinics and groups around the country. These clinics are often run by nurses and usually combine the use of Nicotine Replacement Therapy (NRT, commonly called Patches) and group meetings to support quitters. Again they mainly attract the over 18s but some effort is now being made to provide special groups for children under 18. A check on the internet will help you to locate local groups.

Some of these groups are now starting to try to work with people who have problems with cannabis, many of whom are also long-term smokers of tobacco.

Heavy tobacco use in children can easily escalate into other forms of drug misuse, so parents should not think that tobacco is not a serious drug of addiction.

Acupuncturists

This ancient Chinese form of treatment, using tiny needles placed around the body, does have some success in treating addictions. Some of the drug services and smoking cessation groups offer an ear acupuncture technique for detoxing clients. Acupuncture can be used for stress relief – which is often an issue for problem drug users. I personally have had acupuncture many times to address different issues and it has had some amazing results. It even works on animals and is used by some vets and dentists as well.

Hypnotherapists

Forget what you have heard about stage hypnotists getting people to do daft things for the amusement of a theatre audience, because professionally trained hypnotherapists can offer a range of help to people with drug problems. They can assist with stress management, sleep disorders, phobias and addictions to tobacco, drugs or alcohol. They can also work with clients to help them to deal with withdrawal from drugs and to develop a strong motivation to address their drug problems. Sometimes they produce tapes, CDs and other audio media for clients to take away to use at home, to deepen and sustain the power of the trances they induce in people.

Most hypnotherapists have to be paid for privately and usually cost around £70 for a consultation of around an hour. This is money very well spent if it works for you. What you learn from this is a self-hypnosis technique, which once paid for can be used as often as you like, perhaps for the rest of your life. It is sometimes possible to be referred to hypnotherapists through the NHS. There are some problems about working with young children and around 5% of adults are so resistant to hypnosis that it will not work for them.

Private addiction clinics

There are many of these clinics available in the UK but the cost can be thousands of pounds per week for residential detox and drug problem treatment. GPs and drugs services can refer patients to some of these services, but only if they can provide the funding. Some of the best known clinics are used by famous celebrities who can clearly afford their services. I have never heard of children being referred to them in the UK. One advantage of using residential services is that they are often located well away from the community that a drug user lives in, so it gets them well away from all their normal temptations. However, at the end of the treatment, most users will have to return to where they came from and that often causes serious relapses.

The four stages of recovery from drug misuse

For many problem drug users there are issues about the physical dependence or addiction to a particular drug, but also emotional and psychological issues to be addressed. For some, criminal charges may be pending and there may be family or personal relationship problems to be worked on. Regardless of how many, or how few of these issues anyone has, there are four main stages of the recovery journey, that everyone must face, to achieve the best outcome for them.

The four main stages of recovery are:

1. Acceptance of the problem

Individuals must accept that they have a problem and are willing to address it.

2. Finding the Motivation

Individuals must find the mental strength and willpower to

motivate themselves, not only to seek the help they need, but to carry them through the long process of reducing, stopping, controlling or giving up their drug use.

3. Finding the right form of treatment

Each individual must find the most suitable form of treatment to match their particular drug problem, their personality and their unique needs. Such treatment must include a safe, well monitored method of withdrawal from the drugs they use.

4. Addressing why they became a problem drug user

Understanding the reasons for being a problem drug user is essential if someone is to work towards a life without the overwhelming control that drugs have had on their lives. This is about exploring their past, seeking to understand the causes of their problem and then making plans for living a different life to the one that had overwhelmed them in drug misuse.

To successfully go through these four stages of tackling a drug problem, is never easy. It is unlikely that anyone will move smoothly through this process without falling by the wayside, perhaps many times. So it is important not to start on this journey thinking that there are any quick-fixes, because there are not.

It has normally taken many years, even decades, for someone to develop a serious drug problem, so it will normally take a long time to resolve it.

Success comes one day at a time. Days become weeks, then months and eventually years of good health without drugs.

There is continual debate on how successful residential drug and alcohol rehabilitation is. Wealthy celebrities who can easily afford it can and do successfully detox from drugs in these clinics, and then appear to resume their highly lucrative careers. These highly paid celebrities can afford the anonymity that such exclusive clinics offer, so if their treatment sometimes fails, it is not always reported in the media, so we may falsely believe that these services have very high success rates. This can never be never guaranteed.

More ordinary citizens who do successfully complete residential drugs rehabilitation, often relapse quite quickly because when they then return to the much less glamorous life with no work, no home, no prospects, a broken family and a pile of outstanding bills, and perhaps court cases to face, relapses are very common. This is not a situation conducive to a successful recovery. The very expensive residential treatment may offer them an escape from the reality of their lives during the most painful stages of the recovery. However, the crunch comes when they return to families and communities full of temptation and revert to their old habits. It is for this reason that completing a recovery programme in the community that people normally live in has some advantages.

Acceptance of the problem

This happens in a multitude of ways. It can come in a flash for some people because of life-changing circumstances. For others it is a long, slow realisation that their life is not all it could be. Not being able to accept that we have a problem is often caused by us having got so used to living with a problem that we find it more comfortable to live with the devil we know, than dare to think that there may be a better way. Being nagged by people to change our ways does nudge some people to seek change, but for others this just makes them even more determined to stick with what they know. Once acceptance of a problem does come, the sooner we can get started on seeking help the better. This is particularly true of helping children to address their problems, because the sooner they address them, the less the long-term damage done and the higher the chances are of a successful recovery.

Finding the Motivation

Research across the world suggests that the most important thing that ex-smokers say helped them to succeed in quitting this highly addictive habit was their motivation at the start of that journey. For some it may have been the death of a relative from smoking, for others pregnancy was the motivator. Losing a job and realising how much they spend each week on tobacco may be the trigger for some and for others their children pestering them to quit is enough. Dealing with not being able to smoke in public places has been a big motivator for many people. So finding a strongly motivating reason for seeking help with any drug problem is vital. We are all different so what will motivate each of us will be different. Finding the motivation for a child is perhaps even harder, but I have seen some successes.

I worked with one young female heroin user for many years whose final motivation to stop using was becoming pregnant. She did appear to have an addictive personality having worked her way through many addictions. Her final and very safe addiction has become motherhood, with a brood of three children at the last count.

One example of how a very powerful motivation works for some people was brought home to me when I heard about the rehabilitation programme for problem drug users who work in the caring professions. The recovery programme they used seems to have an unusually high success rate of around 90%. Most other programmes would claim a much lower success rate of perhaps 10%-20%. This example of motivation is based on a fairly small group of people who all work in caring professions, such as dentists, vets, pharmacists, and doctors. This group of professionals have set up their own private rehabilitation programme and if they admit that they have a serious drug use problem then they have to sign up to a very motivating method of solving their problem. We need to learn from successful programmes.

Firstly, they have to accept that they have a problem and agree to stop their professional work until they have recovered. This could mean losing perhaps £100,000 a year of income.

Secondly, they may have to agree to pay towards the cost of treatment. However in some instances treatment costs are borne by their professional organisation or a hospital trust.

Thirdly, they agree that they cannot return to their highly paid work until they have become drug free.

These people have high status in society, they are high earners and they are in caring professions, so want to get back to doing that work. They earn enough to be able to afford to contribute financially to their treatment, so for many this is motivation enough to complete the course. The residential rehabilitation programme they follow is not very different from that provided to most people who are fortunate enough to find the funding for a place on a residential programme. It is basically what is called the 12 steps programme with some additions. It is a programme that requires people to become abstinent from the drugs they have problems with.

Unfortunately, the vast majority of the general public who go into residential drug rehabilitation have a far less attractive life or career to go back to, so it is not surprising that their motivation may be very much lower. Understanding this does however reinforce the point that we need a very, very strong motivation to achieve a successful recovery.

Securing the right form of treatment

After talking with a doctor, who remember is the gateway into most recovery programmes, it is also useful to talk to other people who have been through this already. All the drug services have booklets or fact sheets explaining what they do and how to apply, so gather them all up and study them. They may also be able to arrange for you to meet someone who has been on their programme.

Medical supervision is essential for the safe withdrawal of many drugs, as it can be dangerous to come off some drugs too quickly. This process is called detoxing, or detox, and under the right sort of supervision the psychological and physical pain of withdrawing can be greatly eased and need not take a long time. Some people do 'cold turkey' all on their own. With the exception of quitting tobacco, which most smokers do manage very successfully without any assistance, it is dangerous to try to detox from many other drugs on your own.

Addressing why you were a drug user

Coming off drugs is hard enough, but the real work starts after someone has managed to reduce their use to manageable levels or have stopped using altogether. Many people fail at this point because they think they have got it sorted and try to go back too quickly to living their life as before. Unfortunately for many that is a road to disaster. Returning too soon to the community that supported them in their drug habit, with all the social pressures that are there, only takes users back into the stresses and strains of the life that drove them to drugs in the first place.

Time out with the right sort of support is essential if people are to understand why they got into drug use. Exploring what it is about their personality, their family circumstances or how their lifestyle led them into using drugs, is an essential part of a successful recovery. Unless people have developed such an understanding, and found ways to protect themselves from the pitfalls that could entrap them again, they are not ready to face the world. The good news is that there are many techniques and strategies that can help people to start to find a new and more positive lifestyle – not dependent on using drugs.

Some rehabilitation programmes, however, do not include exploring why the user has a problem as they do not believe this is necessary or helpful to a person in recovery.

Waiting lists

Whatever service is your ideal choice for treatment, you will have to accept that there are still waiting lists to be joined, assessments to be done to establish what the problem is, and time required matching clients to the most suitable and available treatment. The Scottish and UK governments have put in place vast sums of money for tobacco cessation and illicit drug treatment programmes, but much less for dealing with alcohol problems. Targets have been set by the government to make sure that people do not have to wait too long, so waiting lists are getting shorter all the time.

Recovery programmes and young people

Parents should be aware that the number of agencies that can offer appropriate help to young people, especially those under the age of 16 is much more limited than for adults, unless people can afford to go private. [see the 'Resources and Services' list in chapter 10 to find the help you need]

Once the right sort of help is found this can, for instance, help people to unearth the underlying problem that led to someone's drug use, perhaps a lack of self-confidence, which needs to be worked on. If the problem is a failure to make and keep helpful relationships, then that too needs to be tackled. If there are issues of any form of abuse then these need to be resolved, so that the user does not need to self-medicate again, to live with the emotional pain and hurt, that has driven them to drugs in the first place.

Even something as simple as taking regular exercise they enjoy can make an enormous difference to the mental wellbeing of someone and may improve their chances of staying drug-free and having a happier, more stress-free life.

It is only in very recent years that it has been recognised that many problem drug users have underlying, undiagnosed mental health problems. Where there are undiagnosed or untreated mental health problems, then these must be explored and suitable treatments offered if the user has any hope of continuing drug free.

Existing mental health problems are often the reason that people start using drugs. However, using drugs can also be the trigger for some forms of mental ill-health, especially in immature children and young people. Cannabis is a common example. Self-medicating on drugs not prescribed by a health professional to handle mental health problems can be very dangerous. Dual-diagnoses is the term used to describe people who have both a drug and a mental health problem.

Prisons have an enormous number of people who suffer from dual-diagnoses. Prisons are not hospitals; they are not designed to be places to help people resolve such complex issues as a drug or mental health problem. There are now big efforts being made in prisons and young offenders institutions to help people with drug and alcohol problems, but still little or nothing is being done about the mental health epidemic in our prisons.

It is estimated that at least a third of prisoners have serious learning difficulties, including dyslexia or Attention Deficit Disorder, are unable to read, write or deal well with numbers.

These problems all reduce their opportunities of finding suitable work. Unless these issues are addressed, many more, extremely vulnerable people will be incarcerated in our prisons and abandoned to solving their own problems. Imprisonment now costs more than £35,000 per year for each prisoner, money that could be better used in treatment and education programmes in the community.

Importance of Family, Friends and Peers
Finally, it is important to remember that for most young people their family, friends and peers are the most important influences on their lives. People often see peer influence in relation to drug use as being a negative thing, where individuals are led astray by their friends to become involved in drug misuse. In reality peers are just as often the very people who are most powerful in pulling children back from danger and supporting them to modify their behaviour and to help to keep them safe.

We should not underestimate the power of community networks of help and support. Only about 13% of those with serious drug problems use treatment services to help them in their recovery.

Believe it or not but most problem drug users recover without any assistance from specialist treatment service. This is what is known as natural recovery.

Around 90% of smokers seem to manage to quit unaided.

International studies on recovery from addictions consistently tell us that a third of those seeking treatment got better. A third stay the same as they were and a third get worse. Regardless of what sort of treatment they followed.

I make this point not to depress parents who are seeking help for a child with a drug problem but to remind us all that prevention is better than cure. The more we can all do to prevent children from coming to harm from their drug use the better.

10.

Sources of advice and help
where to get help if you or members of your family have a drug problem

Confidentiality

It is important that if someone uses any of the following organisations to discuss a drug problem that they are aware of the level of confidentiality that is on offer. When you visit your doctor you are by law given complete confidentiality. The doctor cannot reveal to anyone what you discuss with them without your permission. This also applies to children. Your medical records can however be shared with other qualified medical staff.

If you are in any doubt then make sure that you ask the organisation you contact about what level of confidentiality they offer. If you are not happy then choose another organisation.

The following is a range of helpful websites and helplines covering every part of the UK. Be careful about consulting websites in the USA, as they may be suggesting solutions that are not easily available in Britain, or only available to those who can pay privately.

In the list that follows I have made it clear if the organisation covers the whole of the UK or only some parts of the country such as Scotland.

Searching for information online – general guidelines

When it comes to health issues, such as drugs, the internet is one source of public information that is enormous. However there are problems in knowing if the information is accurate, up-to-date, factual or just based on the views of an organisation or enthusiast whose motivation could be for the common good or for private gain or profit. Examples include those on cannabis or 'legal highs'. In the case of cannabis there are many sites run by people who are pro-legalisation of cannabis, which is fine as long as we are aware that this is their bias. Other cannabis sites do provide very useful medical and scientific papers explaining the most up-to-date facts.

When it comes to the sites on 'legal highs' my search has so far only found sites that are linked to organisations that are selling these completely unknown drugs. Their very clever marketing omits to tell people of the dangers of these dodgy chemicals and drugs.

Here are some useful questions to ask yourself:

- Do you trust the information you found? Why?

- Do you know how the information is produced, is it from a trusted source? Remember that anyone can upload onto sites and YouTube.

- Do you know who the information is written by? Was it an official organisation, business, an individual, a government, charity, commercial body, personal – who is the author?

- Are those operating that site qualified to provide information on the subject?

- Are their aims and contact details clearly displayed?

- Are they providing biased or neutral views on the health topic?

- Do you know how up-to-date the information is?

- Check if links work and which sites they link to?

- Is there a particular reason why the information is produced? For example newspapers, sponsored advertisements on social networking sites, propaganda, product placement in film and TV.

The last part of the web address may indicate if information is from the UK or not, e.g. SDF.org.uk.

Foreign sites are likely to provide information on methods of treatment that are not available in the UK.

Press and media reporting on drugs

The press and media have a tendency to report only tiny snippets of information on the latest research about drugs. Shock stories about children swallowing methadone, LSD being found in playgrounds and ecstasy causing brain deaths abound. As does advice on drinking and smoking during pregnancy or red wine being good for us all. Bear in mind the notes above on searching the internet and apply the same caution to accepting at face value what you see reported in the press and media.

DRUGS
resources and services

Drug Scope (UK-wide) www.drugscope.org.uk

They do not operate a public help-line.

Drug Scope is the UK's leading independent centre of information and expertise on drugs. Their aim is to inform policy development and reduce drug-related harm to individuals, families, and communities.

They provide very high quality drug information; promote effective responses to drug use, undertake research, advise on policy-making and good practice, encourage informed debate (particularly in the media) and speak for their members working in drug treatment, education, and prevention.

This website includes a very useful facility called D-world, for children in the 11 – 14 age group which is both interactive and child friendly. It is useful for advice and to assist children's school drugs projects. There is an A to Z drug search facility for anyone wanting to find out more up-to-date details about specific drugs.

This is the leading UK organisation for professionals seeking information on drug education and the latest trends in drug use. They have an extensive publications list of materials which are constantly updated.

DrugScope has a range of very well researched and produced drugs guides for teachers, trainers and students. These are bibles of drugs information which are regularly updated a valuable resource for anyone trying to keep up to date with their knowledge of alcohol and drugs.

The Essential Guide to Drugs and Alcohol – 2010 edition £14.95
The Esssential Student Reader £12.95
The Essential Guide to Working with Young People £14.95
All available from HIT www.hit.org.uk

Scottish Drugs Forum (Scotland) www.sdf.org.uk

Scottish Drugs Forum provides similar services to Drug Scope but with a Scottish agenda. They have been established for well over 20 years and have supported the development of a national network of drugs services, research and give advice to the Scottish Government on drug policy developments.

Their website has links to the online Directory of Drug Services in Scotland. It lists all the services, what they do, how to contact them, how you can sign up for help and they explain the sorts of treatment that are on offer. They also have an A to Z drugs search with links to the talktofrank website noted below.

talktofrank (England & Wales) www.talktofrank.com

Telephone Helpline. 0800 77 66 00

This is a free and confidential telephone service.

This is the UK national drugs helpline. It is available 24-hours, seven-days a week, all year.

They offer advice and information for those who are concerned, or have questions, about drugs. This site includes a directory of all the drug services in England only. Wales and Ireland have their own services.

The website includes an excellent A-Z of drugs information.

Know The Score (Scotland) www.knowthescore.info

This is Scottish Government's official website for information on drugs and the sources of help. It links to the other organisations already noted above.

Re-solve (UK-wide) www.re-solv.org

They are dedicated to the prevention of solvent and volatile substance abuse such as glue sniffing.

National Information Line 01785 810762 9am to 5pm on Monday to Friday (excluding public holidays).

They offer a series of information leaflets for free download.

The interactive website www.sniffing.org.uk is an excellent site for 11-14 year olds.

Crew 2000 (Scotland) www.crew2000.org.uk

Tel: 0131 220 3404 Office hours. Standard phone charges.

Email: admin@crew2000.org.uk

This is an independent voluntary organisation involved in drugs education and advice services specifically for young people. They are based in shopfront premises in central Edinburgh where young people can drop in for help and support. They also undertake outreach work in the youth dance scene, music festivals and other venues where large numbers of young people are present. Their website is always kept well up-to-date and is an exceptionally good source of the very latest trends in drug use and young people. They are well worth contacting for free, independent and very reliable information on all forms of drug use by young people.

West Lothian Drugs & Alcohol Service (Scotland)

Tel: 01506 430225 (Office hours only)

This innovative voluntary organisation was established in 1985 and has successfully provided preventive and caring services in drugs, alcohol, tobacco, HIV/Aids and sexual health. They have been in the forefront of pioneering ways of working with children and young people through education work in schools and their counselling services.

This is a local service serving the Livingston area of West Lothian but they are happy to speak to parents seeking advice on children with drug problems.

Over-counter drugs Information Agency (UK)

www.over-count.org.uk.

Tel: 05602 266335 BT Standard rates, mobiles may vary.

7-10pm on Tuesdays only.

Email: info@over-count.org.uk

Based in Dumfries (Scotland), this is the only professional organisation of its type in the world. They are happy to take calls from anyone in the UK. They are concerned about the serious misuse of over-the-counter drugs and the over-prescribing of drugs by doctors. They have very useful information on all of this, and can direct callers to important sources of support and help.

UK Narcotics Anonymous www.ukna.org (UK)

Tel: 0300 999 1212 Low cost call, but check for mobile charges

Operates 24 hrs.

Narcotics Anonymous is a free fellowship or society of men and women for whom drugs have become a major problem. They are recovering problem drug users who meet regularly to help each other to stay clean of drugs. Their website is full of useful information. They can direct people to where local groups are meeting across the UK and have a well-established network in Scotland.

Cocaine Anonymous www.cauk.org.uk (UK)

Tel: 0800 612 0225 (10 am to 10 pm every day)

Free calls from landlines.

If calling from a mobile use: 800 612 0225 Check with your provider for charges.

Scottish helpline 0141 959 6363

Email: helpline@cauk.org.uk

The Cocaine Anonymous website has loads of information on

the drug cocaine, the problems associated with it, and how to get help in the UK if you have a cocaine habit. They have a self-help checklist to help individuals to understand if they are a problem cocaine user. They also explain what the 12 steps rehabilitation and recovery programme is all about.

ALCOHOL resources and services

Alcohol Focus Scotland (Scotland only)

www.alcohol-focus-scotland.org.uk

They state: Our long-term aim is to achieve a culture change in Scotland where far fewer lives are affected by alcohol misuse, and moderate, responsible drinking is the norm.

The website has fact sheets and information on alcohol legislation in Scotland and links to many other organisations concerned about alcohol misuse.

You can search for help with an alcohol problem using a post code.

They do not operate a helpline. Call Drinkline Scotland noted below.

Email: enquiries@alcohol-focus-scotland.org.uk

Alcohol Concern (England and Wales)
www.alcoholconcern.org.uk

They do not operate their own helpline.

This is a voluntary organisation working on alcohol misuse.

The principal aims of this organisation are: to campaign for effective alcohol policy and to improve services for people whose lives are affected by alcohol-related problems.

Drinkline Scotland (Scotland only)

Helpline 0800 7 314 314

Available 24 hours.

Free from landlines and call boxes, but some mobile services may charge.

Provides information on alcohol use and misuse and where to find suitable sources of help in Scotland.

Drinkline UK (England and Wales)

Helpline 0800 917 82 82 (Freephone).

Available 24 hours.

This line offers similar service to the Drinkline Scotland noted above.

The Helpline operates for the whole of the UK. No age limits.

Drinking NHS (UK) www.drinking.nhs.uk

They do not operate a helpline.

This website (change4life) has a wide range of information on alcohol use and misuse. It includes videos with advice on sensible drinking, tips on cutting down on drink. Excellent question and answer section for common questions about alcohol. Has a 'unit of alcohol calculator' and an interactive 'Alcohol Myth Buster'.

Alcoholics Anonymous (UK) www.alcoholics-anonymous.org.uk

National Helpline 0845 769 7555

Calls charged at local BT rates mobiles may vary.

Alcoholics Anonymous is a fellowship of men and women who share their experience, strength and hope with each other that they may solve their common problem and help others to recover from alcoholism.

The only requirement for membership is a desire to stop drinking. There are no dues or fees to be paid for AA membership; they are self-supporting through their own contributions.

The website offers advice, information and will help enquirers to find where local AA groups are meeting in their area. AA also has groups for families (Al-Anon) and (Alateen) for teenagers.

Book on Alcohol

Alcohol Nation – How to protect our children from today's drinking culture Dr Aric Sigman
£13.99
Published in June 2011 this is a very useful read for anyone wishing an insight to the problem of children and alcohol. It emphasises the need for parents to understand about alcohol and to spend time discussing it with their children. Reveals new thinking on why children should be encouraged to drink alcohol as late as possible in life and the links between alcohol use and depression.

SMOKING resources and services

SMOKELINE (UK)

Tel: 0800 84 84 84 (12 noon to 12pm)

For information, advice, counselling and support to quit smoking.

NHS free Smoking Helpline (UK)

Helpline 0800 0224332: Free from landlines, may not be free from mobiles.

It operates 7 days a week, 12 noon to midnight.

They are there to assist people to quit smoking. As well as offering advice and referral to the nearest smoking cessation clinic, they will send you an information pack and DVD on quitting smoking.

www.canstopsmoking.com (Scottish site)

www.smokefree.nhs.uk (Rest of UK)

Helpline 0800 022 4 332 Free from landlines, may not be free from mobiles.

Operates Mon – Fri 9am to 8 pm and Sat-Sun 11am to 5pm.

You can also use this site to chat on line with an adviser.

ASH: Action on smoking and health (UK) + (Scottish organisation)

www.ash.org.uk

www.ashscotland.org.

This organisation campaigns on the smoking issue.

They have both a UK and a Scottish office.

A very useful website, includes fact sheets, briefing notes and information on the latest research into smoking and health. A reliable source of materials for schools pupils and students' projects.

Books on smoking

How to Stop SMOKING, Now, and Forever
Dr Harry Alder and Karl Morris.
£7.99 slightly more than the price of a pack of cigarettes.

From www.howtobooks.co.uk or any good bookshop.

This is an up-to-date, readable self-help book.

It says that a smoker has two problems to overcome: the first is stopping using the drug as painlessly, as possible; the second, and more difficult problem, is making changes in your life that replace that unhelpful habit with other things that you enjoy more.

Allen Carr's Easyway to stop smoking
£8.99 from bookshops or online.

This book has sold 10 million copies across the world. It has an edition for women and another on How to stop your Child Smoking. There are also Easyway Allen Carr stop smoking classes in 50 countries for those that want to quit along with others. They even offer a money back guarantee to those that sign up. That is how confident they are.

www.easywayscotland.co.uk   www.allencarseasywy.com

Mental Health resources and services

Penumbra (Scotland) www.penumbral.org.uk

This is an organisation with presence in the Scottish Borders and in Edinburgh. They are supporting mental health and wellbeing of children and young people. They are also able to advise on finding similar organisations around the UK.

Tel: 0131 475 2380

Email: enquiries@penumbra.org.uk

Young Minds (UK) www.youngminds.org.uk/parents

Parents Helpline 0808 802 5544
Free from landlines and mobiles.

Operates 09.30 – 4pm Mon to Fri.

They cover the whole of UK.

A UK charity committed to improving the emotional wellbeing and mental health of children and young people and empowering their parents and carers.

They offer advice and information mainly to parents but will talk to those under 18.

Parents can book a 50 minute confidential, personal telephone consultation if they feel they need it. Only available to those living in the UK.

Breathing Space (Scotland) www.breathingspacescotland.co.uk

Tel: 0800 83 85 87 Free.

Mon – Thurs 6pm to 2am; Weekend from 6pm Fri to 6am Mon.

A free confidential phone line for people living in Scotland, where you can call when you are feeling down, depressed or are worried about something that you need to talk to someone about.

Sane (UK) www.sane.org.uk

Tel: 08457 67 8000

6pm to 11pm daily.

This is a premium rate call from landlines and mobiles.

They provide practical help to improve quality of life for those affected by mental illness.

The information on the website is very comprehensive and well worth viewing if you have concerns with stress, mental health issues and alcohol.

They have a service called 'SANEmail' aimed at young people which will respond to their questions in a text chat.

www.sane.org.uk/SANEmail

Childline (UK) www.childline.org.uk

Helpline: 0800 1111

It is important that children know that this line is Free and it will not show up on a telephone bill.

They offer confidential telephone support and counselling to children, mainly under the age of 18. This is a highly trusted helpline for children and is used by 500,000 callers each year. Their highly trained counsellors are happy to discuss anything that is worrying a child – drugs, sexual abuse, mental health, family break ups, bullying, exam stress, gangs, racism, self harm and alcoholism are just some of the many topics that callers enquire about.

Confidentiality Promise: It is always our intention to keep calls to ChildLine confidential, but if we are very worried about your safety because the situation you say you are in makes us think your life or the life of someone else is being threatened, we will talk to you about the need for other people to know. Your ChildLine counsellor will only take action if they feel it is an emergency.

Samaritans (UK) www.samaritans.org

Tel: 08457 90 90 90

Operates 24 hours every day.

Email: joe@samaritians.org

Write: Chris
PO Box 9090
Stirling
FK8 2SA

Samaritans provides confidential non-judgemental emotional support for people who are experiencing feelings of distress or despair, including those that could lead to suicide. This service is UK wide. When you call you will be directed to the advice centre closest to you.

Youth Information Services

Youth Information services have been developing in Scotland, the UK and Europe since the 1980s. They include drop-in shops, offices in youth centres, websites and other ways of contacting young people who are in need of information to help them to sort out things for themselves.

Young Scot (Scotland) www.Youngscot.org

This is Scotland's national youth information website and portal, through which children and young people of 11 to 25 years can access masses of useful information on the things they need to know to enjoy their lives. Topics include health, education, money, careers, the law, volunteering, travel and much more.

They also have a youth magazine, a youth discount card to help young people to spend their money wisely. This is an organisation that is interested in youth opinion and the empowerment of children and young people, so they run regular opinion polls to keep up to date with the changes in youth culture, as well as competitions with prizes to be won. A great organisation to inspire children and young people to find alternative activities to using drugs. Young Scot also supports the Scottish Youth Parliament which advises the Scottish Government on youth issues.

The Site (England and Wales) www.Thesite.org

A website for the 16-24 age group. It is the England and Wales equivalent, of Young Scot, noted above. This organisation provides a similar wide range of help and support for young people.

They also host the national volunteering database: www.do-it.org.uk

Through this website you can access an excellent system for finding organisations across the UK who are seeking volunteers. By typing in your particular interests and your postcode you can access the relevant information.

Get Connected (UK) www.getconnected.org.uk

Helpline: 0808 808 4994

Free from landlines and mobiles.

Free and confidential service for the under 25s.

This organisation covers the whole of the UK. It does not offer advice but talks through issues with a young person and then assists them to find the organisation that is best suited to help them resolve their problem.

YouthNet (England and Wales) www.Youthnet.org

Covers England and Wales and provides the same range of services noted above for Young Scot. YouthNet aims to create a socially inclusive environment where young people living in the UK are engaged, informed and inspired to achieve their ambitions and dreams. They deliver high-quality information, signposting, and frontline emotional support primarily through the Internet, but increasingly through mobile phones, digital interactive TV, and hand-held devices – the tools that are central to the way young people communicate.

All the resources noted above have connections to hundreds of other organisations so spending time studying them is a very good starting point to finding the help that your children need. They also offer much needed support to parents and carers.

Other health resources and services

NHS 24 (Scotland) www.nhs24.com

Tel: 08454 242424

Calls are charged at local rates, mobiles may vary.

Available 24 hours every day of the year.

This is a national online and telephone based health information and advice line. They can also be contacted if you think you may have a medical emergency and are not sure who to contact.

NHS Direct (England and Wales) www.nhsdirect.nhs.uk

Tel: 0845 46 47

Calls are charged at local rates, mobiles may vary.

Available 24 hours every day of the year.

ParentLine (Scotland) www.parentline.scotland

This service is run by Children 1st Scotland. It offers help and support for any adult caring for a child with any problems no matter how big or small. If you have a concern about a child anywhere in Scotland you can call this line.

Tel: 0800 828 2233

This is a free and confidential helpline. From the website you can email them for confidential advice is you prefer not to speak to someone.

ParentLine (England & Wales)

www.ParentLine.org.uk

www.parentline.net/

They offer help for parents who have children with special needs.

www.weightlossresources.co.uk

This website includes a facility to view the calories in a wide range of alcoholic drinks.

Hypnosis Books

I Can Make You Smarter
Paul McKenna
£10.99

Particularly useful for children who are studying as it has 2 CDs. One is about relaxation and improving ability to think. The seond CD is about de-stressing children who are studying for exams.

Epilogue
for decision makers
and politicians

The Westminster parliament has twelve bars. They do not require a drinks licence and are not restricted to the opening hours of other licensed premises in the UK. They are heavily subsidised by the taxpayer so a glass of wine costing £3.85 in a typical English pub only costs MPs £1.80. [SOURCE Alcohol Nation p17]

Considering all the discussion that is going through the Westminster Parliament about alcohol being so cheap and that it must be increased in price to stop binge drinking, is it not time that MPs looked no further than their own workplace to start showing us all that they are serious about alcohol pricing and health.

I am told that across the USA there are billboards with the negative messages that says 'you cannot quit smoking on your own'. Sponsored by nicotine patches companies.

In Switzerland the positive messages on the government's public health display boards remind the public 'that around 90% of smokers quit smoking without any assistance from anyone'.

There is constant talk of solving the problem of binge drinking in young people by following the French or Italian way that it is claimed introduces children to alcohol from a very early age by offering them watered down wine. This is an idea very much favoured by the alcohol industry.

Is it not curious though that nobody is suggesting that we should teach young children to smoke sensibly, or that if they were introduced to heroin or cocaine when they were young, so they would not have a problem later in life?

Mistakes of the past should not to be repeated
Having worked on the drugs problem for nearly 50 years I have seen all sorts of initiatives by governments to solve the problems. Many of the efforts have involved importing ideas from other countries, most

often from the United States of America. One thing we should learn from this is that ideas that work in one culture seldom, if ever, work in another country without major adjustments to suit the local culture. When we have religiously followed such ideas we find that they do not work so we lose valuable time and squander public money.

Here are some of the mistakes that I remember and which I hope politicians will take heed of so that they never repeat them.

- **Selling off school playing fields** to boost councils' budgets has left us bereft of facilities that would encourage more children to play sports and would have reduced the problem of childhood obesity. We cannot now afford to replace these facilities.

- **Youth curfews**, such as the one piloted in Hamilton in Lanarkshire, had no effect on youth disorder. It was financially unsustainable as it required such a high police presence that it could not be afforded in all the areas with youth disorder problems. I know of no other UK authority that has adopted this scheme. It has failed time and again in the USA.

- **Re-classifying cannabis twice on police advice**, this mistake proved that knee-jerk reactions to a perceived problem is a bad idea, and it often causes other problems that were not predicted. In this case in the short time that elapsed between re-classifying cannabis downwards from class 'B' to 'C' the type of cannabis on the streets changed to a stronger, potentially more dangerous form (Skunk) which appeared to cause serious mental health problems. So the police had to quickly ask the government for a return to 'B' classification.

- **Just say No to drugs** was an American drugs education campaign launched by Nancy Reagan when her husband Ronald was campaigning to be president. It failed in America and was taken up in Scotland as SAD (Scotland Against Drugs). It was heavily supported by the police, politicians and health promotion services. It was eventually abandoned as the message was too simplistic and had no measurable impact, especially not on teenagers.

- **Be all you can be**. The slogan used by the American army to recruit young men into the military to fight in Vietnam was adopted as another drugs education theme. This was supposed to get people doing alternative things to drinking and taking drugs. Another simplistic message that was quickly ignored and soon discarded.

- **3 strikes and you're out** – another American import, this one from Mayor Rudy Giuliani in New York, aimed at getting criminals off the streets and behaving themselves. It worked for New York because it cleared the gangs and street criminals out of the city. However the citizens of nearby Brooklyn were none too happy when the criminals turned up on their doorstep instead. We have done similar things in Scotland.

- **Police heroin clampdowns just move the problem to other communities**. These have the same effect as 3 strikes and you're out – they move the problem elsewhere. In the 1990s Strathclyde police had a 3 months campaign to clear heroin off the streets of Glasgow. It was highly successful as the stocks dried up very quickly. Unfortunately dealers still have a living to make so they just move their business to lucrative new areas of Scotland. The fishing community of Fraserburgh in the north of Scotland and Stranraer in the rural south suddenly found they had a heroin problem that they never had before. This example should warn politicians of the need to think through policies and laws that can only be measured as successful by moving problems on to other communities.

- **Cutting smoking use may create new problems**. Like the examples above we need to learn that consequences always follow from the actions we take. Increasing the price of tobacco and cutting smoking in public places has been in many ways a considerable success. But, the price hike in tobacco has seen massive imports of highly dangerous black market fags from China, so those that continue to smoke have increased their health dangers. There are also now more home smokers polluting the environment of children.

- **Get Knife Crime off the streets** is another example of moving problems to where you do not want them to go. The police have identified this problem as one of the main outcomes of the public campaigns to tackle street knife crime. The problem has gone from the streets and into homes, where the police cannot control it or detect it, until they are called in to investigate another serious assault or death.

- **Demanding ID from under-25s** to buy alcohol. The same problem as above is starting to be the case with youth drinking. Demanding ID before they can enter pubs, clubs or buy drink in supermarkets or off-licences has resulted in more hidden and uncontrolled drinking in homes. Drinking in well-managed licensed premises does offer a social setting and allows at least some adult supervision of young drinkers. Politicians need to be aware of unwanted consequences from such heavy police and licensing authorities' actions.

- **Going too far in hiking the price of alcohol and raising the age for buying alcohol**, or making it more difficult for those over 18 to buy alcohol will have consequences. The dangerous consequence could be that drinkers and especially young drinkers will switch to using many more illicit drugs which are far cheaper than alcohol already. This is already impacting on crimes of violence, domestic abuse and murders which have moved from the streets and into homes.

- **Expecting school teachers to deliver effective drugs education** has not been a great success. Almost all the drugs education that has been provided in the last five decades has been directed at school aged children. Teachers are highly skilled at teaching topics they know about and are trained to teach. Regrettably teachers have been given the minimum of training in illicit drugs, very little on tobacco and alcohol, so they have only been able to offer highly diluted information that is too often well out-of-date. This has sadly given drugs education a bad name with research constantly suggesting that it has a very limited effect. Teachers are a vital resource who should be able to to deliver better drugs education if only we could invest in training them better and updating their training regularly.

- **Drug misuse is mainly to be found in post-school aged young people and adults**. Almost no work has been targeted on educating these people at the very time when they are most likely to be misusing substances. They are also at an age when if they had any drugs education at school they will long since have forgotten it. They need top-up drugs education appropriate to their age and stage of life.

- **Stop cutting funding for youth work**. This of course is a hobby horse for any professional youth worker such as me. But, the fact is that decade after decade we have cut and cut funding to youth work. We have also reduced the age of children that we target youth work at. As it got more difficult to work with 16-18 year olds we moved downwards to now calling children's work with 10 year olds youth work. It is not, because they are not youths.

Well trained youth workers have an almost unique role to play in the lives of young people as they are neither teachers nor parents. They can work in less authoritarian and less restricted ways with the most difficult of young people. **Abandoning the over 16s in youth work has removed very important role models from thousands of very troubled youths**. The recent successful police-led initiatives with gangs in Glasgow prove this point. Clearly investing time and money on diverting young people with multiple disadvantages away from crime is a very sound investment.

The most shocking example of politicians abandoning success-ful youth work was the cutting of funding to the Airborne Initiative in Lothian after bad publicity from television documentaries about that approach. Airborne had around a 10% success rate in working with the most difficult group of young men that anyone could ever try to work with. In 50 years in youth work I have never seen another youth organisation working so well to turn around these seriously out of control and damaged young men. It is estimated that every £1 spent on good youth work saves around £13 to the state which would be spent on negative activities such as imprisonment. These young men rejected by Airborne had no where to go but back to our failed prisons system.

• **Stop tinkering with drug laws**. For any law to be successful it has to be drafted well to serve the purpose it was created for. It then has to be enforceable and enforced consistently. It must also be revised as circumstances change. In the chapter on law I have highlighted this but would add this caution, that the alcohol laws in particular have been tinkered with for decades with little effect so that they no longer protect children from coming to harm. New research is clearly moving us towards having to consider that the older we start to use alcohol regularly the better. Many countries already have 21 as the age that people are legally allowed to use alcohol. If the research is to be believed then we urgently need to consider redrafting our alcohol laws to prohibit children and young people under either 18 or 21 from regularly using alcohol. Present laws do not stop adults, including parents, from colluding in the drinking of alcohol by children and young people.

• **Don't con the public into thinking you are listening to them** in public consultations. Politicians are said to be worried that they get a bad press, fewer and fewer people vote or believe that they can have any influence on any decisions that governments make. There are good reasons for that and the Scottish Parliament has demonstrated this perhaps more than Westminster. The Holyrood parliament has gone out of its way to invite the public to join in the debates and round table discussions on every topic they can.

Having availed myself of the opportunity to participate in many such consultations, regrettably, I like many others have almost given up on this as too often it seems that the agenda has already been set, policies had already been drafted and if any new ideas are taken up they get watered down, so they become ineffective.

One example will illustrate this well. The suggestion was made at one consultation on alcohol that free water should be provided in all situations where alcohol is sold – pubs, bars, restaurants or clubs. This would have been a healthy thing to do and would, over time, have reduced the amount of alcohol that people consume. It would have cost the government nothing.

The idea was taken up and included in the alcohol bill. However, what the new legislation says is 'if you ask, you must be provided with free water' in licensed premises. This puts the onus on the customer to negotiate this, which is not a normal part of our heavy drinking culture. If as happens in other countries across the world, water was automatically provided to customers then this would be culturally the new and healthy norm, so no embarrassment would be felt, there would be no need for customers to ask and very quickly just like the no smoking ban, the public would get the message and drink more safely. When officials were challenged about this watering down of the suggestion they said that the drinks industry did not want to lose out on sales of bottled water so persuaded the legislators to compromise. Sadly this concession to the drinks industry who are the major drivers of the alcohol misuse problem in Scotland will mean that it could take decades before drinking water along with our alcohol becomes a healthy norm. **The Scottish Government's aim of 'changing our drinking culture' has been badly set back by their lack of courage to take on the vested interests of the drinks lobby.**

Appendix on legalising drugs

The following submission was made to the Westminster parliament but not followed up by the committee on drug use.

The House of Commons Home Affairs Committee on Drugs.
Review of the UK drugs policies.
by Max Cruickshank – Youth Worker and Health Issues Trainer

1. My submission as an individual is based on 50 years of work as a professional youth worker with a special interest in the health issues of young people. Most of my experience has been in Scotland, which the committee will be aware has major drug misuse problems and some success to share with the whole of the UK. Much can be learned from how Scotland has been affected by all drug misuse and what we have been able to do or failed to do about it.

Executive Summary:

2. The general approach of the government to drugs policy has been the right one. With an emphasis on Enforcement, Reducing Demand, Recovery & Rehabilitation. However this approach was only applied to illicit drugs, when it should also have included tobacco and alcohol.

3. In my opinion the first mistake that has been made, in dealing with the drug problems of the UK in the last five decades, has been that governments until very recently have not accepted that tobacco and alcohol are drugs.

4. My submission highlights how children and young people are affected by all drug misuse, including tobacco, alcohol, prescribed medicines, over-the-counter drugs and illicit drugs. I will argue that there are links between how children progress from one drug to another. Addressing how we can reduce the harm from drugs to children will, in the long-term, determine the sort of drug problems adults will have in generations to come.

5. The second important mistake has been to separate legal and illicit drugs into different government departments and committees, whose remits were health or criminal justice issues. I see drugs misuse as primarily a health and mental health issue which has an impact on criminal justice.

6. The third problem has been that drug policies have presumed that misuse would be about adult use. We now know that children too use and misuse drugs and that children are not adults. Now we are starting to understand how early drug use can cause harm to children. I consider children to be those under the age of 25 as is the norm in Europe.

7. The fourth mistake has been that the government has been far too closely involved with the tobacco and the alcohol industries and this has prevented the government from taking the necessary actions to protect public health interests, without being accused of undermining commercial interests and the potential for tax income to the government.

FACT: 80% of the cost of cigarettes goes to our government.

My main concerns:

8. That enforcement has largely failed and did not include the legal drugs tobacco and alcohol.

9. Demand Reduction has failed because we have not done enough to educate adults and this undermined the drugs education of their children.

10. Recovery & Rehabilitation has made some progress but has failed to address the enormous mental health problems associated with drug misuse. We have failed to provide appropriate recovery options for children and young people.

11. The existing UK drug laws protect adults and businesses. They fail miserably to protect children and young people.

FACT: You can drink alcohol from 5 years of age, there is no age at which you cannot smoke tobacco. The Dangerous Drugs Acts do not mention at what age illicit drugs can be bought or consumed. Any new review of drug policies must urgently address this issue.

12. New and more effective drug policies must include what we can learn from the past. Who for instance would have predicted that

legalising tobacco and alcohol would have led to the enormous and costly problems we are facing today?

13. I will argue that the already legalised drugs of tobacco and alcohol are our biggest problem. This is evident from examining the facts from Scotland.

FACT: 90% of men and 86% of women in Scotland use alcohol, but only about 6-7% of adults use illicit drugs. It would seem that the alcohol industry is much more successful than the international drug barons at getting their products to their market.

14. I will argue that we must not presume that by legalising or decriminalising illicit drugs the government will gain any real control of the problem.

15. If drug-related deaths are important indicators of success in solving our drug problems, then the latest facts from Scotland speak volumes:

FACT: 13,473 from tobacco (2004), 1282 (2009) from alcohol and 574 from illicit drugs(2011). These figures are normally about 10% of the UK totals. Clearly our strong emphasis on tackling the illicit drug problem has been a big mistake.

16. FACT: The illicit dugs trade across the world has developed over the last 60 years. It operates in every corner of our land, 24/7 and has never been controlled by any police force, army or government. There are no quality control systems, no customer services department to complain to and they are free to market and produce new products at will.

17. Even our most senior police officers now accept that they have failed in their duty to control access to tobacco and alcohol by children and young people. Our priority should now be to do everything we can to reduce the demand <u>for all drugs</u>, by children, through the revision of the laws, innovative public education and by targeting the top echelons of the illicit drugs trade.

18. Too many politicians have accepted the quite incorrect view that drugs education does not work.

I will argue that drugs education has been more successful than we think, but that we have concentrated that work for too long mainly on school children, not post-school young people. We have failed miserably to provide any drugs education to parents and carers of children. This major omission has undermined the drugs education of children and allowed misinformation and myths to be a major source of the public's understanding of drugs.

The arguments FOR legalising or decriminalising illicit drugs:

19. That over the centuries humankind in most societies, have used drugs and always will.

20. That drug misuse is endemic in the UK so we have to accept that it is here to stay and should concentrate on policies to reduce the harm caused to the minority of users.

21. That it will save the government money in police time and criminal justice costs.

22. That fully grown adults should have the right to do what they want to their own bodies. It is not clear what the definition of an adult is in this context. (16, 18, 21 or 25?)

23. That the quality of illicit drugs used by the public will improve, and health information could reduce some of the harm.

24. That the government would gain tax income which, if ring-fenced, could tackle the damage to people and pay for treatment and rehabilitation for those damaged by drugs.

25. That it will remove the production, distribution and profit from illicit drugs away from criminals and into the hands of legitimate licensed and trustworthy business people.

The arguments AGAINST legalising or decriminalising illicit drugs:

26. Although it is true that over the centuries humankind have always used drugs of one kind or another, in the ancient past such use of drugs were mainly to do with rituals, like coming of age ceremonies or to strengthen the will of men going to war or hunting. Drugs were not sold for massive profits.

27. The more stressed the population of a country is, the higher the consumption of all drugs.

28. Children are not adults. They are not physically fully grown until around 19 years of age and their brains are not fully wired until later. For females this may by 21 but for males it could be two or three years later according to research. Misusing drugs can inhibit mental development. We should define in law that children are those who

are under the age of 25 as in Europe.

29. Children must be protected from using substances that are likely to damage them physically or mentally and could cause damage to their normal growth. Foetal Alcohol Syndrome (FSA) is one example of this.

30. The two main legalised drugs, tobacco and alcohol have been very damaging for humankind, costing the UK far more in government expenditure than the tax income justifies.

31. That when any substance or drug is sold for profit the people involved will always push to the limit the opportunity to maximise profits and so they exploit people for personal gain.

32. It is argued that fully grown adults should have a right to do what they want to their bodies. However the cost to the state is now so high that it could damage the economy, e.g. in liver transplants, cancers and the 13,473 deaths from smoking in Scotland are an avoidable expense.

33. That drugs education is so ineffective that we cannot depend on it, or the sellers of drugs, to ensure that they will assist the users to stay safe.

34. That humankind does not need drugs to provide the extraordinary experiences claimed to result from the use of illicit drugs.

35. That our failure to deal with the major mental health problems of our nation has driven people to self-medicate using both legal and illicit drugs.

36. That current drug laws do not protect the vulnerable and children, only adults and businesses.

37. That we have done very little to curb the access to drugs by prisoners, perhaps because staffing is too low in prisons and this form of social control is cheaper.

38. That decades of evidence shows that we cannot depend on the police to control drug selling by criminals, because that job is extremely dangerous and the police have been too easily corrupted by fear or greed.

39. That the police, licensing authorities and consumer protection authorities have not seen the importance of applying some of the drug protection laws as a high priority. For decades there were no

prosecutions for the sales of tobacco and alcohol to minors. This laxity has helped to create 10 million smokers in the UK and 10 million ex-smokers in the UK with a population of only 62 million.

40. There are alternative ways of blowing people's minds that are not drug induced and so are safer, especially for children. The achievements of our incredible sports people, our brilliant musicians, poets, artists and the use of spiritual practices of meditation, or the secular use of hypnosis, can all provide safer, cheaper, more positive mental experiences.

41. That drugs prescribed by doctors have to undergo rigorous testing before they are allowed to be used by the public, but we still know very little about many of the illicit substances. Legalising cannabis would be damaging to children and lunacy.

42. That mental ill-health can be caused by drug use or made worse by it. Allowing the public to buy and use what are now hundreds of different substances, would be extremely irresponsible.

43. That it is estimated that 40% of children in America are now addicted to drugs prescribed by their own doctors. This is yet another example of the ability of the pharmaceutical industry to persuade GPs to over-prescribe medicines, especially to children.

44. That Methadone has been commonly used to treat heroin problems with very mixed results and many people have died from using it, under prescription, and from buying it from street dealers.

45. That smoking patches, such as Nicorettes, only have about a 2% success rate across the world. Yet these ineffective products make high profits for their manufacturers and are the main treatment provided by government funded smoking cessation clinics. Some users of patches get addicted to the patches. So why are they in use when their success rate is so low?

46. That the most common and most successful way for people to quit smoking is that they just decide to do it, with no intervention from doctors or anyone else. The myth that quitting smoking is so difficult needs to be blown away. A fortune is being made out of selling and prescribing treatments for stopping smoking that are neither necessary nor cost effective.

Conclusion:

47. In my opinion legalising or decriminalising drugs would be a defeatist action by our government.

48. The solutions lie in addressing the issues of massive mental ill-health exacerbated by drug use.

49. Providing new and effective laws to protect our children from harm from all drugs is both urgent and essential.

50. We should now be concentrating on drugs education for adults, especially parents to ensure that they are better informed about how drugs affect them and their children. Knowledge is power. It has already been demonstrated to work with tobacco use. Education can be used as an effective tool to reduce demand for dangerous substances.

51. None of these solutions have been consistently applied to the issue of drug use and misuse. We already know how to do all of this and it is unlikely to cost any more than the failed activities of the last five decades.

52. If these courageous actions were taken by our political leaders we could ensure that the tobacco industry and criminals across the world would no longer need to put into action their plans to sell legalised cannabis and other illicit substances.

My relevant qualifications in submitting these suggestions are:

Fifty years of innovative youth work practice;

Member of the board of Scottish Drugs Forum for 21 years;

Member of the Scottish Parliament's Futures Forum on Drugs and Alcohol;

Member of the Independent Enquiry into Recovery from drug misuse;

I have delivered 4,000 health workshops to young people and adults.

Max Cruickshank, Youth Worker, Health Issues Trainer

Feedback Page

The purpose of this book is to empower parents with the knowledge they need to understand the facts and myths about drug use and children.

If you have found this book useful you could take several actions to ensure that the knowledge you have gained is passed on to others so that in time the action of thousands of parents and carers of children will accumulate into a powerful movement to reduce the harm that all drug use is doing to children in Scotland and across the world.

Those who seek to profit from drugs depend on ignorance to ensure their products continue to make them a profit.

Other actions you could take:

• If you liked the book lend it to a friend or neighbour.

• Buy another copy for someone who you think would never have thought about buying such a book.

• Ask your local library to stock the book.

• Recommend the book to your local school, children's group or youth group.

• Feedback your comments and constructive criticisms to the author, they will all be read and learned from.

• Follow up issues in the book that you feel need political action by speaking to your MSP, your MP or councillors.

• Phone in to any radio or television programmes discussing children and drugs.

• Write letters to the press when you can to keep this issue in the public domain.

Comments can be sent by email to:

oldmaxski@gmail.com

Index